This memorial wall in the "Valley of the Communities" at Yad Vashem in Jerusalem bears the names of about half the 21 communities about which this book was written.

Preserving Our Litvak Heritage
Volume II

A History of
21 Jewish Communities
in Lithuania

by Josef Rosin

Published by JewishGen, Inc. League City, Texas
An Affiliate of
The Museum of Jewish Heritage - A Living Memorial to the Holocaust

Preserving Our Litvak Heritage - Volume II

A History of 21 Jewish Communities in Lithuania

By Josef Rosin

Copyright © by Josef Rosin and Joel Alpert 2007

First Printing: February 2007, Shevat 5767

Editors: Don Loon and Joel Alpert
Proofreader: Susan Levy
Layout: Joel Alpert
Cover Design: Adina Alpert

JewishGen, Inc
2951 Marina Bay Drive Ste 130-472
League City, TX 77573

Printed in the United States of America by Lightning Source, Inc.

Library of Congress Control Number (LCCN): 2006937096
ISBN: 0-9764759-1-X (hard cover: 330 pages, alk. paper)

Cover photograph of artistic carved Aron Kodesh from the synagogue of Vizhun (Vyzuonos)

This book is dedicated to the
memory of
my father Yehudah-Leib Rosin,
my mother Hayah nee Leibovitz
and
my little sister Tekhiyah
who were murdered by the Nazis and their
Lithuanian helpers

Map of Lithuania

TABLE OF CONTENTS

Map of Lithuania
Contents
Town Names in Lithuanian, Yiddish, Latitude and Longitude
Preface
Introduction by Professor Dov Levin   i
About the Author, Josef Rosin   xvii
Common Sources Used   xviii
Acknowledgements   xx
Notes to the Reader   xx
Glossary of Non-English Words   xxi

[Yiddish]	[Lithuanian]	
Alsiad	Alsėdziai	2
Antalept	Antalieptė	10
Balbirishok	Balbieriškis	20
Dorbyan	Darbėnai	32
Gruzd	Gruzdžiai	44
Kelem	Kelmė	50
Kovarsk	Kavarskas	78
Mazheik	Mažeikiai	86
Payure	Pajuris	102
Plungyan	Plungė	108
Rogeve	Raguva	142
Salok	Salakas	152
Salat	Saločiai	162
Shirvint	Širvintos	166
Shukyan	Šaukėnai	178
Ushpol	Užpaliai	186
Vizhun	Vyžuonos	194
Vorne	Varniai	206
Ezhereni	Zarasai	222
Zhager	Žagarė	242
Zhezhmer	Žiežmariai	280

Because <u>Preserving Our Litvak Heritage,</u> which dealt with the history of 31 towns was so well received, Josef Rosin continued his efforts, and provides us with Volume II covering an additional 21 towns in Lithuania. In order to fully appreciate and understand the history of each town, the reader is urged to first read the **INTRODUCTION**, written by the eminent scholar of Lithuanian Jewish History, Professor Dov Levin, retired chair of the Department of Oral History at the Hebrew University, Jerusalem.

Both Dr. Levin and the author, Josef Rosin, are natives of Lithuania, raised in Jewish communities and therefore entitled to be called "Litvaks," a title they both proudly wear. Levin grew up in Kovno and Rosin in Kibart, each living in their hometowns until the start of World War II. They met in the Kovno Ghetto where they were active in the anti-Nazi underground and later in the forests of Lithuania as partisan fighters against the German and Lithuanian Nazis. Both men, now retired, have devoted many years to collecting and assembling information on Litvak history.

In 1996 Yad VaShem published their work, <u>Pinkas Hakehilot. Lita</u> in Hebrew (<u>Encyclopedia of the Jewish Communities in Lithuania</u>); it is a monumental work of more than 750 pages detailing the specific history of over 500 Litvak towns. Professor Levin was the editor and Josef Rosin, who wrote about 80% of the entries, was the assistant editor. Unfortunately this significant work is not accessible to the English reading public because it is written in Hebrew. This book by Josef Rosin provides an account of an additional 21 communities, even more detailed than that presented in *Pinkas Hakehilot. Lita* (Encyclopedia of the Jewish Communities in Lithuania), as the author is now able to elaborate and offer details that could not be included due to space limitations. Further, Rosin mined the memories and photograph albums of many residents of these towns now living in Israel and elsewhere, to compile an even more comprehensive picture of these communities. It is truly fortuitous that he accomplished this task in good time, because today, in 2007, those survivors who were young adults in 1941 are now well past their 80th birthday. As we discovered, the younger generations are finally starting to search for their history as it existed in their Litvak past, and so we are all extremely fortunate to be able to benefit from the thorough research on which this book is based.

It is our distinct honor and pleasure to have been able to work with Josef Rosin and Professor Dov Levin and thus bring this book to the English reading public.

Don Loon and Joel Alpert, Editors
Erev Rosh HaShanah, 5767, September, 2006

On the eve of the Shoah the Jewish population of Lithuania, including the Vilna region and the refugees from Poland, numbered approximately a quarter of a million souls. Although this represented only around 0.9% of world Jewry during the twenty years of independent Lithuania, it was long recognized as a specific religious-cultural unit as compared to the neighboring Jewish centers of Poland, Belarus and Ukraine. Lithuanian Jews were distinguished by their intellectual and rational attitudes. For good reason the Lithuanian Jews were not only nicknamed Litvak, but also *Tseilem Kop* ("Cross Head"), suggesting that the Lithuanian Jew would be ready to strike out vertically and horizontally (in the form of a cross, G-d forbid) in order to achieve his goal, or alternatively to cross-check his findings in order to reach absolute truth.

These attributes and others not only had implications in daily life, but also resulted in various phenomena, currents and systems in the socio-cultural strata, for example the reservation of the majority of Lithuanian Jews to the concepts of "False Messiahs" and their opposition to *Hasiduth* (Chassidism). Their diligence was exemplary in studying the Torah in the Synagogues (*Batei Midrash*), the *Yeshivoth Ketanoth* (Junior Yeshivoth) and especially in the Great *Yeshivoth*. Jewish Lithuania was famous for the great *Yeshivoth* of Slabodka, Telzh, Ponivezh and Kelm* (* *indicates that this town is one of the 21 towns covered in this book*), where hundreds of foreign students also studied. The Salant community was also well known, because it was from here that the *Musar* (Ethics) movement began and spread through Rabbi Yisrael Salanter. The *Musar* principles were based on the use of intellectual activity and knowledge to correct and improve the behavior of the individual. Lithuanian Jewry was also known for fostering the *Hibath Zion* movement and later for practically adopting the Zionist idea, while exhibiting an almost simultaneous openness to the challenge of the *Haskalah* (the Enlightenment Movement), whether it be in Yiddish, Hebrew, Russian or German.

The city of Vilna (also called the "Jerusalem of Lithuania") not only became a worldwide center of Jewish religion but was also the abode of such famous persons as Rabbi Eliyahu (the Vilna Gaon), Rabbi Hayim-Ozer Grodzensky and many others; moreover it was the cradle of the religious Zionist movement (*Mizrahi*) on the one hand and of the socialist workers movement (*Bund*) on the other. In due course the Institution of Yiddish Culture (YIVO), now established in New York, was born in this city.

Historically it seems that these impressive attributes and achievements, as well as the special character of Lithuanian Jewry within the Jewish world, developed alongside prolonged struggles for their economic and civil rights among their ethnic Lithuanian neighbors, and this in spite of frequent changes of rulers.

The first settlement of Jews in the Great Lithuanian Duchy, also named *Magnus Ducatus Lithuaniae*, began in the fourteenth century by invitation of the Grand Dukes Gediminas and Vytautas (Witold). In 1388, one year after the Christian-Catholic religion was introduced throughout Lithuania, the Jews were also granted a preferred civil status and incomparable bills of rights in many different spheres, such as protecting their bodies and property; freedom to maintain their religious rituals; significant alleviation in the field of commerce and money lending, in relation to Christians. There was also a particular regulation protecting Jews against blood libels. But in 1495, only three years after the expulsion of Spanish Jewry, Grand Duke Alexander expelled all Jews, then numbering more than 6,000, from Lithuania and confiscated their property. Eight years later, when he was elected King of Poland according to the joint rule of these two countries, he allowed Lithuanian Jews to return to their homes and gave them back some of their property. Most of the privileges granted by Vytautas were left intact: for a long period after this event they were of some importance in preserving the legal, civil and economic status of the Jews.

This situation often caused envy among the Christian townspeople, mostly Germans, who were organized in merchant and artisan unions (*cechy*) and who for a long time had enjoyed the Magdeburg Rights according to the precedent granted to merchants in the town of Magdeburg in Germany; they now perceived the Jews as competitors who had to be fought. For example, they managed to have an edict proclaimed (*De non tolerandis Judaeis*) forbidding Jews to settle in Vilna, the capital of the duchy, and to trade there. In time this interdict lost its significance. However, insults to Jews by urban Christians, including students at theological seminars in this town and others, continued for centuries.

This was not the same problem that confronted the Jewish population in the northwestern region of the Lithuanian Duchy known as Zemaitija or Samogitia (the Jews called it Zamut). In contrast to the eastern region, Aukstaitija, and the south-eastern parts of the duchy, most of this region was settled by ethnic Lithuanian tribes who, in contrast to most of their brethren, had accepted the Christian-Catholic religion relatively late (1413) and, because of their religious background, had not yet been stricken with Judophobia.

The first Jewish settlers in Zamut earned their living by customs and tax collection. A further wave of Jews settled in this region following the expulsion of Jews from Vilna (1527) and Memel (1567). At this time there were already Jewish settlements in Zamut – in Alsiad* (Alsedziai), Utyan (Utena), Birzh (Birzai), Zhager* (Zagare), Yurburg (Yurbarkas), Palongen (Palanga), Plungyan* (Plunge), Pokroy (Pakruojis), Keidan (Kedainiai), Kelm* (Kelme), Shadeve (Saduva) and other towns.

INTRODUCTION

A considerable improvement in the condition of the Jewish population and in the relationship between Jews and the entire population occurred during the period of the unification of the Great Lithuanian Dukedom with Poland within the framework of the Polish Republic *Rzeczpospolita* (1569-1795).

Then and for many decades after, feudalism reigned in Lithuania. Most of the population continued to make their living from agriculture as before and from breeding cattle and poultry, from fishing in the rivers and lakes and from harvesting trees. A few, mainly Jews, were peddlers, while even fewer Jews dealt with the import and export of agricultural products. Very few Jews, generally those close to the establishment, were granted the privilege of leasing the collection of levies. With the improvement of roads and sailing routes on the rivers, most of which flowed into the Baltic Sea, there was a gradual increase in commercial activity, especially the exporting of timber, flax, grains, poultry, cattle and dairy products. As a result taverns and storehouses were established near the crossroads and at river ports. These small settlements developed into villages and towns where many Jewish artisans and merchants settled. Until the eighteenth century in the area of ethnic Lithuania, recognition as a town was granted to 83 settlements and rights to commercial trade to 87 settlements. In fact there was no significant difference in rights between a small and a big town.

An additional factor for Jews becoming firmly established in the economic sphere was the significant growth in the number of Jews employed by nobles and estate owners to manage their estates, and also in the leasing of barrooms and taverns in rural areas. As a result, the Jewish bartender or manager was exposed to the hostility of the rural population, which regarded him as an agent of the noblemen who wished to exploit them.

Although most ethnic Lithuanians were already Christians, the belief in devils and ghosts had not yet disappeared and now the Jew replaced these evil symbols. It was not difficult for the Lithuanians to believe in the veracity of the blood libels, a phenomenon that continued to exist until recently.

Despite this, Western Lithuania, and in particular the Zamut region, became a relatively safe haven for thousands of Jewish refugees who survived the Period of Tribulation (1648-1667) that started with the mutiny of the Cossacks headed by Bogdan Khmielnitsky, and ended with the occupation of Vilna by the Russian army. At the same time, the Black Plague ravaged the population of the region.

The *Va'ad Medinath Lita* (The Lithuanian Jewish Council) played an important role in maintaining good relations between the general population and the Jews, as well as among the Jews themselves. This *Va'ad* was a quasi-autonomous authority of the union of Jewish communities in the Polish Republic *Rzeczpospolita*. During the 138 years from 1623 to 1761, this authority effectively and honorably represented the day-to-day interests of about 160,000 Jews in the Lithuanian Dukedom vis-a-vis the rulers and also managed to protect their physical safety and dignity against hostile elements in the Christian population. After the *Va'ad* was organized, the communities of the Ethnic Lithuania region were included in an administrative unit called *Galil* Zamut. Later this was renamed *Medinath* Zamut which included several sub-units in Birzh, (Birzai), Vizhun* (Vyzuonos), Plungyan* (Plunge) and elsewhere.

Far-reaching changes in the legal and civil status of the Jews occurred during the third division of Poland in 1795; then, most of Lithuania was annexed to Russia and became known as The North-Western Zone, thereby becoming an integral part of the Russian empire. In addition to the provinces (*guberniae*), Vilna in the northeast and Grodno in the south, the provinces of Kovno in the north-west and Suwalk in the southwest were also added. This arrangement continued more or less until World War I.

Of the twenty-one Jewish communities reviewed in this book, eleven were situated in the Aukstaitija region which during Czarist rule was in the Vilna *Gubernia,* with the other ten in the Zemaitija region in the Kovno *Gubernia* (see map).

At the end of the eighteenth century there were several areas in this region where half of the population was Jewish, while in a few the Jews enjoyed a decisive majority. In urban settlements, Jews usually tended to concentrate in a defined area, a Jewish quarter, sometimes called "The Jews' Street". Jews who were scattered or lived outside this area were strongly linked to and remained in close contact with those living within the Jewish quarter.

As in other areas in western Russia at this time, this region was also proclaimed as belonging to the *Tehum HaMoshav HaYehudi* (The Jewish Pale of Settlement), where many restrictive edicts and harsh limitations were imposed on the Jewish population, resulting in great hardship and which continued almost until World War I.

At the same time the government was troubled by the isolation of the Jews and tried to deal with this problem in different, sometimes contradictory ways. Thus in 1804 Jews were forbidden to live in the villages and to sell alcohol to peasants, but they were allowed to live as peasants on land allocated to them by the government. Schools were opened for Jews, and in Vilna, a *Beth Midrash* (Seminary) for Rabbis was permitted. In fact these institutions served as centers for the development of a strata of learned men who spoke Russian, which gave them entry into the lower echelons of the social and academic establishments. Most Jews, whose main living was based on contact with peasants and the poor and who lived in the villages and in small towns, managed to survive with a minimal knowledge of the Polish and Lithuanian languages. However, among the narrow layer of Lithuanian intelligentsia, still loyal to a great extent to Polish culture and statehood, there were accusations that these Jews were, in fact, causing the spread of Russian culture on behalf of the ruling class. As a result the Jews found themselves "between the hammer and the anvil" in times of war, as during the invasion of Lithuania by Napoleon in 1812. Some of them, favorably impressed by their contacts with French officers, supported the provisional authority established by the French army and even helped to provide information. But the majority remained patriotic to mother Russia. The Jews were thrown into even more critical situations during the Polish uprisings against Russian rule in 1831 and in 1863: on the one hand they were suspected of sympathy with the rulers and some of them were murdered, whereas on the other hand the Cossacks, who had been sent by the rulers against the Poles, abused the Jews after expelling the rebels.

During the 1905 Russian revolution, progressive circles among Lithuanian Jews expressed their support for the Lithuanians, requesting national autonomy in ethnic Lithuanian regions; i.e. in most of the areas of the Vilna and Kovno *Guberniae* and, in particular, in the Neman (Nemunas) and Vilija (Neris) river basins.

In view of the elections to the all-Russian parliament (*Duma*) which took place in the years 1906-1917, preliminary agreements for were arranged collaboration between Jews and Lithuanians: as a result three Jewish delegates were elected from the Kovno and Vilna *Guberniae*. At approximately the same time the local branch of the social democratic party in Lithuania published a proclamation in Lithuanian denouncing pogroms against Jews in these *guberniae*.

From the start of World War I the Russian army organized attacks on Jews in several towns in Lithuania, including Kuziai, on the pretext that they supplied information to the German army. Despite this libel being strongly refuted by a committee on behalf of the Duma, the military authorities did not retract their accusation. Furthermore, in the summer of 1915, before their retreat from the Kovno *Gubernia* when under pressure by the German army, they exiled 120,000 Jewish citizens into remote Russia.

The German military administration (*Oberost*) imposed strict adherence to orders on Jews as well as on other residents, but their relationship to Jews was correct and they even made allowances for Jewish cultural requirements.

This attitude was prompted by the presence of several Jewish officers in the German army. Also the identity cards issued to Jews were printed in German and Yiddish. For political reasons the Germans did not allow the establishment of an autonomous framework for Jews, despite the intercession of noted German Jews. A deputation of prominent local Jews, including the chairman of the Vilna community, Dr. Ya'akov Vigodsky, Rabbi Yisrael-Nisan Kark from Kovno and others, represented Jewish interests. Some of them advocated collaboration with Lithuanian delegates regarding the establishment of an independent Lithuania.

Considerably closer relations between Lithuanian Jewry and Lithuanians at the political level could be seen at the end of World War I when Lithuania was proclaimed an independent state. Being interested in acquiring the support of world Jewry, the Lithuanian government granted a broad cultural autonomy to the Jewish minority. Despite the massive participation of Jews in the independence war of Lithuania and their empathy in the struggle against the seizure of the Vilna region by the Polish army, many Jews were nevertheless wounded in pogroms by Lithuanian soldiers in Ponevezh (Panevezys), Vilkomir (Ukmerge), Kovarsk* (Kavarskas) and other places. Frequent organized offensives against Jews, such as smearing tar on signs written in Yiddish on shops and on the premises of liberal professionals, were carried out in the temporary capital of Kovno (Kaunas) and in other towns.

In the short period 1920-1925, which can be called the Golden Era of Lithuanian Jewry and the peak of its autonomous status, public Jewish issues were managed by local community committees: these were supported and guided in their daily functions by such central institutions in Kovno as the Jewish National Council, the highest institution of the autonomy, and the Ministry for Jewish Affairs.

The education system in Hebrew and Yiddish, serving about 90% of Jewish children and the network of popular banks (Folksbank) in 85 settlements, were some of the many achievements during the autonomy period. In most towns, branches of Zionist parties and Zionist youth organizations were active.

Left: Stamp of the Minister for Jewish affairs.

Right: Stamp of the National Council of Lithuania's Jews.

Between the two World Wars a considerable number of Jews emigrated to *Eretz-Yisrael*. Hayim-Nakhman Bialik, when visiting Lithuania and hearing Hebrew spoken in the streets, was so impressed that he called Lithuania the *Eretz-Yisrael* of the Diaspora.

In contrast to the Zionists, the radical religious camp (*Agudath Yisrael*) and the Yiddishist camp (Folkists, Bundists and Communists) were numerically fewer. Although Hebrew was spoken in educational institutions, in youth organizations and also in a number of houses, the daily language was Yiddish, which was also the language of the six daily newspapers and other publications.

According to the census of 1923, its 156,000 Jews (7.6% of the entire population of Lithuania) was the largest minority in the state. The Lithuanian majority numbered 1,701,000 persons (84%). Most Lithuanians were peasants. More than half of the Jews dealt in commerce, crafts and industry and the remainder worked in transportation, liberal professions and agriculture. Two thirds of the Jews lived in the temporary capital city of Kovno (Vilna and a region around it were annexed to Poland during this period) and in cities such as Ponevezh, Shavli (Siauliai) and Vilkomir, while the rest could be found in 33 smaller cities and in 246 smaller towns and rural villages.

In spite of the high degree of loyalty which Jews showed to Lithuania and their willingness to fulfill their civil obligations to the state, by the end of the 1930s a considerable sector of the Lithuanian public and authorities decided to restrict the economic livelihood of the Jews. A prominent role in a defamation and incitement campaign on this subject was carried out in cities and towns by members of the association of Lithuanian merchants and artisans, *Verslininkai*. In their journal *Verslas* they even advocated the prohibition of the employment of Lithuanian women by Jews.

At the same time the number of blood libel incidents, the so called use of blood of Christian children for baking matzoth, increased. Assaults on Jews increased, on students in Kovno University, and also on people in the streets. Given that specific malicious incidents, such as shattering windows in synagogues and setting fire to wooden Jewish houses, were carried out in several villages simultaneously, one can conclude that they were organized country-wide. It eventually became clear that some nationalist circles, which favored these actions, had close contacts with various groups in neighboring Nazi Germany, in spite of the fact that at about the same time (March 1939) Germany annexed the Lithuanian port of Klaipeda (Memel), through which numerous Jewish residents narrowly escaped.

This situation, as well as economic depression during this period, which affected the Jewish sector in particular, strengthened left wing political circles among the Jews. Due to international tension and the prospect of war, emigration to America, South Africa and *Eretz-Yisrael* was restricted.

With the return of the Vilna *Gubernia* to Lithuania at the beginning of World War II (October 10th, 1939), the Jewish population, including war refugees from Poland, increased to 250,000. Despite the difficult situation, Lithuanian Jews came to the assistance of the Polish refugees and warmly welcomed the return of Vilna Jews, with whom contact was renewed after 19 years. This stopped to a great extent on June 15th, 1940 when all Lithuania fell to the Red Army and Soviet-Communist rule was implemented, with all that this implied. Despite the misgivings of many Jews, mainly business owners and those from the Zionist sector, the new regime was accepted positively, particularly when the alternative was that Nazi Germany could have taken over instead.

Despite Soviet rule in Lithuania lasting for only one year, from June 1940 until June 1941, the Jews experienced severe changes to their social and economic status. With Sovietization they were adversely affected by the nationalization of the commercial (83%) and industrial (57%) sectors; by the elimination of the Hebrew education system and the religious institutions, the pride of Lithuanian Jewry; by reduction of the Yiddish press and the closing of all public and political organizations except those connected to the Communist party. A section of Jewish youth, particularly former members of Zionist youth organizations and Hebrew educational institutions, organized secret underground circles, where they maintained intellectual and social activities in Hebrew in a national spirit.

During that year the Soviet government imprisoned several Jewish leaders, local Zionist activists and merchants. All were exiled to Siberia and to other remote areas in the Soviet Union. Others who were destined for the same fate, but had meanwhile been overlooked for some reason, changed their addresses. During this period about 7,000 Jews, including refugees from central Europe and Poland (among them Menahem Begin, the future Prime Minister of Israel) were detained and exiled.

Even though Soviet rule caused obvious suffering to the Jewish population, the Lithuanians blamed the Jews for the loss of their independence, calling for revenge. Meanwhile the Lithuanian national underground (L.A.F. – the Lithuanian Activist Front) which had been established in Berlin on November 17th, 1940, strengthened its secret contacts with Nazi Germany and incited Jews, preparing for an uprising against Soviet rule in expectation of an invasion by the German army.

And indeed, during the first days of war between Germany and the Soviet Union in June 1941, many Jews were cruelly murdered by their inhumane Lithuanians. Only a small number managed to escape to the Soviet Union, where some fought against the Nazi German army in the Lithuanian Division of the Red Army.

Since the German army managed to overrun Lithuania in a few days, the majority of Lithuanian Jews remained under Nazi occupation, while the hostile Lithuanian population stepped up their bloody pogroms, raping and robbing their Jewish neighbors.

Very often these terrible events occurred long before the soldiers of the German army arrived at the settlements where Jews had lived for generations. Salat* (Salociai) was such a settlement.

Thousands of Jews all over Lithuania were imprisoned in jails and in other locations which would later serve as mass murder sites, following a precise German plan which was executed with great enthusiasm by the Lithuanian military, the police force and local volunteers. The "Organized Murder Units" would appear in villages where Jews lived, usually after the first pogroms. The scared and hapless Jews were brutally concentrated into synagogues (which became, in fact, torture sites), in market places, on isolated farms or in other buildings. From there they were led, first the men, then the women and children, to the mass murder sites. Here they were forced, while being tortured, to hand over jewelry and other valuables they had carried with them, to undress and to descend into previously prepared pits where they were shot by gun and machine-gun fire. The wounded and those still alive were buried together with the dead in mass graves; their clothes and property were plundered by the murderers and local residents.

About 40,000 Jews who survived the mass murders in the summer and autumn of 1941 and who were destined to serve as a temporary labor force for the German war effort, were imprisoned in ghettos in Vilna, Kovno, Shavli, Shventsian (Svencionys) and in several labor camps in eastern Lithuania. The despairing Jews were subject to inhumanly organized murders, euphemistically called "Actions", and many were deported to countries outside Lithuania. With the Soviet-German front drawing nearer at the end of 1943 and in the first half of 1944, the ghettos and labor camps were liquidated and their remnants transferred to concentration camps in Estonia and Germany. When the Red Army returned to Lithuania in the second half of 1944, there were then about 2,000 Jews in Soviet partisan units and the same number in hiding places, where they had not been discovered. Others had found shelter with non-Jews, mostly in villages far from the central towns of Lithuania. If one adds the number of Lithuanian Jewish survivors to those who escaped or were exiled to Russia, and to those who survived the concentration camps in Germany, Estonia and elsewhere, it would seem that 94% of the 220,000 Jewish residents fell victim to the Nazi occupation, the greatest percentage in all Europe. It is not surprising that most of the remnants of the *Shoah* left Lithuania's blood soaked earth: a considerable number of these survivors emigrated to *Eretz-Yisrael*.

One of those privileged to arrive in *Eretz-Yisrael* before the State of Israel was established, was engineer Josef Rosin, the author of this book: he alone survived when his entire family was murdered in 1941 together with all the Jews in Kibart (Kybartai), western Lithuania.

Fifty years after the complete destruction of his community, Josef Rosin decided to commemorate the loss of his family and community by producing the Yizkor Book *Kibart*, which was published in Haifa in 1988 by the The Association of former Kibart Citizens in Israel. In October 2003 a second extended and updated edition of this book was published, including more impressive photographs of Kibart community members, their institutions, their houses and important documents of community life.

This Yizkor book and thirty more articles on other Lithuanian Jewish communities, some of them situated not far from his home town, were included in his next book of 703 pages.

PRESERVING OUR LITVAK HERITAGE
A History of 31 Jewish Communities in Lithuania
by Josef Rosin.
Edited by Joel Alpert. Introduction by Professor Dov Levin.
Published by JewishGen, Inc. 2005

Now, in this second volume, the author again presents his material in a similar manner to that of the Hebrew book "*Pinkas Kehilot Lita*" (The Encyclopedia of the Jewish Communities in Lithuania): the history of every community is divided into the three main periods in which it grew and developed. These periods were:

1) From the settlement of the first Jews (often during the fourteenth century) until after World War I in 1918.

2) The period of independent Lithuania between the two world wars, 1918 to 1940.

3) The duration of World War II and the fate of Jewish communities at the hands of the Lithuanians and the Nazis, with losses of about 94%. Also described in this period is the fate of the few known survivors to date.

The history of Lithuanian Jewry from its flourishing beginning until its bitter and tragic end may be described as "From zenith to nadir" or literally, "From the highest pinnacle to the lowest depth."

Population statistics presented in the following tables show the early growth of Jewish communities in the 21 towns, their reduction during the second period, and finally their absolute destruction. This also applies to all the 21 communities in this book. Furthermore, a graphic picture (table 1) of their impressive growth to the end of period 1, their shrinking in period 2 and their absolute destruction in period 3 is given in the two tables below.

Table 1 includes data of the Jewish population gleaned from the three census surveys of 1847, 1855/57 and 1897 carried out in Lithuania under Czarist Russian rule. In addition to the absolute growth of the number of Jews in almost all of the 21 towns, they were the absolute majority in 14 of these centers by the end of the century and this despite the great emigration of Lithuanian Jews to overseas countries during this period.

INTRODUCTION

Table 1. The Jewish Population according to the census surveys of 1847, 1855-57, 1897.

Town	1847	%	1855-7	%	1897	%	Remarks
Alsiad	---	--	---	---	295	27	
Antalept	---	--	---	---	474	85	
Balbirishok	---	--	1,167*	48	925	45	*1861
Dorbyan	---	--	---	---	1,129	55	
Ezhereni	453	--	909	26	3,348	53	
Gruzd	---	--	---	---	482	41	
Kelm	759	--	---	---	2,710	69	
Kovarsk	342	--	---	---	979	63	
Mazheik	---	--	---	---	435	21	
Payure	---	--	---	---	---	---	
Plungyan	2,917	--	---	---	2,502	56	
Rogeve	852	--	---	---	1,223	69	
Salok	---	--	---	---	1,582	66	
Salat	---	--	---	---	---	---	300 in 1914
Shirvint	216	--	---	---	1,413	76	
Shukyan	569	--	---	---	624	63	
Ushpol	515	--	---	---	691	93	
Vorne	1,084	--	---	---	1,226	39	
Vizhun	---	--	150*	23	445	79	*1859
Zhager	2,266	--	---	---	5,443	60	
Zhezhmer	---	--	1,372*	74	1,628	58	*1867
Total:	**9,973**				**27,554**		
Over 50% of Population				1		14	

(*) In 1923 the first census in independent Lithuania was carried out.

Table 2. Jewish population of all 21 towns during the period of Independent Lithuania (1918-1940), according to the census of 1923.

Yiddish Name	Jewish Population	% Total Population		
	*1923		1945*	After 1945
Alsiad	199	19	0	
Antalept	367	63	0	
Balbirishok	560	72	0	
Dorbyan	601	59	0	
Ezhereni	1,329	35	0	65 Jews in 1959, 45 in 1970
Gruzd	142	10	1	
Kelem	1,599	55		21 Jews in 1959
Kovarsk	436	42	0	
Mazheik	682	16		+ 1 Jew in 1959
Payure	280	58	0	
Plungyan	1,861	44		138 Jews in 1959
Rogeve	593	58	0	
Salok	917	49	0	
Salat	174	28	0	
Shirvint	1,053	46		2 Jews in 1959
Shukyan	324	41	0	
Ushpol	551	36	0	
Vizhun	367	27	2	
Vorne	843	43		6 Jews in 1989
Zhager	1,928	41		7 Jews in 1959
Zhezhmer	1,205	55	0	
Total	**16,011**		**3**	

(*) In 1923 the first census in independent Lithuania was carried out.

(**) In January 1945 all Lithuania was liberated from the Nazis.

(+) The Jewish population increased compared to the census of 1897, whereas in all the other towns it diminished.

Table 2 shows data of the Jewish population in the 21 towns during the period of independent Lithuania revealed by the census of 1923. It would seem that their numbers had decreased to a noticeable degree in most of the towns. Only in one town, Mazheik* (Mazeikiai) did the Jewish population increase to some extent. In spite of administrative manipulations by the authorities, the Jews retained their majority in   seven towns: Antalept* (Antaliepte), Balbirishok* (Balbieriskis), Dorbyan* (Darbenai), Kelem* (Kelme), Payure* (Pajuris), Rogeve* (Raguva) and Zhezhmer* (Ziezmariai).

There is no doubt that the diminishing numbers of Lithuanian Jews was a result of the increasingly hostile attitude to Jews in the Lithuanian provinces. This foreshadowed the impending slaughter of Jews in Lithuanian towns in the summer of 1941 long before the first German soldier appeared.

A laconic but very reliable expression of what happened from then until the end of 1945 when Lithuania was liberated from the various murderers of the Jews, is given in the penultimate column (1945) in Table 2 where the conventional arithmetic symbol "Zero" is scattered over most of the table, serves as a grim reminder that 100% of the Jews were exterminated in those places.

The reader will understand the considerable differences between relatively large communities where there were more than a thousand Jews in the period of independent Lithuania (e.g. Kelm*, Plungyan*, Ezhereni* (Zarasai)) and smaller communities which numbered only several hundreds (e.g. Gruzd* (Gruzdziai) or Salat*).

Despite this difference and others, the Jewish Popular Bank (Folksbank) had branches in almost all the communities described in this book.

Regarding the religious and cultural aspects, several eminent communities should be recalled, namely Vorne*, Zhager*, Plungyan* and Kelm*.

Note that while Jewish numbers rose in most communities, they were above 50% of the population in fourteen of the towns, despite the great emigration during this period.

The basic way of life of the communities reviewed in this book shows community life directed first of all to fulfilling religious commandments, e.g. *Hevroth Kadisha* (burial societies), cemeteries, synagogues and different *Minyanim*. In bigger communities there were prayer houses for groups of worshipers of the same profession, such as artisans, merchants, shop owners, synagogue beadles etc. Special institutions for studying the Torah were established: *Batei Midrash* for adults, *Hadarim* for children and *Yeshivoth Ketanoth* (small *Yeshivas*) for youngsters. In most of the communities various groups of volunteers, acting under different names, worked in welfare organizations, including *Bikur Holim* for medical help and hospitalization; *Linath Hatsedek* to support the poor and sick and to supply free medicines; *Gemiluth Hesed* providing small interest free loans to the needy; *Zokhrei Petirath Neshamah,* for commemoration of the deceased.

Although the *Hasiduth* was not accepted by the majority of Lithuanian Jewry, the struggle between them and the *Hasidic* minority became moderate. In towns like Ezhereni*, Antalept*, Salok*, Kupishok (Kupiskis), Rakishok (Rokiskis), Ushpol* (Uzpaliai), Utyan and others in the northern part of the country and in Kovno, *Hasidic* communities and the *Mithnagdim* communities acted side by side de facto and in peace.

Several communities established Volunteer Fire Brigades. These brigades, on more than one occasion, fulfilled an effective role in protecting Jewish communities in times of pogroms and riots. Here it must be noted that almost every town in Lithuania was ravaged by fire. Since most houses and synagogues were constructed of wood, most of the Jewish population was at some time rendered homeless. In such cases, the community Rabbis would publicize the disaster by mail, messengers and in later years also in the Jewish press in Hebrew and Yiddish, pleading for aid from near and far communities. On the whole help arrived as requested, and similar methods were adopted when other disasters struck, such as a virulent cholera epidemic.

It is worth mentioning here the Jewish solidarity in the communities of Vorne*, Vizhun*, Zhager*, Zhezhmer*, Mazheik*, Kovarsk*, Rogeve*, Shukyan* and others, that expressed itself in donations of money to Jewish communities outside Lithuania, as far away as Persia (Iran) and certainly *Eretz-Yisrael*.

To illustrate this phenomenon, hundreds of donors' names are listed in this book. They were published in the pages of HaMagid from 1872 (566 names) and Hamelitz (828 names) from the late nineteenth century to the beginning of the twentieth. This may be valuable for descendants seeking reference to their ancestors whose tombstones in the cemeteries of Lithuania have been ruined by weathering or vandalism.

I am privileged to have known Josef Rosin for more than sixty years, since 1943 in the Kovno ghetto: there, we became partners in social and cultural activities in the underground organization of survivors of the Zionist-Socialist youth organization HaShomer HaTsair. Already then Josef was outstanding for his knowledge of different subjects and his moderate and balanced point of view. In particular, he gave us immeasurable pleasure in the depressing atmosphere of the ghetto - he would play his wonderful music on his *Garmoshka* (Mouth organ). Later his melodies soothed us in the heavily forested partisan woods of eastern Lithuania, where we were privileged to be partners in the fight against the German Nazis and their local allies. This pleasant tradition continued, when in October 1945 we were together on an Italian fishing vessel, which transported 171 illegal Shoah survivors to *Eretz-Yisrael*. During those seven very difficult and trying days on board ship, he was given the job of allocating the scarce drinking water to the passengers. (It is doubtful that he then foresaw that, about half a dozen years later, he would hold the position of a department head in TAHAL - The Water Planning Authority for Israel!).

We arrived safely in *Eretz-Yisrael*, having evaded capture by the British police as illegal immigrants. Both of us joined Kibbutz Beth-Zera in the Jordan valley and there we worked for some time in the banana plantations. Even after he went to study at the Technion in Haifa and I at the Hebrew University in Jerusalem, we would meet at least annually with other friends who had shared our ideals and life in the Kovno ghetto. And, of course, we and our families would again enjoy the music from his ever-present mouth organ.

In due course we came to cooperate even more positively at this scientific-literary level. This happened at the beginning of the nineties, when I was elected by the directorate of Yad Vashem to serve as chief editor of the book *Pinkas Kehilot Lita*.

Knowing well his involvement and expertise concerning Jewish life in Lithuania and also his accuracy when writing, it was natural to approach Josef Rosin to accept the assignment of assistant editor. I am glad to state that from that time until the publication of the first edition of the *Pinkas Kehilot Lita* in 1996, we were blessed with productive and beneficial working relations, which, if indirectly, gave rise to this book.

I wish to praise him for his great efforts in obtaining documentary and photographic evidence from many places in the world in order to enrich the visual and historic dimensions of our people and the main events referred to in this book.

The author also deserves appreciation for his care in including with awesome reverence most of the names of his hometown Jews. In view of the terrible tragedy that the Jewish people experienced, it is essential, in my opinion, to repeatedly mention the Jewish names of villages and even more so the names of Jews, particularly those who did not leave relatives or descendants. We hope that, in this way, their names, at least, will not be lost.

Finally, it is appropriate to mark with gratitude and appreciation the professional work of the outstanding American-born Litvak, our mutual friend Mr. Joel Alpert, who invested much energy in preparing this book with all its components and appendices which also have great historical value and human importance. This is an act of true kindness (*Hesed shel Emeth*) for the hundreds of people of Kibart and the other twenty Jewish communities that were destroyed, never to rise again.

Professor Dov Levin, The Hebrew University of Jerusalem
Yerushalayim, 15ᵗʰ of Shevat, 5766, 13 February 2006

ABOUT THE AUTHOR, JOSEF ROSIN

I am a native of Kybartai (Lithuania). I was born on January 24th, 1922 to Hayah (nee Leibovitz) from Marijampole and Yehudah Leib Rosin from Sudargas (Lithuania). They were the owners of a paper and stationary shop in Kibart (the Yiddish name of the town).

I received my elementary and high school education in Kibart, Virbalis and Marijampole. During the years 1939 to 1941 I was a student at the Civil Engineering Faculty of the Kovno (Kaunas) University.

I left my home for the last time on Friday, June 20th, 1941, just two days before the German invasion into the USSR began. My parents and my sister stayed in Kibart and were murdered together with all the Jews of the town, in July of the same year. I was in the Kovno Ghetto for more than two and a half years until the beginning of February 1944, when I escaped into the woods (first into the Rudniki forests and later into the Naliboki forests in Belarus). I remained there until the liberation by the Red Army. In August 1944 I returned to Kovno. At the end of March 1945, I joined a group of young Lithuanian Jews who determined that we should leave Europe and make our way to *Eretz-Yisrael*; we became part of the movement that became known as the *Brikhah* (Flight) movement. I left Lithuania and after the tribulations of illegal travel through Poland, Slovakia, Rumania, Hungary, Austria and Italy, I arrived in *Eretz-Yisrael* on October 24th, 1945 on a ship of *Ma'apilim* (Illegal Immigrants). During the stay in Rumania I married Peninah (nee Cypkewitz) from Wloclawek, who had made a similarly difficult journey from Poland.

We lived in Kibbutz Beth-Zera in the Jordan Valley for nine months. In the autumn of 1946 we left the Kibbutz and moved to Haifa, with the aim of continuing my studies at the Civil Engineering Faculty of the Technion. I was accepted in the second course (as a second year student) and after a delay of yet another year because of the War of Independence, I completed my studies in 1950 with the degree of Engineer. In 1958 I received the M. Sc. in Agricultural Engineering from the Technion.

During the War of Independence I served in the Air Force in the Aerial Photography Unit and was discharged with the rank of Staff Sergeant. I served in the Army Reserves until the age of 54.

During the years 1950-1952 I worked at the Water Department of the Ministry of Agriculture and with the establishment of Water Planning for Israel (Tahal), I joined this firm, where I worked until my retirement on the April 1st, 1987. For more than twenty years I held the position of Head of the Drainage and Development Department of that firm.

In 1989, I published my Memoirs in Hebrew, and in 1994 in English.

Between 1987 and 1994 I wrote many entries for the Hebrew book Encyclopedia of the Jewish Communities in Lithuania *(Pinkas Hakehilot Lita)* and participated in publishing this book as the Assistant Editor. This book was published by Yad Vashem in 1996, edited by Professor Dov Levin.

In 2001 and 2002 I was the assistant editor for the publication of the Memorial Book of the Jewish Community of Yurburg, Lithuania - Translation and Update.

In 2005 I authored Preserving our Litvak Heritage - A History of 31 Jewish Communities in Lithuania.   This current book is a continuation of that effort.

I have a married son and a married daughter and four grandchildren.

****

This book contains articles on the history of twenty-one Jewish communities, half of them in the Zemaitija region (Mazeikiai, Zagare, Plunge, Kelme etc.) and half in the Aukstaitija region (Zarasai, Vyzuonos, Ziezmariai, Sirvintos etc.) (see **Map**).

The pictures included in the articles come from various sources: for pictures provided by individuals, their names are printed beneath the pictures. Others are taken from the four volumes of *Yahaduth Lita* (Lithuanian Jewry) published by The Association of Lithuanian Jews in Israel, Tel Aviv, and the Archives of the Association and *Yahaduth Lita Lita* (Lithuanian Jewry)published by *Mossad HaRav Kook*, Jerusalem. Pictures of the massacre sites and the monuments erected on them are taken mostly from The Book of Sorrow, Vilnius 1997.

COMMON SOURCES USED

Yad Vashem Archives, Jerusalem.

Central Zionist Archives, Jerusalem: 55/1788; 55/1701; 13/15/131; Z-4/2548.

YIVO, NY-Lithuanian Communities Collection.

Kamzon Y.D.: *Yahaduth Lita* (Lithuanian Jewry) (Hebrew), *Mossad HaRav Kook*, Jerusalem 1959.

Yahaduth Lita (Lithuanian Jewry) (Hebrew), Tel-Aviv, 1960-1984, Volumes 1-4.

Cohen Berl: *Shtet, Shtetlach un Dorfishe Yishuvim in Lite biz 1918* (Towns, Small Towns and Rural Settlements in Lithuania till 1918) (Yiddish), New-York 1992.

Pinkas haKehiloth Lita (Encyclopedia of Jewish Communities in Lithuania) (Hebrew). Editor: Dov Levin, Assistant editor: Josef Rosin, Yad Vashem. Jerusalem 1996.

Masines Zudynes Lietuvoje (Mass Murder in Lithuania) vol. 1-2 (Lithuanian), Vilnius 1941-1944.

The Book of Sorrow (Hebrew, Yiddish, English, Lithuanian), Vilnius 1997.

The Lithuanian Encyclopedia (Lithuanian), Boston 1953-1965.

The Small Lithuanian Encyclopedia (Lithuanian), Vilnius 1966-1971.

From Beginning to End (The History of *HaShomer HaTsair* Movement in Lithuania) (Hebrew).

HaMeilitz (St. Petersburg) (Hebrew).

Dos Vort, Kovno (Yiddish).

Folksblat, Kovno (Yiddish).

Di Yiddishe Shtime, Kovno (Yiddish).

Particulars of each town are printed at the end of each article.

ACKNOWLEDGMENTS

Many thanks to my relative and friend Joel Alpert for initiating, compiling, proofreading, editing and organizing the publishing of this book.
To my good friend Professor Dov Levin for his encouragement and advice.
To my friends Sarah and Mordehai Kopfstein who edited my poor English in half of the articles.
To my cousin Fania Hilelson-Jivotovsky for editing the English in the other half of my articles.
To Peninah, my beloved wife for almost sixty years, for her wise and sensitive remarks.
To Don Loon for editing and Susan Levy for proofreading the manuscript.
To the JewishGen organization for their willingness to publish this book and specifically Carol Skydell for her enthusiastic cooperation and participation in this effort.

J. R.

NOTES TO THE READER

1. All the Yiddish and Hebrew names were transliterated anew according to the rules issued by YIVO for this purpose.

2. Dates in the book are written according to the European standard, as day-month-year, so that, for example, Dec. 15, 1955 would be abbreviated as 15.12.1955.

3. The Lithuanian names of the towns and places are printed without the particular Lithuanian letters and symbols due to technical difficulties.

GLOSSARY OF NON-ENGLISH TERMS

Agadah - Homiletic passages in Rabbinic literature
Agudath-Yisrael - Orthodox anti-Zionist organization
Aliyah (Ascent) - Immigration to Israel
Aron Kodesh - The Holy Ark in the Synagogue
Ashkenazi - Jew from Central or Eastern Europe
Benei-Akiva - Religious Zionist youth organization
Berith-Milah - Circumcision
Beth Midrash - A Synagogue for praying and studying the Torah
Bikur-Holim - Welfare Society for Helping the Ill
Beitar (Brith Yosef Trumpeldor) - The Revisionist youth organization
Bimah - Platform, mostly in the middle of the Synagogue, for reading the
Torah
Bund - Jewish anti-Zionist workers organization
Ein Ya'akov - collection of legends and homilies from the Talmud
Eretz-Yisrael - The Land of Israel
Ezrah (Help) - welfare society who took over the functions of the
Community Committees after their liquidation in many communities
Gabai, (pl. Gabaim) - Manager of a Synagogue
Gemara - Talmud
Gemiluth Khesed - Small loans without interest to the poor
Gordonia - Zionist Socialist youth organization
Grosmanists - Jewish State Party led by Meir Grosman
Gubernia (Russian) - Province
Hakhnasath Kalah - Welfare society for helping poor brides to get married
Hakhnasath Orkhim - Welfare society for accommodate passers-by
Halakhah - Legal part of Jewish traditional literature
Hamelitz - an Hebrew weekly newspaper founded in 1860 in Odessa, later a
daily newspaper in St.Petersburg, was closed in 1903
HaMagid - an Hebrew weekly newspaper, founded in 1856, was printed in
Prussia near the border with Russia, was closed in 1890
HaNoar HaZioni - The youth organization of the General Zionist party
HaPoel - the sport organization of the Z.S. party
HaShomer-HaTsair - leftist Zionist youth organization. In Lithuania its
official name was: "The Young Guard Organization of Hebrew Scouts"
HaShomer-Hatsair-Netsakh - a splitting of the main organization of "The
Young Guard Organization of Hebrew Scouts"
Havatseleth HaSharon - Lily of the Sharon. A beautiful flower growing in
the Sharon region of Israel
HeKhalutz (Pioneer) - Organization with the goal to enable its members to
move to Eretz-Yisrael after first undergoing a serious course of training
particularly in agriculture
Ivrith uThekhiyah - Hebrew and Revival

Khalutz or **Halutz, (pl. Halutsim, Halutsoth)** - Pioneer

Hitakhduth - Federation of several Zionist Socialist parties

Humash - First Five Books of the Bible (Pentateuch)

Kadimah - Forward.

Kadish - Liturgical doxology said by the mourner

Kahal - Assembly

Karaite - member of Jewish sect originating in the 8th century, which rejects the Oral Law

Khalah, Halah - Loaf of bread made of white flour, prepared specially for Shabath

Khevrah-Kadisha (Hevrah) - Burial Society

Kheder (pl. Hadarim) - Religious Elementary School

Kheder Metukan - Improved Kheder in which secular subjects were also taught

Khupah - Marriage ceremony

Keren Kayemeth Le'Yisrael (KKL) - The Jewish National Fund. Its goals were buying land, planting groves and other reclamation works in Eretz-Yisrael

Keren Tel-Hai - The fund of the Revisionists after they split from the Zionist Organization

Keren Ha'Yesod - Jewish Foundation Fund

Khibath Zion (Love of Zion) - a 19th century movement to build up the Land of Yisrael before the establishment of the Zionist organization

Khovevei Zion - Members of the above-mentioned movement

Khasidim - a sect in Judaism founded by Rabbi Yisrael Ba'al Shem Tov

Khevrah - Society

Kibutz Hakhsharah - Training Kibutz for the Halutsim before their Aliyah to Eretz Yisrael

Klois - a small prayer room

Kultur Lige - Culture League, association of Yiddishists

Lekhem Aniyim - Welfare society for supplying bread to the poor

Linath HaTsedek - Welfare society for helping the ill

Magdeburg Rights - the Constitution of Magdeburg was an example of almost full autonomy for many towns in Eastern Europe

Magen David (The Shield of David) - The national emblem of the Jewish people

Malbish Arumim - Dress the naked

Maoth - Money

Maoth Khitim - Charity Fund for the poor for buying flour for Matsoth

Matsah (pl. Matsoth) - Unleavened bread for Passover

Matsah Shemurah - Guarded Matsah of wheat kept dry from the time of reaping

Melamed (pl. Melamdim) - Teacher in a Kheder

Meshulakh - Emissary for collecting money for different institutions in Eretz-Yisrael

Midrash - Homiletic interpretation of the Scriptures

Mikveh - Ritual bath

Minyan (pl. Minyanim) - Ten adult male Jews, the minimum for congregational prayer

Mishnah - Collection of Oral Laws compiled by Rabbi Yehudah haNasi, which forms the basis of the Talmud

Mithnagdim - Opponents to Hasidim

Mizrahi - Religious Zionist party

Mohel - Circumciser

Moshav Zekeinim - Home for the Aged

Oleh (pl. Olim) (Ascending) - Immigrant to Israel

Olim LaTorah - called up to the weekly bible portion

Orakh Hayim - The first column of the Shulhan Arukh of Rabbi Josef Caro

ORT Chain - International organization for spreading vocational education among the Jews

OZE (Initials of the Russian name) - International organization for improving the public and personal hygiene of the Jewish population, in particular of the school children

Pinkas - Notebook, Register

Pesakh - Passover

Poalei Zion (Workers of Zion) - Socialist workers party

Poale Zion-Smol (Workers of Zion-left) - Radical leftist party, was forbidden by the Lithuanian government

Rosh Yeshivah - Head of a Yeshivah

Sepharadi - Jew of Spanish stock

Shamash - Synagogue beadle

Shas (Abbreviation of Shisha Sidrei Mishnah) - The six books of the Mishnah

Shekhitah - Ritual slaughtering

Shekel (pl. Shekalim) - the membership card of the Zionist organization that granted the privilege to vote at the Zionist Congresses

Shokhet (pl. Shokhtim) - Ritual slaughterer(s)

Shtibl (pl. Shtiblakh) - Small prayer room for people of the same profession

Shul - Synagogue

Shulhoif-The backyard of the Synagogue

Shulkhan Arukh (The prepared table) - authoritative code of Jewish laws, written by Yoseph Caro (1488-1575)

Sidur - Prayer book

Somekh Noflim - Loans without interest for people who lost their business or property

Suvalkija - the Region of Lithuania on the left side of the Nemunas (Nieman) river

Tallith (pl. Tallithoth) - Praying shawl
Talmud - The commentaries on the Mishnah
Talmud Torah - Religious school
Tarbuth Chain (Culture) - Zionist Hebrew chain of elementary schools
Tehilim - Psalms
Tefillim - Phylacteries
Tifereth Bakhurim - Orthodox boys organization
Tomkhei Tsedakah - Charity
Tsair - Young
Tseirei Zion - Young Zionists party
Tsedakah Gedolah - Charity
Va'ad - Committee
Va'ad Kehilah - Community committee
Va'ad Medinath Lita - Autonomous organization for Jewish communities in Lithuania (1623-1764)
Verslas - Lithuanian Merchants Association
WIZO - Women International Zionist Organization
Yavneh Chain - Religious Zionist Hebrew schools
Yeshivah (pl. Yeshivoth) - Talmudical college
Yeshivah Ketanah - Small Yeshivah
Yiddishist - Ideological fan of Yiddish
Z.S. - Zionist Socialist Party
Z.Z. - Tseirei Zion Party - Young Zionists

THE 21 TOWNS

Lithuanian	Yiddish [Y], Russian [R], Polish [P], German[G], etc	Coordinates
Alsėdziai	Alshad[Y], Alsiad[Y], Olsiadi[R], Olsiady [P]	56 °02' / 22 °03'
Antalieptė	Antalept[Y], Antolepty[P]	55 °40' / 25 °51'
Balbieriškis	Balbirishok[Y],Bal'verzhishki[R],Balwierzyszki[P]	54 °32' / 23 °53'
Darbėnai	Dorbian[Y], Dorbyany[R], Dorbiany[P]	56 °01' / 21 °15'
Gruzdžiai	Gruzd[Y], Gruździe[P]	56 °06' / 23 °16'
Kelmė	Kelm[Y, G], Kelmy[R], Kielmy[P]	55 °38' / 22 °56'
Kavarskas	Kovarsk[Y, R], Kowarsk[P]	55 °26' / 24 °55'
Mažeikiai	Mazheik[Y], Możejki[P],Mažeiķi [Latvian]	56 °19' / 22 °20'
Pajuris	Pajure[Y]	55 °26' / 22 °51'
Plungė	Plungian[Y], Plungiany[R], Pluņģe [Latvian]	55 °55' / 21 °51'
Raguva	Rogeve[Y], Rogów[R]	55 °34' / 24 °36'
Salakas	Salok[Y], Sołoki[P]	55 °35' / 26 °08'
Saločiai	Salat[Y], Sałaty[P]	56 °13' / 24 °24'
Širvintos	Shirvint[Y],Shirvinty[R], Szyrwinty[P]	55 °03' / 24 °57'
Šaukėnai	Shukian[Y], Shavkyany[R], Szawkiany[P]	55 °48' / 22 °53'
Užpaliai	Ushpol[Y], Uszpole[P]	55 °39' / 25 °35'
Vyžuonos	Vizhun[Y], Vizhuny[R], Wiżuny[P]	55 °36' / 25 °30'
Varniai	Vorne[Y], Vorni[R], Wornie[P]	55 °45' / 22 °22'
Zarasai	Ezhereni[Y], Novo-Aleksandrovsk[R],Jeziorosy[P]	55 °44' / 26 °15'
Žagarė	Zhager[Y]	56 °21' / 23 °15'
Žiežmariai	Zhezmir[Y], Zhizhmory[R], Żyżmory[P]	54 °48' / 24 °27'

Source: JewishGen Communities Database

http://www.jewishgen.org/ShtetlSeeker/ShtetlMaster.asp

Alsėdžiai (Alsiad)

Alsedziai (Alsiad in Yiddish) is situated in the northwestern part of Lithuania, in the heart of the Zamut (Zemaitija) region, about 14 km. (8 miles) northwest of the administrative district center of Telsiai. The village is surrounded by hills, groves and lakes and the Sruoja stream flows through it.

Its distance from a railway line and from the Siauliai-Klaipeda main road prevented its development. The nearest railway station was at Mazeikiai, situated a distance of about 45 km. (28 miles) from Alsiad. Only during the period of independent Lithuania was the railway line connecting Siauliai to Klaipeda constructed, and the nearest station at Lieplauke was thus only 9 km. (5 miles) distant. This influenced the economy of the village, reinforcing its connections with the big cities of Lithuania.

Alsiad is an old settlement, having been mentioned in historical documents since 1253. The first church was built in 1471. The estate and the village, including the adjacent lake, was owned by the Bishops of Zamut who dwelled in a magnificent palace until the nineteenth century.

In 1702, King August the Second authorized an annual fair, and in 1790 King Stanislaw August expanded this edict to allow two per year.

During Russian rule (1795-1915) Alsiad was first included in the Vilna Province (*Gubernia*) and later in the Kovno Province. During the period of independent Lithuania (1918-1940) Alsiad was a county administrative center.

Jewish Settlement until World War I

According to statistical data from 1662, there were four Jews, two men and two women (not including children) in Alsiad. Their number increased and before World War I there were about 300 Jews in the village. In 1897 there were 1,088 residents of whom 295 (27%) were Jews.

In 1908 fourteen Rabbis of the region assembled in Alsiad by invitation of the Telzer Rabbi Eliezer Gordon in order to discuss Jewish education. The resolutions included one stipulation that secular subjects in the *Hadarim* would not exceed an hour and a half per day, another that a daily newspaper in Hebrew and in Yiddish would be published.

Some Alsiad Jews emigrated to *Eretz-Yisrael* in the 1870s. One of them was David, the son of Benjamin, who died in 1880 and whose headstone exists in the old cemetery in Jerusalem.

It was published in *HaMelitz* #184 (1893), that Avraham-Yits'hak Bolnik and his new wedded wife Rachel Broida (on the 3rd of Elul) donated money, probably for the settlement of *Eretz-Yisrael*.

During the period of independent Lithuania the number of Jews in the village decreased. According to the first census conducted by the government in 1923, there were then 1,049 residents including 199 Jews (19%). Before World War II only 30 Jewish families remained. The Jews made their living from commerce, mainly grains and flax, crafts and agriculture. The government survey of 1931 showed that there were several shops in Alsiad owned by Jews. These were groceries, textile outlets, a butcher, a pharmacy and a barber shop and a few more small shops not included in the survey.

A bride, groom and guests at a Jewish wedding in Alsiad in 1930s

In 1937 four Jewish artisans worked in the village; a baker, a hatter, a shoemaker and a butcher. Jews also owned four flour mills in the adjacent villages, two workshops for processing leather (owned by the Kalvaria and Faktor Brothers) and a factory for blocks (for shoe making) and wooden nails (owned by Zundel Klein and sons) which, even before World War I, sold its products all over Russia.

Many Alsiad Jews made their living from agriculture, the weekly markets and the now quarterly fairs being the basic livelihood for most of them. However, many lived in dire financial straits and needed help from relatives abroad. Over the years, many of the village's Jews emigrated to South Africa and to *Eretz-Yisrael*.

In 1920 a fire broke out in Alsiad and 35 of the 45 Jewish houses burned down. Donations from outside the town and loans from the Joint Distribution Committee (the "Joint"), enabled the reconstruction of the vicitms' houses, including the Beth Midrash.

In 1939 there were nine telephones in the village, three of them owned by Jewish families.

Among the Rabbis who served in Alsiad were Zvi Broida (at the beginning of the nineteenth century) and Avraham-Aba Zak (1890-1941) who was murdered by Lithuanians. There were also societies for studying the *Talmud*, *Mishnah* and *Orakh Hayim*.

Rabbi Avraham-Aba HaCohen Zak

The Hebrew Elementary School 1933

Jewish children received their elementary education in a *Talmud Torah* and in the Hebrew school of the *Tarbuth* network.

The Synagogue

(Picture taken and supplied by Gilda Kurtzman, July 2005)

Many of Alsiad's Jews were Zionists and were supporters of most of the Zionist parties. The division of votes at the elections for the Zionist Congresses in the 1930s is presented in the table below:

Cong No.	Year	Total Shek.	Total Voters	Labor Party Z"S Z"Z	Rev	G.Z. A B	Gr.	Miz.
18	1933	--	14	11	---	2 --	--	1
19	1935	--	60	17	--	1 15	--	27
21	1939	21	19	4	--	4 -	**Nat Blk** -	11

Shek.-Shekalim; Cong.-Congress; Rev.-Revisionists; G.Z.-General Zionists; Gr.-Grosmanists; Miz.-Mizrahi; Nat. Blk.-National Block

There was a branch of Maccabi with an annual average of 25 members.

The following were the Alsiad reporters who sent articles to the Hebrew press of the nineteenth century; Z. Klein and Yom-Tov Lipman to *HaMeilitz* and Shimon Zak to *HaZeman*.

A class of the Hebrew School 1937-38

During World War II and Afterwards

When Lithuania became a Soviet Republic in 1940, shops and factories were nationalized, some of them Jewish owned. All Zionist parties were disbanded and the Hebrew educational institutes were closed.

The German army entered Alsiad a few days after the outbreak of war between Germany and the Soviet Union. Even before the Germans entered, a local Lithuanian group was organized, headed by the local blacksmith Baltis, which began to plot against the Jews, on whom a penalty of 50,000 rubles each was twice imposed.

On July 5th, 1941, the Jews were imprisoned in a ghetto which included the Beth Midrash, the bathhouse and two other houses. Every morning a parade was arranged; the men were forced to run head down in circles while Lithuanian policemen whipped them. After that they were forced to do different types of labour, such as weeding gardens and cleaning latrines.

On July 24th the above Jews were ordered to prepare themselves to proceed to another ghetto which had been established for Jews of the area in the village of Geruliai, about 10 km. (6 miles) from Telz. Prior to this, armed Lithuanians who had come from Telz in order to murder Alsiad Jews were stopped by the local priest Dambrauskas, who told them that they could do so only after shooting him first.

Before the Jews were transferred to Geruliai the Lithuanians forced them to hand over all their money, their silver and gold jewels and other valuables. Each was allowed to keep only 100 rubles for expenses. The eighty-three years old Rabbi A.A. Zak and the remaining old people were loaded into a car, the others onto carts. On the way they were robbed of most of their belongings. Arriving in Telz the men were left there and the women were sent to Geruliai. Next morning the men did not find their shoes or their garments, but were then ordered to dress in worn out uniforms of Lithuanian soldiers and sent to work. The Lithuanians forced them to destroy the big Beth Midrash of Telz and to transfer the building materials to the railway station. Thirty-six of Alsiad's young men, who were left in Telz, were sent to spread lime onto the mass graves in Rainiai, where Jewish men from Telz had been murdered on July 15th (the 20th of Tamuz).

On August 14th, 1941, these thirty-six men were sent to dig a large pit: they were told that this pit was intended for a German aircraft which had crashed in the vicinity. Several days later, on the 23rd of Av, the men of this group, together with two Jews from the village of Makushki and two from the village of Geilishok, were shot and buried in this pit. Three were killed elsewhere.

The older men who were left were transferred to the Geruliai camp, joining the other Jews from Telz and its surroundings who were concentrated there. On Saturday, August 30th (7th of Elul) all Jews were ordered to leave the camp with their belongings. That same day, after the young women had been separated and taken away, all were massacred with machine guns between 8 a.m. and 12 noon. Thirty-eight Alsiad Jews were among the dead.

Some Alsiad women were among the 400 young women from Geruliai who were transferred to the Telz ghetto, while others worked for farmers, harvesting potatoes.

Before the liquidation of the Telz ghetto, at the end of December 1941, the farmers who employed these Jewish women were ordered to return them to the ghetto for "medical inspection." All were executed.

In order to take revenge on the priest who had opposed murder, the Lithuanians brought thirty women and children from the Telz ghetto to Alsiad, shot them and buried them near the priest's home. This happened on the day of the liquidation of the Telz ghetto, December 24th, 1941 (6th of Teveth 5702). Only one woman managed to escape.

The monument on one mass grave in Geruliai

The monument on another mass grave in Geruliai

The family of Alsiad's *shokhet*, Josef-Ber Faktor, owners of a leather processing factory, were allowed to stay in the village, in order to finish processing the stock. Shortly before the work was complete, the family escaped from the village. They found shelter with a Lithuanian acquaintance until the liberation by the Red Army in the autumn of 1944. Before their escape Mr. Faktor managed to remove the Torah scrolls and other holy books from the Beth Midrash, giving them to the priest Dambrauskas for preservation. The latter then transferred them to another priest in Laukuva. After the Germans were expelled and the Russians returned, the priest returned the books to the Faktor family. The Faktor family survived and was privileged to emigrate to *Eretz-Yisrael*.

Sources:

Gotlib, *Ohalei Shem* (Hebrew), page 10

Devar HaShavua (Hebrew) Tel Aviv, 9.4.1953

Di Yiddishe Shtime (Yiddish), Kovno, 25.4.1938

Hamelitz (Hebrew), St. Petersburg, 5.4.1885; 8.1.1886

Yedioth Yad Vashem (Hebrew), Nr. 8-9, Mars 1956

Folksblat (Yiddish), Kovno, 5.9.1930

Antaliepté (Antaliept)

Antaliepte (Antaliept in Yiddish) lies in northeast Lithuania, about 25 km. (15 miles) from the administrative district center of Zarasai (its previous names were Ezerenai and Novo Alexandrovsk, the latter before World War I) and the same distance from the railway station at Utyan (Utena). The town is situated 9 km. (5 miles) from the main road from Daugavpils (Dvinsk) to Vilnius (Vilna). It has beautiful scenery and is surrounded by hills covered with pine trees and lakes and the Sventoji River that flows through it.

Antaliept - General View

Antaliept was probably built in the sixteenth century. In 1675, it had already reached the status of a town. In 1730 Carmelite monks built a monastery on its riverbank. and during the years 1732 to 1760 they built a Baroque style church in the town. In 1832 the Carmelite monastery was closed down and in 1893 a Pravoslavic one was established. The main function of this monastery was to proselytize the Pravoslavic faith among Lithuanians and Poles who were Catholics.

Jews probably began to settle in Antaliept at the end of the seventeenth century. In 1723 the rabbi, of the Galil (district) Vizhun, Avraham Katsenelenbogen of the *Va'ad Medinath Lita,* granted permission to repair the Jewish cemetery of Antaliept. In 1897, there were 554 inhabitants in Antaliept, including 474 (85%) Jews.

As in most of the Lithuanian towns and villages where houses were built of wood, fires were common so much so that the town was almost entirely destroyed over the years. In 1893, 42 Jewish homes were lost in the fires. Early in May 1898, another large fire broke out and many Jewish homes burned down along with all the possessions. Jews from the neighboring town of Dusiat (Dusetos) collected funds and clothes for the victims.

In 1905, during the revolution, meetings and demonstrations against the Czarist rule were organized in Antaliept. In 1919, a revolutionary committee representing the Bolshevik rule was formed. Following political stabilization, a weekly market was held on Mondays and fairs were organized semi-annually on a regular basis.

There was one flour mill, run on water power, owned by a local Jew; a dairy powered by steam; a private fish processing plant existed along with a state-owned fish shop. In 1924, the town built its own power station.

Before World War I, there were about 80 to 100 Jewish families (about 400 persons) among them ten shopkeepers and many peddlers. Their businesses were supported by the Provoslavic monastery, which housed 100 nuns. Jews served the monastery as shopkeepers, millers, construction workers and tradesmen who worked on repairs.

Among the tradesmen there were three to four shoemakers, two to three millers, two to three etchers, one tanner and one tailor. There were no factories in town, except for a brush-manufacturing workshop. Most Antaliept Jews were poor.

The Beth Midrash

As in all Lithuanian towns, the Jews of Antaliept led traditional religious lives. There was a wooden *Beth Midrash* in town and two small prayer houses run by the *Hasidim*. Because of the small community, the rabbis who served in Antaliept were not paid, and they made their living by selling yeast, *ethrogim*, special flour for *Matzah-Shemurah* (special Passover Matzah) and other religious items. These were their only sources of livelihood, and they were very poor. As a result an implied term was coined for them: "Rabbinate of Antaliept".

During the years 1875 to 1885 there were 21 subscribers to rabbinic literature in this town.

During the German occupation that occurred in World War I, the situation became worse. The nuns left the monastery and the German army personnel took over the building. Nevertheless, the Jews remained in town with the exception of two families who moved to Russia.

During the Period of Independent Lithuania

After World War I, during the period of independent Lithuania (1918-1940), there were changes in the lives of Antaliept Jews. Many left and emigrated to South Africa, America and Uruguay, and the number of Jews in the town decreased. According to the first census conducted by the new Lithuanian government in 1923, there were 581 residents in Antaliept, including 367 (63%) Jews. Many young people left town for economic reasons or because they didn't see a future for themselves in a small town. Quite a few emigrated to *Eretz-Yisrael*.

Important changes occurred in the education system of the children. It is true that some continued studying in the open *Hadarim*, but some parents began sending their children to study in other towns. During the Czarist rule there were children who were sent to study at the elementary school not far from Antaliept. In 1937, a Hebrew school was opened in town and the lifestyle became more modern.

בי״ס עברי, אנטליפט חרף תרצ״ז.

Children of the Hebrew Elementary School - winter 1937

Children on an excursion in 1937

According to a trade survey conducted by the state in 1931, the town had a textile shop and a heat utility shop owned by Jews.

Several Jews worked in agriculture and one Jewish person was the owner of the flourmill in the area. There were 15 Jewish tradesmen among them: five butchers, four metal workers, three carpenters, two tailors and one shoemaker. In 1939 there were nine telephones in town, none owned by a Jew.

At the sixteenth Zionist Congress, which took place in 1929, only two Antaliept Jews bought *Shekalim*. At the elections for the eighteenth congress in 1933, 15 people voted: 10 for the Labor Party, 3 for *Mizrahi*, 2 for the General Zionists A party. At the elections for the nineteenth congress in 1935, the number of voters increased to 114 voters: 59 for the Labor Party, 55 for *Mizrahi*. In Antaliept, a branch of *Hashomer-Hatsair* was active as well.

Guests at a wedding in town

Members of *Hashomer Hatsair*

Among the Rabbis who served in Antaliept, Yehudah-Tudl (in the second half of the nineteenth century) was famous for his knowledge of the Torah and for his wisdom. In 1858, Nathan, the son of Moshe Levin was the rabbi of Antaliept. The last rabbis were Zalman-Tuviyah Markovitz, Yitschak Nosel and Yehudah Levin. Rabbi Markovitz was murdered in the Fort IX in Kovno together with his son Hayim-Shimshon, who was well known for his phenomenal memory, along with Yits'hak Nosel and Yehudah Levin.

Rabbi Yits'hak Nosel

Antaliept youths at an outing in the snow

During World War II and Afterwards

In 1940 Lithuania was annexed to the Soviet Union and the Antaliept Jews were compelled to conform to the new rulers.

The German army entered Antaliept on June 26th, 1941, four days after the German invasion of the Soviet Union. The Lithuanians, former members of the *Sauliai* (Gunmen Society), were quite well organized by then and began their constant persecution of the Jews. Particularly active were Jonas Masilauskas, the son of the local bell-ringer, and other peasants in the vicinity.

Shortly after the German invasion, Jews were ushered to the church square and the torture began. One of the most respected merchants in town, Yitschak Berelsky, was made to run back and forth from the square to the river carrying two buckets filled with water all through the day until he collapsed. The Germans forced the healthier young men to work for the local farmers. One farmer whose farm was about 2 km. (1 mile) from the town took in a group of Jews to work for him, but he kept them without food and in such shocking condition that none returned alive.

Monument at the massacre site with the inscription: "Let us do everything so that this tragedy is never again repeated."

At the end of August 1941 all Jews were brought to the Paziemiai grove, situated about 3 km (2 miles) southeast of the village Baltriskiai, 500 meters (1600 feet) off the Deguciai-Dusetos road, where they were massacred on August 26th, together with the Jews of Zarasai - 2,569 men, women and children.

After the war, the Lithuanians would not let the victims rest in peace. During these years, gold seekers exhumed the bodies looting for gold and other valuables.

Among the few youths who managed to escape from the Germans to the Soviet Union in the summer of 1941, ten served in the Lithuanian Division and in the other units of the Red Army. Kalman Shur of Antaliept was decorated with the highest order - "Hero of the Soviet Union." In the 1970s he emigrate to Israel.

A ditch filled with the remains of the slain Jews

The monument on the mass graves

Sources:

Yad Vashem Archives: 0-57 A, testimony of Mosheh Barkan (according to the story of Yehudah Levinas).

Bakaltchuk-Felin, M., Yizkor Book of Rakishok and Vicinity, Johannesburg, 1952, pages 346-349.

Hamelitz (St.Petersburg) 20.5.1898.

Antaliepte by Rafi Julius "Pinkas Hakehiloth-Lita" Yad Vashem, Jerusalem 1996.

Balbieriškis (Balbirishok)

Balbieriskis (Balbirishok in Yiddish) is situated in southwestern Lithuania, on the west bank of the Nemunas River, about 18 km. (12 miles) north west of the railway station in Alite (Alytus). The town developed alongside an estate established by a noble Russian family at the beginning of the sixteenth century. Over the years the owners changed and in 1846 it became the property of the daughters of Graf Tishkevitz. Balbirishok received the rights of a town in 1520.

Balbirishok was part of the Polish-Lithuanian Kingdom until 1795, when the third division of Poland by the three superpowers of those times, Russia, Prussia and Austria, resulted in Lithuania becoming partly Russian and partly Prussian. The area of the state which lay on the west bank of the Neman River (Nemunas) was handed over to Prussia while the other area became a part of Russia. Thus Prussia ruled from 1795-1807 and the rights of the town were annulled because of its small population.

After Napoleon defeated Prussia and according to the Tilzit agreement of July 1807, Polish territories occupied by Prussia were transferred to what became known as the Great Dukedom of Warsaw, which was established at that time. The King Friedrich-August of Saxony was appointed duke, and the Napoleonic code became the constitution of the dukedom, according to which everybody was equal before the law, except for the Jews who were not granted any civil rights.

During the years 1807-1815 Balbirishok was included in the Great Dukedom of Warsaw. In 1815, after Napoleon was defeated in Russia, all Lithuania was annexed to the Russian Empire; this included Balbirishok (Balverzhishki in Russian,) which was in the Suwalk Province (*Gubernia*). Under Russian rule the town grew and became an important commercial center. Its merchants developed business connections with Leipzig and other towns in Germany, the main export item to that country being timber.

At the end of the nineteenth century, with the construction of the railway to Alite and Pren (Prienai), these two towns began to grow, to the detriment of Balbirishok.

During World War I Balbirishok was occupied by the Germans, who ruled it from 1915 until 1918. During the period of independent Lithuania (1918-1940), the town was the administrative center of the county.

Jewish settlement until World War I

Balbirishok was one of the 246 towns in the Polish Kingdom where there were no restrictions on Jewish settlement. Probably most Jews moved to Balbirishok and its environs during the middle of the seventeenth century.

They dealt in timber and grain. Wealthy Jewish tradesmen exported goods to Germany by rafts and barges on the Nieman (Nemunas) River.

In 1843 Balbirishok comprised 1,153 Jews (about 154 families), and by 1861 the total population had grown to 2,424 including 1,167 (48%) Jews.

The old synagogue and the young Jew

Building the new synagogue

A pogrom against Balbirishok Jews erupted in 1881. On a market day on the eve of Yom Kippur, peasants attacked Jewish shops, looted everything they could, before dousing the buildings with kerosene and setting them on fire. The windows of Jewish houses were shattered, pillows and cushions were torn open and the feathers dispersed, and Jews were savagely attacked. One died and twenty were badly injured. The rioters broke into the synagogue and the *Beth Midrash*, destroying everything. The local priest tried to help and rang the church bells, but to no avail. All this carnage occurred because a Jewish merchant apprehended a peasant who had not paid for goods in his shop!!

In the period before World War I, the Jewish children of Balbirishok were educated in *Hadarim* and *Talmud-Torah*. There were also young learned people thirsting for general knowledge, and the Propagators of Knowledge society in Russia sent them secular books. Reuven Hurvitz, representing Balbirishok youth, had a letter published in *HaMelitz* on January 2, 1883, in which he thanked the society for sending six books.

In 1881 the *Hevrah Kadisha* comprised nine clerks and superintendents: three were elected, the others being three *Gabaim*; a bookkeeper, a superintendent and a senior *Shamash* (beadle). There were two Jewish cemeteries, the old and the new, which were established early in the nineteenth century.

In 1898, just after the first Zionist congress, funds were raised for settlement in *Eretz-Yisrael*. *HaMelitz* of that year published a list of donors, and *HaMelitz* # 40 dated 1897 gave a list of eighteen donors from Balbirishok (see **Appendix 1**). From 1861 until 1933 there were 64 subscribers to rabbinic literature.

At the end of April 1915 Balbirishok Jews were exiled far into Russia by the retreating Russian army.

During Independent Lithuania (1918-1940)

After the war ended Balbirishok Jews returned to their town, which was then included in the Marijampole administrative district. Following the law of autonomies for minorities issued by the new Lithuanian government, the minister for Jewish affairs, Dr. Menachem (Max) Soloveitshik, ordered elections to community committees *(Va'adei Kehilah)* to be held in the summer of 1919. In autumn 1919 the elections for the community committee of Balbirishok took place and nine members were elected: two General Zionists, two Tseirei Zion, two Mizrahi, two non-party men and one orthodox Jew. Tuviyah Cohen-Tsedek was elected chairman.

Those active in economic, social and cultural spheres were: Aharon-Yits'hak Charny (headmaster of the school), Aba Frank, Michael Chizikovsky, Rabbi Yits'hak Bernstein, Kalev Cohen-Tsedek, cantor Aryeh-David Berezovsky (member of the *Mizrahi* center), Eliezer Tatz, David Charny and Hanokh Cohen-Tsedek.

A survey, carried out by the committee at the request of the Ministry for Jewish Affairs revealed that sixty-one men made their living from commerce, twenty-four from crafts and five from agriculture. The artisans included six tailors, three carpenters, three blacksmiths, two oven builders, two glaziers, two shoemakers, two carters, two painters, a hatter and a watchmaker. Eight of them worked in villages. Among the agrarians, two cultivated plantations, two grew grain and one grew vegetables. In commerce thirty-two men were shop owners and twenty-five peddlers. Eight of the latter had horses and the others would walk from village to village with their goods. Fifty-four families had small farms near their homes and fifty-six families each owned a cow.

By 1921 the town had 780 residents, of them 560 (72%) Jews, comprising about 130 families.

Most of the town's trade was in Jewish hands. According to the government survey of 1931, Balbirishok had ten shops, eight of them Jewish-owned. There were also thirteen light industry enterprises, ten of them Jewish: two flour mills, two bakeries, a power station, a metal workshop, a brick factory, a spirit factory, a sawmill, a leather factory, a furniture workshop and a shoe workshop.

In 1937 twenty-one Jewish artisans made their living there: four butchers, three tailors, three dressmakers, three bakers, two shoemakers, two watchmakers, one barber, one painter, one photographer and one leather worker. There were two weekly market days and three annual fairs.

The management of the Folksbank (1934)

The Folksbank played an important role in Jewish economic life of Balbirishok, having 100 members in 1929. Its director was Aharon-Yits'hak Charny and members of the management were David Charny, Michael Chizikovsky, Kalev Cohen-Tsedek and Aba Frank. By 1939 there were twenty-three telephone owners in the town, ten of them Jewish.

Due to the slump in economic activity and competition from Lithuanian consumer cooperatives, the standard of living of many Jews deteriorated and their numbers declined from about 200 families before World War I to about 100 before World War II. Many emigrated to Canada, Mexico, Uruguay, Argentina and South Africa. By 1939, 53 persons had emigrated to *Eretz-Yisrael*. Most remaining youths were unemployed.

Balbirishok Jewish children studied in the Hebrew school and some of its graduates continued their studies in the government gymnasium.

The Hebrew elementary school

Students of the Gymnasium

During the 1920s a repertory group performed in town

The repertory society 1921-1923

(Pictures courtesy of the Archives of The Association of Lithuanian Jews in Israel)

The religious life of Balbirishok Jews centered mainly around the synagogue and the *Beth Midrash*. (For the list of rabbis who served here see **Appendix 2).** All of the customary welfare institutions in Jewish communities, such as *Ezrah* and *Linath Hatsedek*. were also active.

Among personalities born in Balbirishok were Rabbi Gavriel Fainberg (1825-1905) who officiated as rabbi of Memel until his death; doctor Yits'hak Fainberg (1822-?), who published many articles on medicine in German and Russian scientific journals and who established the famous Mapu Library in Kovno; Mordehai Rozenstein, a journalist, who later on lived in London and America and Reuven Hurvitz, a correspondent for *HaMelitz*.

Many Balbirishok Jews were Zionists. There were followers of all Zionist parties and most of these had branches in the town. Many participated in the elections for the Zionist congresses and the table below reveals the division of the votes for each party:

Cong No.	Year	Shek	Total Voter	Labor Party		Rev.	Gen. Zion		Gro	Miz
				Z"S	Z'Z					
14	1925	25	----	----	----	--	----	----	----	----
15	1927	30	26	6	4	10	4	----	----	2
16	1929	83	44	11	1	21	3	----	----	8
17	1931	52	39	14	1	19	2	----	----	3
18	1933	---	94	46	30	---	5	----	4	9
19	1935	---	119	72		---	1	2	25	19

Key: Cong No. = Congress Number, Tot Shek = Total Shkalim, Rev = Revisionists, Gen Zion = General Zionists, Gros = Grosmanists, Miz = Mizrakhi

There were also several Zionist youth organizations: *Gordonia, Maccabi* and *Betar*.

World War II broke out with the German invasion of Poland on September 1st, 1939, and its effects on Lithuanian Jews in general and Balbirishok Jews in particular were felt several months later.

In agreement with the Ribbentrop-Molotov treaty on the division of occupied Poland, the Russians occupied the Suwalk region, but after delineation of exact borders between Russia and Germany, this region fell into German hands. The retreating Russians allowed anyone who wanted to join them to move into their occupied territory, and indeed many young people left the area together with the Russians.

The Germans drove the remaining Jews out of their homes in Suwalk and its vicinity, robbed them of their possessions, and then directed them to the Lithuanian border, where they were left destitute. The Lithuanians refused to allow them to enter Lithuania and the Germans did not allow them to return. Thus they stayed in this swampy area in cold and rain for several weeks, until Jewish youths from the border villages smuggled them into Lithuania by various routes at great personal risk. Altogether about 2,400 refugees passed through the border or infiltrated on their own, and were then dispersed in the Suwalk region including Balbirishok which absorbed fifty refugees.

In June 1940 the Soviet Union annexed Lithuania and it became a Soviet Republic. Under the new rules, the majority of the factories and shops belonging to the Jews of Balbirishok were nationalized and commissars were appointed to manage them. All Zionist parties and youth organizations were disbanded and Hebrew educational institutions were closed.

The German army entered Balbirishok on the first day of its invasion of the Soviet Union, June 22nd, 1941. Immediately on the arrival of the German troops, a group of Lithuanians, local students and workers was organized to attack and mistreat Jews. Thus began the assault on and persecution of the Jews. Initially the Lithuanians detained all Jewish men and concentrated them in the house of the local committee where the guards forced them to do different types of labor both indoors and outdoors, all the while continuing the abuse and physical assault. On August 17th, 1941, all the men (about 100) and six women were led on foot to the town of Pren, where they were all shot, probably on August 22nd, 1941 (4th of Teveth 5701); they were buried in the north of Pren, on the west bank of the Neman River.

Several hundred women and children were kept in Balbirishok for some time and later transferred to Mariampol (Marijampole), where they were murdered together with local Jews and those of the surrounding towns and villages on September 1st, 1941 (9th of Elul 5701).

The site of the mass grave and the monument in Pren (Prienai)

The monument

The mass grave and the monument in Mariampol near the barracks

The inscription on the monument in Yiddish and Lithuanian reads: "Here the blood of about 8000 Jewish children, women, men and of 1000 people of different nationalities, was spilled. The Nazis and their local helpers cruelly murdered them all in September 1941."

A group of survivors from Mariampol and its surroundings near the monument

Sources:

Yad Vashem Archives: M-1/Q-1341/145

YIVO, New York, Collection of Lithuanian Communities, Files 106-110, 1377, 1560

HaMelitz, St.Petersburg, 11.10.1881; 1.11.1881; 2.1.1883

Di Yiddishe Shtime, Kovno, 18.8.1919

Folksblat, Kovno, 3.8.1935; 2.9.1935; 25.9.1935

Appendix 1

List of 18 donors from Balbirishok (From *Hamelitz* 1895-97)

(Jewishgen Organization-Databases, by Jeffrey Maynard)

Surname	Given Name	Comments	Source	Year
BLEICHMAN	Malka		Hamelitz #40	1897
BLEICHMAN	Tuvia	husband of Sima Goldberg wed 4 Shevat	Hamelitz #40	1897
BLOCH	Note		Hamelitz #40	1897
GOLDBERG	Avraham A		Hamelitz #40	1897
GOLDBERG	Eliahu		Hamelitz #40	1897
GOLDBERG	Sender		Hamelitz #40	1897
GOLDBERG		Sima wife of Tuvia Bleichman wed 4 Shevat	Hamelitz #40	1897
GOLDBERG	Tane		Hamelitz #40	1897
GOLDBERG	Yeshiahu	bridegroom	Hamelitz #40	1897
GOLDBERG	Yitzchok		Hamelitz #40	1897
KOTLER	Shmuel		Hamelitz #208	1895
KOTLER	Shmuel		Hamelitz #40	1897
LODNITZKI	Tzvi		Hamelitz #40	1897
NADEL	Shlomo		Hamelitz #40	1897
NAWIAZKI	Moshe Ari		Hamelitz #40	1897
SALANSKI	Zlate		Hamelitz #40	1897
WILNER	Mordechai		Hamelitz #40	1897
WOZAWINSKI	Menachem		Hamelitz #40	1897

Appendix 2   An incomplete list of Rabbis who officiated in Balbirishok

R' Ozer. died 1819

Tsevi-Hirsh, son of Avraham Kahana.

Shelomoh-Zalman Gordon, until 1858 (later in Mariampol), died 1872.

Efraim, son of Avraham Gabai.

Hayim-Yirmiyahu, son of Avraham Flensberg (1842-1914), in Balbirishok in 1873.

Shemuel-Meir, son of Yits'hak Ash, until 1884.

Eliezer-Yits'hak Algazi.

Barukh Grosbard.

Eliyahu Fink.

Hayim HaLevi Lev, the last rabbi, murdered in the Holocaust

Darbėnai (Dorbyan)

Darbenai (Dorbyan in Yiddish) is situated in northwest Lithuania, in the Zhamut (Zemaitija) region, 13 km. (8 miles) north of the administrative district center of Kretinga and 8 km. (5 miles) from the Baltic Sea. It is surrounded on the east, south and north by forests. The Darba stream flows through the town.

A village named Darbenai was mentioned in documents as early as 1591. The village grew gradually and by 1701 it had become a town, and permission was granted to hold a weekly market and an annual fair.

During the Russian rule (1795 to 1915) Dorbyan was first included in the Vilna Province (*Gubernia*) and later, after 1843, it fell within the limits of the Kovno *Gubernia*. In the nineteenth century the noble Tishkevitz family owned the town and the large estate next to it. During this period and also during that of independent Lithuania (1918 to 1940), the town was considered to be a county administrative center.

During World War I (1915-1918) Dorbyan was occupied by the Germans. In June 1941, at the outbreak of war between Germany and the Soviet Union, the town was badly damaged.

The Jewish Settlement until after World War I

When the Jews were evicted from the village of Laukzeme by order of the nobility in the nineteenth century they settled in nearby Dorbyan. Here they made their living mainly by trading with the surrounding villages. They bought and sold fish, flax, rags etc. Most of the families had a barn for livestock and a house with a garden.

In October 1882, a fire broke out in the town, resulting in forty buildings being burnt down. Of these thirty were Jewish-owned shops. Thirty Christian houses remained. The situation of the homeless victims was critical with winter approaching. The October 21st, 1882 issue of *HaMelitz* carried a request for help for the victims of the fire. Contributors were asked to send their donations to the address of Rabbi Gershon Robinson in Plungyan (Plunge) because there was no post office in Dorbyan. In the fire of 1909, the center of the town, the *Beth Midrash* and the synagogue were completely destroyed and were never restored. Many Dorbyan Jews emigrated to Canada, South Africa, America and *Eretz-Yisrael*.

In 1854 Eliezer-Dov son of David, of Dorbyan, emigrated to *Eretz-Yisrael*. He died in 1896 and his tombstone can be found in the old Jerusalem cemetery.

According to the Russian census of 1897 there were 2,059 residents in Dorbyan 1,129 (55%) of them were Jews.

The list of contributors for the year 1909 contains the names of many Dorbyan Jews who donated money to the settlements of *Eretz-Yisrael*. The fund-raiser was Yisrael-Leib Cohen.

A Street in Dorbyan

From the beginning of the twentieth century, the Zionist Movement and the *Agudath Yisrael* were almost equally strong in Dorbyan.

The list of 30 contributors from Dorbyan who worked to help victims of the Persian famine in 1872 was published in *HaMagid* #10 (1872) (see **Appendix 1**).

The list of contributors to the *Agudah* Fund of 1913 contains the names of 26 Dorbyan Jews (see **Appendix 2**).

Between the years 1835 to 1911 there were 83 subscribers to rabbinic literature from the town of Dorbyan.

During Independent Lithuania (1918-1940)

Following the law of Autonomy for Minorities issued by the new Lithuanian government, the minister of Jewish affairs, Dr. Menachem (Max) Soloveitshik, ordered elections for community committees *(Va'adei Kehilah)* to be held in the summer of 1919. On July 30th, 1919 elections for the community committee of Dorbyan took place and sixteen members were elected. Of 400 eligible persons, only 198 voted. Most of the elected were Zionists and orthodox Jews. At the elections of 1921, nine members were elected to the committee.

Another street in Dorbyan

According to the first census conducted by the Government in 1923, there were 1,018 residents in Dorbyan, of whom 601 (59%) were Jews.

The committee collected taxes as required by law and was in charge of all aspects of community life. It operated until the end of 1925 at which time autonomy was annulled.

During this period Dorbyan Jews made their living in commerce and crafts. Most of them had small gardens at home. A great part of their economic activity centered around the weekly markets and the annual fairs.

According to the 1931 government survey of stores, there were 25 shops in Dorbyan, all owned by Jews:

Type of shop	Owned by Jews
Grocery and farm produce	10
Grains and Flax	1
Butcher and Cattle Trade	4
Textile Products and Furs	4
Leather and Shoes	3
Hardware	1
Heating Materials	2

A survey of factories and workshops showed there were two sawmills, a flourmill, a bakery, a metal workshop, a wool-combing workshop and a factory making soft drinks, all Jewish owned.

In 1937, eighteen Jewish tradesmen worked in town: five butchers, two knitters, two boot makers, two photographers, one tailor, one milliner, one locksmith, one barber, one tinsmith and two others.

The local Folksbank was closed in 1927. It had only 53 members.

In 1939, there were twelve telephones in town, three of them owned by Jews.

After the annexation of the Memel region to Germany in March 1939, several Jewish refugee families from there were absorbed into the Dorbyan community.

The Jewish children in town acquired their elementary education in two *Hadarim*, the *Talmud-Torah* and the Hebrew school of the *Tarbuth* network. These institutions accommodated about 150 children in all. There were two libraries, one for Hebrew books and one for Yiddish books. In 1925 the Zionist Socialist party organized Hebrew lessons.

There was also a repertory group in town.

Among Dorbyan Jews there were many Zionists. The results of the elections for the Zionist Congresses are given in the table below:

Cong No.	Year	Total Shek	Total Votes	Labor Party Z"S	Z"Z	Rev	Gen Zion A	B	Gros	Miz
14	1925	60	----	----	----	--	----	----	----	----
15	1927	32	29	7	---	----	12	----	----	10
16	1929	71	24	3	---	---	8	----	----	13
17	1931	53	42	5	---	9	17	----	----	11
18	1933	---	57	18		1	12	----	---	26
19	1935	---	197	60		---	1	23	---	133

Key: Cong No. = Congress Number, Total Shek = Total Shekalim, Rev = Revisionists, Gen Zion = General Zionists, Gros = Grosmanists, Miz = Mizrahi

Zionist youth organizations of Dorbyan included *Ivrith uTekhiyah* (established in 1920), *HaShomer Hatsair - Netsakh* (from 1930) and other organizations. At the end of 1933 a branch of *HeKhalutz* was established with about forty members. In 1934 an urban training kibbutz of the *HeKhalutz* movement was developed. Sports activities took place at the local Maccabi branch.

Religious life concentrated around the *Beth Midrash* and the *Kloiz*. A *Gemara* (Talmud) Society was active in the *Beth Midrash* while the religious youth were organized in the *Tifereth Bahurim* branch.

Among the Rabbis who officiated in Dorbyan, Aryeh-Leib Shalmen should be noted. He was the rabbi for 40 years and he served simultaneously the three communities of Kretinga, Palanga and Darbenai. Eliyahu Margalioth (1816-1874) served as a rabbi until 1872. Later he was replaced by Gabai of *Yeshivah* Vilna-Zhamut in Jerusalem. He was succeeded by Josef son of Avraham Alexander and then by Yisrael-Iser Levin and Yits'hak Kopelovitz, who served during the period of about 1868-1888. The last rabbi of Dorbyan was Yisrael-Iser son of Shelomoh HaLevi Vaisbord. Most of the rabbis published books or brochures on religious subjects.

HeHalutz HaMizrah **training** *Kibutz*

(Picture supplied from the archives of The Association of the Lithuanian Jews in Israel)

מפ חג הזובל למאה שנה, והסיום הגדול על חש"ם יב כסלו
חברה גמרא דורבין

Members of the *Gemara* Society – 1929

Men Walking to the Synagogue

Welfare institutions serving the town were *Gemiluth-Hesed* and *Linath Hatsedek.*

Dorbyan is the birthplace of Zionist leader David Wolfson (1858-1914). He became the founder of *Otsar Hityashvuth Hayehudim* (The Jewish Colonial Trust Ltd.) and he escorted Theodore Herzl on his trip to the Turkish sultan and to *Eretz-Yisrael*. After Herzl died Wolfson was elected president of the World Zionist Organization. In 1954 Wolfson's coffin was brought to Israel and buried near Herzl's tomb in Jerusalem.

David Wolfson

Other personalities with known roots in Dorbyan were Yehoshua Bloch (1890-1957), who worked as a librarian of the Yiddish division at the New York municipal library and contributed articles to Hebrew, Yiddish and English periodicals; Nathan Slavit who wrote articles for the publication *HaTsefirah* and Gershon Arenzon who wrote for the publication *HaMagid.*

During World War II and Afterwards

In June 1940, Lithuania was annexed to the Soviet Union and became a Soviet Republic. Following new rules, light industry enterprises owned by Jews were nationalized. A number of Jewish shops were nationalized and commissars were appointed to manage them. The supply of goods decreased and, as a result, prices soared. The middle class, mostly Jewish, bore most of the brunt and the standard of living dropped gradually. All the Zionist parties and youth organizations were disbanded and the Hebrew school was closed.

That year there were about 2,200 residents in town; 800 of them were Jews. On June 22nd, 1941, the first day of the war between Germany and the Soviet Union, the German army entered Dorbyan and did not encounter any resistance. Nevertheless, heavy shelling followed and several houses were destroyed and a few people killed. The local Jews, who escaped the shelling, returned home. On their way back they were accosted by Lithuanians, who beat them. Back in town they were forced to sweep the streets, to weed the grass and clean bathrooms with their bare hands. The Germans entered Jewish homes and looted anything they pleased. Jews were not allowed to lock their homes and "night visits" became a frequent occurrence.

On Saturday, June 28th, a fire broke out on the market-square. Immediately, rumors were spread that the Jews started the fire. All Dorbyan Jews were ordered to gather together at the market square, men and women apart. Germans and Lithuanians raided the house of Rabbi Iser Vaisbord, who was in the market-square. They humiliated him, then shaved off half of his beard together with the skin of his face and beat him to death. A few Jews were then ordered to dig a pit and to bury the rabbi and other Jews who were shot for not coming to the square fast enough. All their valuables were looted. Later the Jews were forced to run from Dorbyan to Kretinga, a distance of 13 km. (8 miles). The old people were seated in carts. On the way the Germans and Lithuanians released the horses pulling the carts and harnessed the men to replace them. The Lithuanian guards whipped them incessantly. On arrival in Kretinga they were ordered to return to Dorbyan.

On Sunday morning, June 29th, 1941 (4th of Tamuz 5701) all the men aged sixteen years and over were separated from the women and led to the nearby flourmill, where they were forced to dig a pit. Here, they were shot and buried; some were still alive.

The Jewish women were ushered to the *Beth Midrash*. They were not given any food or water. The crowding was unbearable. The Lithuanian guards would force their way inside during the night and rape the women. After several days the older women and mothers with many children were taken out and murdered. After a month the remaining women and children were killed too. A small group of women was allowed to live; some of them worked for Lithuanian peasants. These murders were carried out on August 15th and 16th, 1941 (22nd and 23rd of Av 5701).

The Lithuanian guards used axes, iron bars, rods and similar weapons. The last group of Jewish women was murdered on *Rosh HaShanah* 5702. In this manner, the life of a Jewish community that had existed for generations ended forever.

Several young Jewish women were rescued by Lithuanians, who hid them, nourished them during all the years of the war, thereby fulfilling their humanitarian obligations.

According to Soviet sources four mass graves were found in the surrounding areas of Darbenai:

1. 100 meters (330 feet) from town on the left side of the road to Lazdininkai; the bodies of 144 men; date of massacre June 29th, 1941.

2. Two graves in the forest on the Balto Kalno (White Mountain).

    2.1   1 km. (0.6 miles) from Darbenai on the right side of the road to Vaineikiai, about 100 meters (110 yards) from the road; 300 Jewish women and children; date - end of July 1941.

    2.2   2.5 km. (1.5 miles) from the town in the direction of the village Kasuciai, about 500 meters (550 yards) off the road; about 100 Jewish men and women; date - beginning of September 1941.

3. Near village Dimitravas 7.5 km. (4.7 miles) from Kretinga, where the concentration camp for prisoners was located; 1,770 Jews, murdered between the second half of 1941 and 1944.

4. Near the Alka Mountain, at the edge of the forest, about 1 km. northwest of Dimitravas; 510 Jewish women and children; dates August 15th and 16th, 1941

It is believed that only Jews are buried in the sites 1, 2 and 4.

The mass grave monument near Dorbyan (Site 1)

The inscription: "All the people died not having understood that innocence was their fault." (by Justinas Marcinkevicius)

The monument on the mass grave at Balto Kalno forest (Site 2.1)

The mass grave monument at the Balto Kalno forest (Sites 2.2 and 4)

Sources:

Yad Vashem Archives, 0-33/979

Unzer Veg (Yiddish), Kovno. 9.11.1925

Dos Vort (Yiddish). Kovno, 24.10.1935

Di Yiddishe Shtime (Yiddish), Kovno, 18.8.1919

Di Tsait (Yiddish), Kovno, 4.12.1933

HaMelitz (Hebrew), St.Petersburg, 21.11.1882; 18.2.1889

Appendix 1

A list of 36 contributors from Dorbyan for the victims of the Persian famine in 1872. It was published in *HaMagid* #10 in 1872. Source: Jewishgen. Org. Databases compiled by Jeffery Maynard

Surname	Given	Comment	Surname	Given
ALTER	Chaim		WOLFZOHN	Yeshiyahu
ALTSHIL	Gershon		WOLFZOHN	Yitzchok
ASS	Eliezer Gordon			Eizik
DONMANN	Dovid		YAKOBZOHN	EizikPrikastzikes
EINBINDER	Tzvi		YAKOBZOHN	Eizik
KOHN	Feivish		YAKOBZOHN	Moshe
KOHN	Meir		YAKOBZOHN	Yakov ben
LESKEN	Boruch			Moshe
LEWIA	Chaim		ZEWIN	Avraham
NACHMAN	Yehuda		ZIMAN	Chaim
ORDONG	Dov		ZIMAN	Henich
ORDONG	Yakov		ZIMAN	Meir
ORDONG	Yudel		ZIMAN	MeirPrikastzikes
PELSHEV	Leib		ZIMAN	Yakov
PINTER	Mendil	wife	ZIMAN	Yosef
SEGAL	Bentzion			Eliezer ben
SHALMAN	Ari Leib	Rabbi Gaon		Avraham
TEITZ	Avraham			Leib Heshil
				Mendil Shneur
				Mordechai
				Sandler
				Tzvi Yakov

Appendix 2   List of contributors to the *Agudah* Fund in 1913

Rabbi Alexander Josef

Berzan Yehoshua-Nakhman

Brutskus Leib

Davidzon H.A.

Davidzon Hayim-Aharon

Ernshtein Ya'akov-Ze'ev

Etis Ze'ev

Fraintil Shemuel

Gilis Eliezer

Gershon Ber

Golos Yehudah

Hailperin Barukh

Kaidon Manakhem

Kil Ber

Klompus Tsevi

Leibovitz Josef-Yits'hak

Levin Shemuel-Iser

Levi Shelomoh-Mosheh

Pekil Avraham-Yits'hak

Ruf Zalman

Sher Eliezer

Shohet

Shevat David

Shpitz Ben-Zion

Taitz Nahum-Mosheh

Tsuker Bunem

Ya'akov Yakov

Gruzdžiai (Gruzd)

Gruzdziai (Gruzd in Yiddish) is located in the Zamut (Zemaitija) region in northwestern Lithuania, about 22 km. (nearly 14 miles) northwest of Siauliai (Shavl) which was the district administrative center. The nearby estate and the land in the vicinity were owned by a noble family named Zubov. From 1858 until the World War I the Narishkin family had ownership. During this period, the town was part of the Kovno Province (*Gubernia*) and was the county's administrative center. It also had this status in independent Lithuania.

Gruzdziai - General View

The Jewish community in Gruzd was established at the end of the eighteenth century, and by the end of the nineteenth century the Jews of Gruzd comprised almost half the town's population. In 1897, there were 1,160 residents in town, 482 (41%) Jews comprising about 120 families.

The majority of the Jewish people were involved in small scale trading. Several families made their living through commercial dealings with the Narishkin estate and, in particular, with the adjoining cattle ranch.

In 1887, the *Beth Midrash*, the only prayer house in town, and 22 Jewish homes burned down. The local rabbi and four honored men of the community appealed to Jewish communities for help through the Hebrew newspaper *HaMelitz*.

The *Beth Midrash* was rebuilt, but the poor economic situation in town forced many families to emigrate abroad, in particular to South Africa, America and Mexico. A few families settled in *Eretz-Yisrael*.

The *Aron Kodesh*

Several of the Jews of Gruzd were activists for the settlements of *Eretz-Yisrael*. Some are mentioned in the 1886 list of donors: "The volunteers for our brothers, the colonists in the Holy Land." M. Shragai was the principal fundraiser. In another list published in 1914, additional names, headed by Rabbi Y. A. Fridman, are chronicled. During this time, a society named *Havatseleth HaSharon* was active in town.

Among the rabbis who officiated in Gruzd were:

Mosheh Shapira for twenty-four years. He died in 1885. Yits'hak-Aizik, son of Josef Fridman (from 1905), was one of the leaders of the *Mizrahi* party in Lithuania and published many books.

Rabbi Zisl Levin.

Under the law of autonomies for minorities issued by the new Lithuanian government, the Minister for Jewish affairs, Dr. Menachem (Max) Soloveitshik, ordered elections to *Va'adei Kehilah* (Community Committees) to be held in the summer of 1919. In Gruzd, a *Va'ad Kehilah* of five members was elected, one a General Zionist, two from the *Tseirei-Zion* party and two non-party men. This committee acted for several years and was in charge of all aspects of community life in the town.

A Street in Gruzd

According to the first government census of 1923, there were 1,354 residents in town of whom 142 (10%) were Jews. During this period, numbers of Jews left Gruzd and emigrated abroad.

The Jews who remained barely made a living. They were involved in small scale trading, mainly from crafts and agriculture at the weekly market, which took place on Wednesdays. According to a government survey of shops in 1931, Gruzd had eleven Jewish shops. There were three grain merchants, one horse merchant, one hardware shop, one grocery store, four textile shops and one sewing machine shop. In 1937, there were seven Jewish artisans in town: two tailors; two barbers; one photographer, one potter and one butcher.

Students and Teachers of the Jewish School

The Jewish cemetery in Gruzd - in the left corner, note the head of the *Hevrah Kadisha*

The Jewish Folksbank played an important role in the town's economic life. In 1920 it had twenty-six members.

There was a Jewish school in Gruzd as well as several welfare societies, namely *Gemiluth Hesed* and *Linath HaTsedek*.

In 1939, of 1,300 residents in Gruzd, 75 (27 families) were Jews.

With the annexation of Lithuania to the Soviet Union in the summer of 1940, the social and economic life of the Jews of Gruzd changed.

On June 29th, 1941, only a week after the German invasion of the Soviet Union, many Jews were detained by local Lithuanian nationalists and imprisoned in the *Beth Midrash*. By order of the Germans who had arrived in town, they were freed the same day. As a result, the Lithuanians were angry and protested vehemently.

On August 5th, 1941 (12th of Av, 5701) approximately fifty people were imprisoned in the *Beth Midrash*. They were led to the Jewish cemetery the next day, where they were shot. The Jewish cemetery was located 1 km. (0.6 miles) south of the town center. The bodies were thrown into a pit that had been prepared beforehand near the eastern gate of the cemetery. The Germans watched and took photographs as the Lithuanians brutally murdered the Jews. Within a month, the remaining Jews of Gruzd were transferred to the town of Zhager (Zagare) where they too were murdered and buried together with other Jews who had been concentrated there. This atrocity took place on *Yom Kippur* 5702.

Pinkhas Ulman was the only Gruzd Jew who survived. A Lithuanian peasant, Augustinas Mazeikas and his family hid him in a nearby village. Pinkhas Ulman later emigrated to Israel.

The mass grave near the Jewish cemetery of Gruzd

The monument at the murder site in Zagare
(Picture taken and supplied by Elkan Gamzu, July 2005)

Sources:

HaMelitz, St. Petersburg - 26.4.1887

Masines Zudynes Lietuvoje (Mass Murder in Lithuania), Vol. 2, page 403

Kelmė (Kelm)

Kelme (Kelm in Yiddish) is situated in the center of Lithuania, on the west bank of the Krazante River, about 23 km. (17 miles) northwest of the district administrative center, Raseiniai. The village began to develop in the fifteenth century alongside an estate of Lithuanian princes. In 1591 this estate along with the nearby village was acquired by a Polish noble family named Gruzhevsky.

After the third division of Poland in 1795 by the three superpowers of that time, Russia, Prussia and Austria, this part of Lithuania including Kelm was handed over to Russia. During the Russian rule (1795-1915) Kelm was first included in the Vilna Province (*Gubernia*) and later in the Kovno *Gubernia*. During the sixteenth and eighteenth centuries, large fires damaged the town. A cholera epidemic ravaged Kelm in 1848, claiming many victims.

The construction of the Siauliai-Tilzit road traversing Kelm in the years 1836-1858 made it an important trade center, famous for its fairs, and in particular for its horse trade. At the end of the nineteenth century it already had several light industry enterprises. During the period of independent Lithuania (1918-1940) Kelm was a county administrative center.

Jewish settlement until after World War I

The Jewish community in Kelm was probably established in the sixteenth century. During the period of *Va'ad Medinath Lita* (1623-1764) the Kelm community was part of the Keidan district (*Galil*).

A street in Kelm, 1916

(*Picture courtesy of the Archives of the Association of Lithuanian Jews in Israel*)

1019 Jews lived in Kelm in 1764, 519 men and 500 women. In 1784 there were 839 Jews, but by 1816 this number had dropped to only 248, 101 men and 147 women. In 1880 the total population numbered 1,800 residents, of whom 1,600 were Jews (89%).

According to the all-Russian census of 1897, there were 3,914 residents in Kelm, 2,710 (69%) of them being Jews.

The Jews were the majority in this town up to the end of the nineteenth century, most of them making their living from commerce and crafts, and their economic situation was sound. They traded in grains, timber, leather, textile, seeds and pig bristles and, to a great extent, were also involved in the processing of skins and bristles. The great weekly market days and the annual fairs supplied a fair livelihood to the Jewish shop owners, whose businesses were concentrated around the Market Square. The skin craft workshops employed five to eight workers and the bristle processing workshops 50 and sometimes more workers. In 1887 there were 28 Jewish grain traders and 85 Jewish shop owners in town.

Another street in Kelm

(Picture courtesy of the Archives of the Association of Lithuanian Jews in Israel)

The grocery wholesalers were Zalman Ziv and Refael Grinberg, the textile wholesaler from 1886, Avraham-Mosheh Hurvitz.

There was a soap factory owned by Girshovitz. M. Lifshitz was the pharmacist and a station for post horses was run by B. Leizer. During the years 1909-1914 the printing press of M. Das (Dath) served the town.

There were Jewish tailors, shoemakers, blacksmiths and builders who supplied both peasants and the estate owners. During these years there was a

Jewish commercial bank and a smaller bank that provided loans to artisans at low interest rates. In the years prior to World War I, the economic situation of most of Kelm Jews was stable, but they suffered from the restrictive edicts and intrigues of Czarist rulers. This resulted in many of Kelm's Jews emigrating to America and South Africa.

Early in the 1880s hoodlums planned a pogrom against Kelm Jews. The Bishop of Zamut (Zemaitija), M. K. Beresnevicius made great efforts to prevent Lithuanians of his domain taking part in this atrocity.

Kelm was not damaged during World War I and its Jews were not exiled to Russia as had occurred in so many other Lithuanian towns. During the German occupation the town housed thousands of Russian prisoners of war as well as German field hospitals and big provision storehouses. The nearby town of Shavl (Siauliai) had burned down almost completely and thus Kelm became the commercial center of the surroundings.

Jewish children of elementary school age studied at the *Talmud Torah* and youngsters from Kelm at the Great Yeshivah, while many students came from far and near because of Kelm's unique moral atmosphere and because it had become a seat of learning. Many students were without means and the community looked after their needs.

The Great Talmud Torah, a *Yeshivah* of the *Musar* (Ethics) trend, was founded in the second half of the nineteenth century by a pupil of Rabbi Yisrael Salanter, Simhah-Zisl Ziv-Broida. This was an upper *Beth Midrash* for selected pupils, aiming for perfection in their knowledge of the *Torah*, in morals and in behavior. The task of this *Yeshivah* was not to produce rabbis, but rather to produce regular citizens who would achieve high personal standards and serve as role models. This institution and its activities became famous throughout the entire Jewish world, as a result of which the Kelm community too became well known.

Zionist ideas had already infiltrated Kelm during the second half of the nineteenth century, even before Jews emigrated to *Eretz-Yisrael* in order to be buried in Jerusalem. There are at least seven tombstones of Kelm Jews in the old cemetery in Jerusalem:

> Hode daughter of Yehiel, died 1863
>
> Hilel, died 1826
>
> Shemuel Beharav son of Ya'akov, died 1827
>
> Bath-Sheva daughter of Hilel, died 1874
>
> Leah daughter of Eliyah, died 1979
>
> Yits'hak son of Yehudah
>
> Barukh son of Ya'akov Broide, a teacher in several *Yeshivoth* died 1896

In a list of donors for the settlement of *Eretz-Yisrael* from 1896, the names of eight Kelm Jews are mentioned (see **Appendix 1**). The local rabbi, Eliezer Gordon, who served between the years 1874-1884, was among those who approved (*Haskamah*) the book <u>Josef Khen</u> written by Nathan Fridland which discussed the issue of settlement of *Eretz-Yisrael*.

A delegate from Kelm participated at the conference of the Russian Zionists of the Vilna and Kovno *Gubernias* in Vilna in 1899. Another Kelm delegate participated at the conference of the Zionist societies of the Kovno and Suwalk Provinces (*Gubernias*) in 1909.

The Correspondence Center of the Zionist societies, in Kishinev at this time, had postal contact with the society in Kelm, one of thirteen in the Kovno *Gubernia*. The *Talmud* (*Shas*) society *Sha'arei Zion* accepted a custom whereby each member had to purchase the Zionist *Shekel*. At the conclusion of each Sabbath its members would gather to read the *Galil Keidan* circular and news of happenings in the Zionist movement.

In a list of donors for settlement of *Eretz-Yisrael* (1896), eight Kelm Jewish donors were mentioned (**Appendix 1**); in 1909 there were seventy. During that year the *Kadimah* society planted trees in the Herzl grove in the Yizrael Valley in memory of its friends Josef-Reuven Shnitz and Zelig Cohen.

124 names of Kelm donors appeared (See **Appendix 3**) in the Hebrew newspaper *HaMelitz* of the years 1894-1902 while in another Hebrew newspaper *HaMagid* #299 of 1872 there is a list of 101 Kelm Jews who donated money to the victims of the Persian famine (see **Appendix 4**).

The first synagogue in Kelm was built in the middle of the eighteenth century with the help of the estate owner Gruzhevsky. He vowed that if Jewish prayers would help and a son would be born to him after the five daughters he already had, he would relieve them of taxes for three years and also build a synagogue. This wooden structure was one of the biggest and most beautiful synagogues in the entire area. One hundred and twenty years later, his great grandson fortified its walls that were beginning to warp. In 1775 Kelm's wealthy Jews donated a new *Aron Kodesh* (Holy Ark), a work of art carved from white timber, created by an artist named Ya'akov, the son of Shelomoh Marsin, who worked on it for two years. In 1820 a candelabrum with 49 columns, planned and produced in Vilna by the same Ya'akov son of Shelomoh, was installed in the synagogue. All Kelm's Jews helped finance this candelabrum, donations being collected in charity boxes in every home.

In addition to the synagogue three *Batei Midrash* were built: "the Great," "the Small" and a *Kloiz*, and later a house for *Gemiluth Hesed*. A large fire, which ravaged three quarters of the Jewish homes in the 1880s, did not affect the prayer houses. These buildings, including the house of the rabbi, were concentrated in the *Shulhoif* (the yard of the Shul), the center of social life in town. After prayers these buildings served as a place for studying the Torah according to the capability of each Jew.

The Synagogue in Kelm

The Bima in the Kelm Synagogue

Left: Chandelier   Right: Aron HaKodesh (Holy Ark)

Above four images by Balys Buracas (1897-1972), were provided courtesy of A. Buracas. For higher resolution images contact anbura@lrs.lt

Among others there were the *Talmud* society and the societies for studying *Hayei Adam, Mishnah Ein Ya'akov, Midrash, Menorath HaMaor* and others.

The *Shulhoif* also served as a place for weddings. When a wedding took place in town most of the Jewish population participated.

Between the years 1839 and 1914 there were 109 subscribers of rabbinic literature in Kelm.

These were the rabbis who officiated in Kelm in the nineteenth and twentieth centuries:

> Eliezer Gutman, the first Rabbi of the community, from 1810
>
> Rabbi Yehezkel (died in 1855)

Elyakum-Getsl haLevi Hurvitz, known by his nickname *Shulhan Arukh* (died in 1873)

Eliezer Gordon

Tsevi-Ya'akov Oppenheim, who was rabbi in Kelm for 43 years till his death (1884-1926)

Kalman son of Yehezkel Beinushevitz (1893-1941), rabbi in Kelm from 1926, murdered by the Lithuanians in 1941.

The welfare institutions included *Malbish Arumim*, *Linath HaTsedek*, *Gemiluth Hesed* and others, with many women helpers.

In a list of donors for the Agudah Fund, *Agudath Yisrael*, in 1913 the names of sixteen Kelm Jews are mentioned (see **Appendix 2).**

Kelm during the period of Independent Lithuania (1918-1940)

Society and Economy

Following the law of autonomies for minorities issued by the new Lithuanian government, the minister for Jewish affairs Dr. Menachem (Max) Soloveitshik, ordered elections for community committees *Va'adei Kehilah* to be held in the summer of 1919. In Kelm the elections took place in autumn 1919, and almost 99% of the accredited voters participated. Most of the votes were given to candidates of *Agudath Yisrael* and *Tseirei Agudath Yisrael*, who were in no hurry to activate the committee. This was because the rabbis had reservations about its establishment, which they believed to be competing with their influence. Due to disagreements within the committee, the minority representatives resigned and only the orthodox remained.

The market place

(Pictures courtesy of the Archives of the Association of Lithuanian Jews in Israel)

The elections in 1921 resulted in fifteen members being elected to the committee: four *Akhduth* (*Agudath Yisrael*), three General Zionists, two *Tseirei Zion*, two Artisans, one worker, one non-party man, two not defined. The committee was active until the end of 1925 when the autonomy was annulled. During these years, it was involved in all aspects of Jewish community life, but only at the discretion of its members. For example, the Hebrew school did not receive financial help from the committee because boys and girls studied together.

According to the first census taken by the Government, Kelm had 2,890 residents in 1923 with a majority of 1,599 Jews (55%). Several of them built new houses, after being helped by relatives from abroad.

Relations with their Lithuanian neighbors were good and generally anti-Semitism was not felt except for a few isolated incidents. For example, in the spring of 1923 anti-Semitic proclamations were widely distributed, and in 1934 there was an attempt to create a blood libel. In the winter of 1937 Lithuanian hoodlums attacked a few Jews, causing protests resulting in a court case which continued for many years. The Jewish population also believed that due to its Jewish majority, Kelm did not obtain the status of a town, but only that of a county administrative center.

During this period Kelm Jews made their living from commerce, crafts, light industry and a few from agriculture. According to a survey performed by the government in 1931 Kelm had 55 shops, 51 (93%) Jewish owned. The distribution according to type of business is given in the table below:

Type of the business	Total	Owned by Jews
Grocery stores	4	4
Grain and flax	16	16
Butcher's shops and Cattle Trade	8	7
Restaurants and Taverns	7	6
Food Products	2	2
Beverages	2	2
Textile Products and Furs	4	4
Leather and Shoes	3	3
Haberdashery and house utensils	2	2
Medicine and Cosmetics	3	2
Watches, Jewels and Optics	1	1
Hardware Products	2	2
Bicycles and electrical equipment	1	0

According to the same survey there were 33 factories, 28 (85%) of them Jewish owned according to the division in the table below:

Type of Factory	Total	Jewish owned
Power Plants	2	2
Concrete products	1	0
Textile: Wool, Flax, Knitting	4	3
Sawmills and Furniture	1	1
Flour mills, Bakeries	12	10
Dresses, Footwear	4	4
Leather Industry: Production, Cobbling	5	5
Others	4	3

In 1937 there were 63 Jewish artisans: eighteen tailors, thirteen butchers, nine shoemakers, seven bakers, three barbers, two hatters, two watchmakers, two stitchers, one oven builder, one carpenter, one printer, one tinsmith, one painter and two others. In 1925 there was a Jewish doctor and a Jewish dentist (although before World War II there had been four Jewish doctors), two Jewish lawyers as well as a Jewish judge (Heiman).

There were Jewish farmers in Kelm and its vicinity (the families Luntz, Milner, Zax, Asher, Holozin, Berman, Kushelevsky, Mendelovitz, Gelman, Meirovitz). Another source of income was the *Yeshivoth*. Their students came from all over Lithuania and even from abroad, so that they needed housing and food, which the local Jewish population supplied.

The Jewish Folksbank comprised 82 members in 1920, and by 1927 the membership had risen to 197. It played an important role in the economic life of Kelm's Jews. There was also the *Gemiluth Hesed* society, established by a donation of $1,000 from former Kelm Jews in Chicago. The Broide family who acted within the framework of the Folksbank donated much help to the needy. In 1939 a *Gemiluth Hesed* society for artisans was established with the help of funds donated by former Kelm citizens living in America.

Over the years, efforts by the Lithuanian merchants association (*Verslas*) to organize a boycott of Jewish businesses became more effective. They established their own bank and cooperatives for marketing goods, and as a result the income of Jewish shop owners decreased. Jewish artisans also suffered from heavy competition and their living standard dropped too. Since there was no alternative, the Jews developed new sources of income, such as leasing vegetable and fruit gardens and establishing transportation companies for people and goods. They owned twenty buses and trucks, and all transportation to and from Kelm was in their hands. This provided Jewish porters and coachmen with a living. But previously felt economic security had disappeared and concern for the future prevailed.

Kelm had seventy telephone owners in 1939, of whom 28 were Jews.

Education and Culture

The Kelm community was one of the first to establish a Hebrew elementary school. This school was established at the initiative of *Tseirei Zion* who later joined the *Tarbuth* network. Some time later the school, guided by teacher Akiva Vankhotsker (Yishai), became a Hebrew gymnasium consisting of two preparatory and five other classes. Some of its graduates continued their studies in the Hebrew high schools in Rassein (Raseiniai) and Shavl (Siauliai), but not many studied at the local Lithuanian high school. When the number of Jewish pupils in this school increased, the local rabbi K. Beinushevitz was appointed a teacher of the Jewish faith. Among the graduates of the Lithuanian high school in 1941, there were three Jews.

There was also a Hebrew kindergarten and a school for boys of the *Yavneh* network, with four classes and about 100 pupils. The graduates of this school also received governmental graduation certificates, which enabled them to be accepted in every high school. The headmaster of the *Yavneh* School was Lis who was succeeded by Likhtenshtein. Religious girls studied in the *Shulamith* School of the *Yavneh* network, which closed at the beginning of the 1930s. The Hebrew gymnasium was located in the same building. The *Tarbuth* and *Yavneh* schools officially had one headmaster. For many years the well-known educator Akiva Vankhotsker held this position, and he eventually became one of the founders of *Ben-Shemen*, a youth village in *Eretz-Yisrael*. In the mid-1930s a modern building was erected for the *Tarbuth* School, which was helped financially by the county committee. Most of the young people spoke Hebrew.

Also during this period there was a *Talmud Torah Gadol* (Great Talmud Torah) directed by Daniel Movshovitz and the *Or Torah Yeshivah* (the Small *Yeshivah*) under the direction of Shelomoh Pyanka. Due to these *Yeshivoth* the town of Kelm became famous in the entire Jewish world as a center of Torah instruction and pupils from the entire Diaspora studied there. The local religious youth organization *Tifereh Bahurim* with dozens of members was quite active, having its own club where they would gather for discussions and for lectures on Jewish issues.

Kelm had a Jewish library of Yiddish and Hebrew books. There was also a repertory group that performed shows for the purpose of raising money for various charities, such as buying heating fuel for the poor.

The Hebrew pro-gymnasium in 1921

***Tifereth Bahurim* branch in Kelm in 1933**

*(This and the next picture are courtesy of the Archives of the
Association of the Lithuanian Jews in Israel)*

Many of Kelm's Jews belonged to the Zionist camp and donated money to
the national funds. All Zionist parties had branches in town. The results of
the elections for the Zionist Congresses are given in the table below:

Cong No.	Year	Tot Shek	Total Votes	Labor Party Z"S	Z"Z	Rev	Gen Zion A	B	Gros	Miz
14	1925	16	----	----	----	--	----	----	----	----
15	1927	80	42	17	11	2	10	---	---	2
16	1929	247	103	40	12	22	19	----	----	10
17	1931	203	177	74	6	73	12	----	----	11
18	1933	----	442	215		162	13	---	---	52
19	1935	550	506	234		--	32	82	5	153

Key: Cong No. = Congress Number, Tot Shek = Total Shekalim,   Rev = Revisionists,
Gen Zion = General Zionists, Gros = Grosmanists, Miz =Mizrahi

Procession of Jewish children in Kelm

Among the active Zionist youth organizations were the *HaShomer-HaTsair*; *HeHalutz*; *HeHalutz HaMizrahi*; *Hehalutz Haklal Zioni*; *Betar* and other movements. There was also the Sirkin Society (the Z. S. party) which had its own club. Near the town *Gordonia* established a training kibbutz and in the town itself there existed an urban kibbutz of *HeHalutz* (1934). The branch of *Agudath Yisrael* in Kelm leased a farm in the vicinity and established a training kibbutz for *Tseirei Agudath Yisrael*. There was also a training kibbutz of *Hehalutz Haklal Zioni* named *HaBoneh* (1935).

Some of the local youth joined these training kibbutzim in order to emigrate to *Eretz-Yisrael*. Many of them achieved this goal and joined the kibbutzim Givath-Brenner, Afikim, Yagur, Degania, Dafna and others. Others emigrated to *Eretz-Yisrael* together with Dr. Lehman and the orphans of the orphanage in Kovno, and settled in Ben-Shemen.

Sports activities were carried out at the local *Maccabi* branch with its 38 members, and also at the *HaPoel* branch.

Most members of the local volunteer fire brigade were Jews, who also maintained a wind instruments band. The heads of the brigade were Eliezer Danin and Hayim Yevner.

Religion and Welfare

Religious life concentrated around the *Shulhoif* where all the prayer houses were located, and in which all activities of the Torah study societies took place. Rabbi Kalman Beinushevitz officiated from 1926. He was murdered together with his community in 1941.

The existing welfare institutions, *Linath HaTsedek* and *Bikur Holim* which were partial substitutes for a Jewish hospital, excelled in their activity during this period. The county committee partially financed the budget of *Bikur Holim*.

These are some of the personagess who were born in Kelm:

Simhah-Zisl Ziv-Broide (1824-1898), founder and head of the *Talmud Torah Hagado*

Mosheh-Yits'hak Darshan, *HaMagid MiKelm* (1828-1899), famous in all of Lithuania as a fiery orator who influenced many to improve their behavior

Aryeh-Leib Frumkin (1845-1916), rabbi, writer and Zionist public worker, who came to *Eretz-Yisrael* in 1883 and was one of the founders of Petakh-Tikvah

Elyakim Goldberg (born 1855), rabbi and doctor in *Eretz-Yisrael*, and later in America

Eliezer-Eliyahu Fridman (1858-1936), a Zionist public worker, published articles in *HaMagid* and in *HaMelitz* as well as several books, died in Tel-Aviv

Shifrah Waiss (1889-1955) poetess, active in the *Bund* in Russia and America

Zevulun Levin (1877-1935), a Yiddish writer in America

Aharon-Hirsh-Adolf Kurlender (born 1816), a religion teacher, moved to Vienna in 1870

Daniel Movshovitz (1887-1941), head of the *Yeshivah Talmud Torah Hagadol*, murdered in the Holocaust

M. Tsvik (1905-1938), a revolutionary who was detained in Lithuania, escaped to the Soviet Union where he was murdered by the government

B. Fridman-Latvis (born 1904), member of the popular *Seim*, fulfilled many functions in the Lithuanian Communist party and during Soviet rule in Lithuania

David Kohav (born 1929) a known economist in Israel, adviser to the World Bank

Yits'hak Mer (Meras), a writer who as a child was hidden by Lithuanians during Nazi rule and later published many books in Lithuanian about that period. Lives in Israel.

During World War II and Afterwards

In 1940 Lithuania was annexed to the Soviet Union and became a Soviet Republic. Following new rules, the factories, most of them owned by Jews, were nationalized. Jewish shops and farms were nationalized and commissars appointed to manage them. All Zionist parties and youth organizations were disbanded and the Hebrew school was closed. The religious institutions found their activities very much restricted. Supply of goods decreased and, as a result, prices soared. The middle class, mostly Jewish, bore the brunt of this situation. The standard of living dropped gradually and some began to look for other income sources: one bought a cart and a horse, another a knitting machine and a third a loom.

The new rulers did not succeed in preventing anti-Semitic outbursts. At an election meeting for trade unions, which took place in Kelm in August 1940, anti-Semitic comments were heard, as a result of which the Jewish workers stood up and left the meeting.

On the day of the outbreak of war between Germany and the Soviet Union, the 22nd of June 1941, most of the Jewish houses in Kelm, including the old synagogue and the other prayer houses were burned down. Jews escaped to Jewish farms in the vicinity and to Lithuanian acquaintances. Many of those who tried to go northwards in the direction of Russia did not get very far, because the Germans preceded them. On the way back to Kelm, Lithuanian peasants murdered several Jews.

The Germans entered Kelm on the 26th of June, four days after the beginning of war, and Lithuanian rule was organized immediately to persecute the Jews. An order was issued according to which Jews had to leave Lithuanian houses and concentrate in Jewish farms. On the first of July an order was published to the effect that all Jewish men aged from 16 to 60 years old had to gather at the barn of Z. Luntz at the edge of the town. Before this these Jewish men were concentrated in the market square, and there a German made an anti-Semitic and poisonous speech proclaiming that Jews should be imprisoned in camps because they were to blame for the war. The barn, encircled by a barbed wire fence and Lithuanian guards, became a labor camp. The imprisoned, who were ordered to wear a yellow *Magen David* on their chests, were led every morning to various types of work, such as cleaning streets of the remnants of the burnt houses and burying the corpses of dead horses. While working, these Jews were maltreated and humiliated in many ways. Some Jews were murdered in the barn.

The Lithuanian guards ordered the Jews to collect all the holy books, *Tefillin* and *Tallitoth* which they had brought along and to burn all of them in the yard. Women, children, the elder and the ill were left on the Jewish farms without any guards. They were employed in agricultural work. The Lithuanian auxiliary police would burst onto the farms and rob at will.

At the beginning of July 1941, eleven men were led to a place near the Jewish cemetery and there they were forced to dig a pit, after which they were shot and buried there. At dawn on the 29th of July (5th of Av 5701), two armed Lithuanians appeared, asking for twenty young and healthy men for agricultural work for a peasant in a nearby village; they promised that the men would be treated well. Many believed them and volunteered, whereupon twenty-five young and healthy men were chosen. The Lithuanians led them to the sandpits near the Gruzhevsky estate where they were forced to dig a large pit and were then shot. The shots were heard in the camp, but its inhabitants did not realize the bitter truth. On that same day a hundred more Jews were taken out of the camp on different pretexts and led to the sandpits, where they too were killed. Only thirty-six men remained in the camp. On this day, the Jews of Vaigeve (Vaiguva) and many other Jews from the farms were also murdered there. All were forced to disrobe down to their underwear. Kelm's rabbi, Kalman Beinushevitz, who had escaped to Vaigeve at the beginning of the war, was brought to the murder site together with the town's Jews and was forced to kneel all day long near the pit and to watch the terrible extermination of his community. He was shot last. The head of the *Yeshivah*, Daniel Movshovitz, when standing with his pupils near the pits, asked the German commander to allow him to say a few words. The German agreed, and Daniel spoke to his pupils in a calm voice as though giving a regular lecture. "Don't panic," he said, "we have to accept the verdict quietly." He then turned to the German and said, "I have finished, you may start".

The garments of the murdered were brought on carts to the yard of the Lithuanian high school and Jewish youth were forced to unload them and to put them into the cellar of the building. During the work they recognized the garments of their parents and relatives. In the evening at the hall of the high school, a big party for the murderers and their families was arranged. The murderers were seated at tables which had been set, and the Jewish youngsters were forced to carry boxes with beer bottles from a nearby shed and serve them to the peasants.

On the 22nd of August, 1941 (29th of Av 5701) the women and children from the farms were brought to the Luntz farm, and from there in groups to the sand pits where they were shot. The massacre continued all day.

Several tens of Jewish men and women managed to escape and were hidden by Lithuanian peasants in the vicinity. However, many were recaptured in a little while as a result of information provided by neighbors or by the peasants themselves. The latter wanted to acquire the property the Jews deposited with them.

A few Jewish young men, Ya'akov Zak and the brothers Holozhin, wandered through the villages. They were armed and managed to supply food for the hidden and to take revenge on the murderers. Just fifteen Kelm Jews managed to survive until liberation. In addition several Jews sought refuge in the Soviet Union. Two sisters hid in a monastery and were converted to Christianity.

According to Soviet sources a mass grave exists 2 km. (1 miles) north of the town and in it are the corpses of 483 men, women and children. According to a cartographic survey of Jewish cemeteries in Lithuania that was performed in 1991, a Jewish cemetery was found in the vicinity of Kelm, in the village Vaitkiskiai.

The Mass Grave at the outskirts of Kelm

After the war some Jews returned to live in Kelm, but their numbers decreased: 1n 1970 there were eleven Jews; in 1979, nine and in 1989 only four Jews.

At the beginning of the 1990s the remnant of the Broide-Ziv family erected a monument on the mass grave, bearing an inscription in Hebrew and Lithuanian (see above).

At the site of the destroyed Jewish cemetery stands a monument with a long inscription in Hebrew and a short one in Lithuanian.

של קדושי עליון חסידי מעלה
ראשי וחכמי ותושבי
העיר קעלם וסביבותיה
שנרצחו ונהרגו על קדוש השם
ע"י הזדים הגאצים הארורים ימ"ש
בשנת תש"א

הונצחו על ידי שרידי
משפחת ברודא זיון
מקעלם

ČIA 1941M. LIEPOS MĖN. 26D.
NACISTINIAI BUDELIAI IR JŲ TAL-
KININKAI NUŽUDĖ 485 KELMĖJE
IR JOS APYLINKĖSE GYVENUSIUS
ŽYDUS

The monument at the massacre site with the inscription in Hebrew and Lithuanian: "In memory of the scholars and residents of the town of Kelm and surroundings, who were murdered by the bloody Nazi scoundrels, damn them, in 5701 (1941)." Immortalized by the remnant of the Broida-Ziv families of Kelm

Sources:

Yad Vashem Archives - M-1/E-1032/930; M-9/15/(6); Koniuhovsky collection 0-71, Files 44, 46, 47, 48

YIVO - New York, Lithuanian Communities Collection, Files 1008-1016,1677

Fridman, Eliezer Eliyahu, Memoirs 1858-1926 (Hebrew), Tel Aviv 1926

Kelm - A Cut Down Tree (Hebrew), edited by Ida Marcus-Karabelnik and Bath-Sheva Levitan-Karabelnik, published by The Association of Kelm Jews in Israel, Jerusalem 1993

The Story of an Underground (Hebrew) page 52 - Zwie A. Brown, M.A. and Dov Levin M.A., Yad Vashem, Jerusalem 1962

Di Yiddishe Stime (Yiddish) - Kovno, 3.10.1919; 4.11.1919; 30.6.1920; 18.10.1920; 1.2.1922; 14.7.1922; 19.1.1923; 12.4.1923; 24.3.1931; 19.10.1931; 8.5.1935; 12.9.1938; 14.2.1939; 5.3.1939; 8.5.1939

Yiddisher Hantverker - Kovno, #2, 1938; #16

Folksblat (Yiddish) Kovno - 20.6.1935; 23.6.1935; 4.6.1937; 1.8.1938; 13.6.1939; 21.8.1940

Dos Vort – Kovno - 17.12.1934

HaNe'eman -Telz, 1928, # 9

Funken - Kovno, # 26, 1931

HaTsofeh - Tel Aviv, 7.8.1940

Shearim, # 63, 3.4.1946

Komunistu Zodis (Lithuanian), Kelme, 11.6.1988

Naujienos (Lithuanian) Chicago, 11.6.1949

Lituanus (English), #27/3, 1981

Appendix 1

A List of Donors from Kelm in 1896 for aid to Jewish Agrarians in
Eretz-Yisrael

Abramovitz Ber-
Menasheh

Getz Faivel

Hurvitz Avraham-
Mosheh

Hirshovitz Eliezer-Ber

Kalmanovitz Meir

Rom Mosheh-Eliyahu

Rom Shelomoh

Yanover Pesakh

Appendix 2

A List of Donors of Kelm for the *Agudah Fund* in 1913

Abramovitz Avraham

Broide Tsevi

Danilevitz Menahem

Goldberg Yosef

Grinberg Refael

Lapyan Eliyahu

Leibovitz Meir

Levitan Mordehai

Mordehovitz Aizik and
Meir

Oshri Ben-Zion

Shmulevitz Ya'akov Meir

Stam Yisrael-Ze'ev

Vitchik Mosheh-Yits'hak

Zaher Shemuel

Ziv Nahum-Ze'ev

Appendix 3

A List of Kelm Donors for the Settlement of *Eretz-Yisrael*

(from Jewishgen Org.>Databases> Lithuania>HaMelitz. Compiled by Jeffrey Maynard)

Surname	Given Name	Comments	Source	Year
ABEL	Leib ben Kalman husband of Eirle Liubowitz	wed 11 Sivan - from Telsiai	*Hamelitz* #142	1897
ABELOWITZ	Sisters		*Hamelitz* #229	1902
ABRAMOVITZ	Dov Menashe		*Hamelitz* #123	1897
ABRAMOWITZ	Dov Menashe		*Hamelitz* #208	1895
ABRAMOWITZ	Dov Menashe		*Hamelitz* #142	1897
ABRAMZOHN	Mordechai	bridegroom	*Hamelitz* #142	1897
ANTIPOLSKI	Shmuel Chaim		*Hamelitz* #56	1899
BERMAN	Zev		*Hamelitz* #123	1897
BERSON	Zev		*Hamelitz* #56	1899
BERTMAN	Aba		*Hamelitz* #56	1899
BIRMAN	Mase	widow	*Hamelitz* #56	1899
BIRON	Tzemach	wed	*Hamelitz* #204	1899
BROIDA	Dvora		*Hamelitz* #123	1897
BROIDA	Moshe father of Sarah		*Hamelitz* #112	1898
BROIDA	Sarah bas Moshe wife of Yitzchok Mordechailowitz		*Hamelitz* #112	1898
BROIDA	Shmuel		*Hamelitz* #56	1899
BROIZ	Etil	*Hamelitz*	*Hamelitz*	1902
CHASID	Yehuda Leib	deceased	*Hamelitz* #240	1894
DRUZINSKI	Chaya bas Moshe wife of Chaim Tzvi Fridman from Girtagole (Girkalnis)	wed in Kelme 14 Elul	*Hamelitz* #229	1902
DRUZINSKI	Dina		*Hamelitz* #229	1902
DRUZINSKI	Dishe		*Hamelitz* #229	1902
DRUZINSKI	Moshe father of Chaya		*Hamelitz* #229	1902
EITZIKZON	Pinchos	came from Africa	*Hamelitz* #123	1897

FEIN	Eli		*Hamelitz* #123	1897
FEIN	Eliahu		*Hamelitz* #56	1899
FEIWELZON	Eli Meir	Rabbi from Kelme appointed ABD Kruk	*Hamelitz* #123	1897
FINKELSHTEIN	Rivka bas Yedidia wife of Moshe Rabinowitz	wed 2 Shevat	*Hamelitz* #56	1899
FRIDLAND	Feie		*Hamelitz* #229	1902
FRIDMAN	Ch		*Hamelitz* #229	1902
FRIDMAN	Chaim Tzvi		*Hamelitz* #56	1899
FRIDMAN	Devorah		*Hamelitz* #229	1902
GOLDBERG	Yosef ben Boruch		*Hamelitz* #132	1900
GORDON	Leib		*Hamelitz* #56	1899
GORDON	Pese		*Hamelitz* #56	1899
GOTHELF	Moshe		*Hamelitz* #56	1899
GRINBERG	Yakov husband of Rochel Shamshewitz from Kovno		*Hamelitz* #151	1898
GUTMAN	Chaim husband of Gitl Rostowski from Varna	wed in Varna	*Hamelitz* #123	1897
GUZMAN	H		*Hamelitz* #229	1902
HATZER	Yehoshua		*Hamelitz* #56	1899
HAWSHA	Shmuel Yosef ben Reuven		*Hamelitz* #132	1900
HIRSHOWITZ	Binyomin		*Hamelitz* #112	1898
HIRSHOWITZ	Mordechai		*Hamelitz* #229	1895
HIRSHOWITZ	Nechemiah		*Hamelitz* #56	1899
HIRSHOWITZ	Sarah		*Hamelitz* #56	1899
HOROWITZ	Avraham Moshe		*Hamelitz* #137	1900
HOROWITZ	Avraham Moshe		*Hamelitz* H #137	1900
HORWITZ	Avraham Moshe Halevi		*Hamelitz* #208	1895
HORWITZ	Yakov		*Hamelitz* #208	1895
KAPLAN	Tzvi		*Hamelitz* #123	1897
KAPLAN	Tzvi		*Hamelitz* #229	1902

KAPLAN	Zev Yehuda	Shub	*Hamelitz* #56	1899
KESLER	Yakov Nachum		*Hamelitz* H #208	1895
KESLER	Yakov Nachum		*Hamelitz* #56	1899
KOSEL	Avraham Yitzchok		*Hamelitz* #123	1897
KOSEL	Yitzchok		*Hamelitz* #56	1899
KOSSEL	Avraham Yitzchok		*Hamelitz* #229	1895
KREMER	Chaim Leib		*Hamelitz* #123	1897
LEIMOWITZ	Tzvi		*Hamelitz* #208	1895
LEIZEROWITZ	Aizik		*Hamelitz* #208	1895
LESTZ	Leah		*Hamelitz* #229	1902
LEWITAN	Bentzion		*Hamelitz* #56	1899
LIUBOWITZ	Eirle wife of Leib Abel	wed 11 Sivan	*Hamelitz* #142	1897
LIWERMAN	Pesach father of Yakov	from Libau	*Hamelitz* #142	1897
LIWERMAN	Yakov ben Pesach fiance of Wital Yanower	from Libau	*Hamelitz* #142	1897
LUNTZ	Boruch	in Shillel	*Hamelitz* #249	1899
LUNTZ	Yosef		*Hamelitz* #230	1895
MEHLMAN	Dov		*Hamelitz* #123	1897
MEIROWITZ	Breine		*Hamelitz* #229	1902
MEIROWITZ	Mordecai		*Hamelitz* #123	1897
MEIROWITZ	Mordechai		*Hamelitz* #56	1899
MEIROWITZ	Mordechai		*Hamelitz* #229	1902
MELMAN	Dov		*Hamelitz* #208	1895
MIRVIS	Moshe Falk - listed with Shmuel Mordechai Zinger	in Baltimore, USA	*Hamelitz* #57	1897
MORDECHAILOWI TZ	Yitzchok husband of Sarah Broida		*Hamelitz* #112	1898
MURINIK	Yosef Ari		*Hamelitz* #208	1895
ODWIN	Moshe ben Yakov Leib of Taurage husband of Rivka baszfon	wed	*Hamelitz* #201	1895
OPENHEIM		widow	*Hamelitz* #56	1899
ORINTZ	Kalman		*Hamelitz* #138	1897
PEREWAZNIK	Mendil		*Hamelitz* #56	1899

PERLMAN	Sarah		*Hamelitz* #123	1897
RABINOWITZ	father of Moshe	Rabbi from Wivokla	*Hamelitz* #56	1899
RABINOWITZ	Gershon		*Hamelitz* #56	1899
RABINOWITZ	Moshe son of Rabbi husband of Rivka Finkelshtein	wed 2 Shevat	*Hamelitz* #56	1899
RAPOPORT	Chana Libe bas Yona Raphel wife of Shmuel Mordechai Zinger	in Baltimore, USA	*Hamelitz* #57	1897
RAPOPORT	Fradil wife of Yona Raphel	in Baltimore, USA	*Hamelitz* #57	1897
RAPOPORT	Yona Raphel husband of Fradil father of Chana Libe	in Baltimore, USA	*Hamelitz* #57	1897
RATNER	Chana		*Hamelitz* #229	1902
ROM	Moshe Eli		*Hamelitz* #229	1902
ROM	Moshe Eliahu		*Hamelitz* #56	1899
ROM	Muse		*Hamelitz* #56	1899
ROM	Sh		*Hamelitz* #229	1902
ROZENBERG	Yosef		*Hamelitz* #56	1899
SHANDER	Chaya		*Hamelitz* #229	1902
SHANKER	Chaya	widow	*Hamelitz* #56	1899
SHAPIRO	P brother of R		*Hamelitz* #208	1895
SHAPIRO	R brother of P		*Hamelitz* #208	1895
SHAPIRO	Shraga		*Hamelitz* #229	1895
SHMARKOWITZ	Beila		*Hamelitz* #56	1899
SHNITZ	Yosef Reuven	from Upyna	*Hamelitz* #56	1899
TERESPOLSKI	Ber		*Hamelitz* #56	1899
TERESPOLSKI	Tzvi	wed 6 Shevat	*Hamelitz* #56	1899
TERESPOLSKI	Yechiel		*Hamelitz* #56	1899
TZEITEL	Moshe Yitzchok		*Hamelitz* #56	1899
WINIK	Sarah		*Hamelitz* #229	1902
WOLFOWITZ	Yitchok		*Hamelitz* #56	1899
WOLFOWITZ	Yitzchok		*Hamelitz* #56	1899
WOLPERT	Dov		*Hamelitz* #229	1902
WOLPERT	Zev		*Hamelitz* #56	1899

YAFE	Nochum		*Hamelitz* #208	1895
YANOWER	Eli father of Wital		*Hamelitz* #142	1897
YANOWER	Wital bas Eli fiancee of Yakov Liwerman		*Hamelitz* #142	1897
YEKUTIELI	Avraham Yitzchok		*Hamelitz* #208	1895
YOSELOWITZ	Devorah	wed 6 Shevat	*Hamelitz* #56	1899
YOSELOWITZ	Tzvi		*Hamelitz* #123	1897
YOSELOWITZ	Tzvi		Hamelitz #56	1899
ZAKS	Michal		Hamelitz #208	1895
ZINGER	Dvora Ite wife of Eliahu	in Baltimore, USA	Hamelitz #57	1897
ZINGER	Eliahu husband of Dvora Ite father of Shmuel Mordechai	in Baltimore, USA	*Hamelitz* #57	1897
ZINGER	Shmuel Mordechai ben Eliahu husband of Chana Libe Rapoport	in Baltimore, USA	*Hamelitz* #57	1897
ZINGER	Yosef Yehuda Leib ben Shmuel Mordechai	in Baltimore, born 1884	*Hamelitz* #57	1897
ZIW	Menachem Mendel		*Hamelitz* #229	1902
ZIW	Mordechai		*Hamelitz* #229	1895
ZOCHER	Shmuel Mordechai		*Hamelitz* #208	1895
ZAKS			Hamelitz #123	1897

Appendix 4

A List of Kelm Donors for the Victims of the Persian Famine in 1872

(from Jewishgen.Org.>Databases>Lithuania>HaMaggid, compiled by Jeffrey Maynard)

Surname	Given Name	Comments	Year
AVAK-MACHIR	Yakov		1872
BABELITZK	Avraham Nachum		1872
BARZINER	Akiva		1872
BOCH	Tzvi		1872
BROIDA	Eli		1872
BROIDA	Moshe		1872
BROIDA	Yosef		1872
CHAYAT	Avraham ben Yakov		1872
CHAYAT	Boruch		1872
CHAYAT	Gershon		1872
D"TZ	Yitzchok	Rabbi	1872
DROZINSKI	Moshe		1872
GOLDBERG	Zelig		1872
GORDON	Ari Leib ben Meir		1872
GORDON	Meir	father of Ari Leib	1872
GROSS	Shmeril	father of Zevulun	1872
GROSS	Zevulun ben Shmeril		1872
HILMAN	Avraham Noach		1872
KA"TZ	Zelig		1872
KATZ	Yakov Nachum		1872
KATZAV	Yakov Eliezer		1872
KIRZNER	Avraham		1872
KIRZNER	Dovid		1872
KONOR	Meir		1872
KORDER	Yisroel		1872
KORKLAN	Tzvi Leib Ka"tz		1872
KUPERSHMID	Tzvi		1872
KUPERSHMID	Yisroel		1872
KURZIN	Abba Meir		1872
LEIZEROWITZ	Aaron		1872

LIEBERMAN	Brothers		1872
LUNZ	Chaim Shaul		1872
MANE	Gershon		1872
MELAL	Reuven		1872
NESHES	Sarah	bride of Tzvi	1872
NIMAN	Avraham		1872
OMANTZEI	Leib		1872
PARIMAN	Zalman		1872
REITZKIN	Shulam		1872
ROM	Eli		1872
ROS	Dovid		1872
ROZENTAHL	Binyomin Beinis		1872
SANDLER	Moshe		1872
SEGAL	Abba		1872
SEGAL	Isser		1872
SHAPIRO	Shmuel Yitzchok		1872
SHEMESH	Yitzchok		1872
SHINDL-DEKEL	Lipman		1872
SHMUELEWITZ	Avraham		1872
SHTOLER	Yitzchok		1872
SHU"B	Zev		1872
SUDANIK	Leizer		1872
SWILPISK	Tuvia		1872
WATIN	Zev	Mechir	1872
WEINSHTOK	Shmuel		1872
WEINBERG	Yitzchok ben Chaim Moshe		
WEITZ	Tzvi		1872
WOLFER	Yitzchok		1872
WOLPERT	Ephraim		1872
YANIVER	Eli		1872
YAWNA	Avraham	brother of Yosef	1872
YAWNA	Yosef	brother of Avraham	1872
YOCHNISK	Yakov		1872
ZACHIR	Reuven		1872

ZAGERER	Chaim		1872
ZEIBERMACHER	Avraham		1872
ZELTZER	Avraham		1872
ZIV	Shaul		1872
ZOHN	Moshe		1872
	Aharon bridegroom of Sheina		1872
	Avraham ben Shalom		1872
	Avraham ben Shlomo		1872
	Chaim Shmuel		1872
	Chaim Yitzchok ben Avraham Noach	bridegroom	1872
	Cheiga daughter of Yitzchok		1872
	Eli ben Kopil		1872
	Eliezer ben Eliezer		1872
	Eliezer Ber		1872
	Eliezer Nechemiah		1872
	Elimelech brother of Leizer		1872
	Esther Ruchel	woman	1872
	Gershon Zalkind		1872
	Hille bridegroom of Fruma		1872
	Kopil ben Moshe		1872
	Leizer brother of Elimelech		1872
	Mordechai ben Yisroel	g"g	1872
	Mordechai Moshe ben Aleksander		1872
	Mordechai Yisroel		1872
	Seime ben Yona		1872
	Shimon ben Leib	bridegroom	1872
	Yakov ben Shaul		1872
	Yedidia ben Shraga		1872
	Yehoshua ben Shalom		1872

Yekil ben Zev		1872
Yisroel ben Zalman		1872
Yisroel Shalom		1872
Yitzchok	Rabbi, son-in-law of the Rabbi ABD	1872
Yoel ben Moshe		1872
Yona ben Ever	boy from Raseiniai (Rashin)...	1872
Yosef	son-in-law of Chaim	1872
Yosef Hillel		1872

Kavarskas (Kovarsk)

Kavarskas (Kovarsk in Yiddish) is situated in the center of Lithuania, 24 km (15 miles) from the district administrative center of Ukmerge (Vilkomir), on the west bank of the Sventoji River.

Kovarsk is mentioned in historical documents from the middle of the fifteenth century. From the start of the sixteenth century the town was owned by several Polish estate families, Oginsky, Tishkevitz, Chichinsky and others. During Russian rule (1795-1915) Kovarsk was at first a part of the Vilna Province (*Gubernia*), but from 1843 it was transferred to the Province of Kovno. By the middle of the nineteenth century the town had grown and developed significantly. Merchants had settled there. There were regular fairs and market days and it had become a county administrative center. During 1915-1918 Kovarsk was under German rule, but during the period of independent Lithuania (1918-1940) Kovarsk reverted to being a county administrative center.

Jewish Settlement until World War II

Jews probably settled in Kovarsk at the end of the eighteenth century. It is known that in the middle of the nineteenth century an organized Jewish community already existed there. It employed a rabbi and a *shokhet* (ritual slaughterer).

Kovarsk Jews made their living by trading in flax, seeds, grains and timber. Timber merchants came to the town, bought up plots of woods in the surrounding areas, felled the trees and transported them to the river where they were floated as rafts. This was a source of income for many Jewish families. The Jews of Kovarsk also exported geese and fruit. They owned large shops selling food products and textiles.

342 Jews were resident in 1847, and by 1897 the population had increased to 1,546, including 979 (63%) Jews.

In 1883 a severe quarrel erupted over an issue concerning the local *shokhet* who had served the community for 20 years. In that same year an extensive fire broke out. The victims were assisted through the generosity of an estate owner named Chichinsky.

In 1898 the community split into two camps over the issue of electing a new rabbi after the demise of Rabbi Yehudah-Leib Grinshtein, who had officiated for 30 years. One camp favored the appointment of Grinshtein's young son to the rabbinic chair, but only after he had been ordained. The other group proposed Yisrael-Yehoshua Segal as the town's Rabbi. After a long quarrel, Rabbi Segal was successful and the community paid young Grinshtein 600 rubles as compensation, whereupon peace returned to the town.

The following Rabbis officiated in Kovarsk thereafter:

> Josef Kanovitz (1878-?), in Kovarsk from 1907 and later in America from 1915

> Hayim Rudnia (1867-?) officiated in 1910

> Avraham-Aba Kriger (1876-?) officiated in Kovarsk in 1913.

During 1891-1892 there were 21 subscribers to rabbinic literature in town.

In a list of donors to the settlement of *Eretz-Yisrael* dated 1909 the following names of Kovarsk Jews appear: M. Lurie, Menahem-Asher Helman, Meir Panavky, Shabtai-Pinhas Shmidt, Josef Shklar, Shneur-Zalman Shifrin, Shemuel-Eliezer Levinson. In another list dated 1914 many names of Kovarsk Jews can be found; the fundraiser was M. Luria. The corespondent of the publication *HaMelitz* was Yehuda son of Mosheh Zilb.

At the end of July 1915, during World War I, Kovarsk Jews were exiled to Russia by the retreating Russian army, which burned down more than half the town. Retreating Cossack battalions carried out a pogrom against them as they robbed, raped and murdered. After the war only half of the exiles returned.

Kovarsk - General View

Following the law of autonomies for minorities issued by the new Lithuanian government, the minister for Jewish affairs Dr. Menachem (Max) Soloveitshik, ordered elections for community committees (*Va'adei Kehilah*) to be held in the summer of 1919, and in Kovarsk seven members were elected. During its years of activity the committee was involved in all aspects of Jewish community life. According to the first government census in 1923 there were 1,041 residents in Kovarsk and 436 (42%) of them were Jews.

At this time Kovarsk Jews made their living from trade, peddling, crafts and small industry. The weekly market and the quarterly fairs contributed a substantial part of their livelihood.

According to a survey of shops performed by the government in 1931, Kovarsk had fifteen stores, eleven of which were owned by Jews.

The distribution according to type of business is given in the table below:

Type of business	Total	Owned by Jews
Groceries	1	1
Grain and flax	3	3
Butcher shops and Cattle Trade	3	3
Restaurants and Taverns	2	0
Textile Products and Furs	2	2
Books and Stationery	1	0
Medicine and Cosmetics	1	0
Heating Materials	1	1
Bicycles and electrical equipment	1	1

According to the same survey seven enterprises were owned by Jews: two wool combing plants, two flour mills, one leather processing factory; one light drink factory and one bakery.

In 1937 there were 24 Jewish artisans: seven tailors, three shoemakers, three potters, two blacksmiths, two barbers, two butchers, one hatter, one knitter, one felt boots maker, one leatherworker, one dressmaker. In 1925 Kovarsk had one practising Jewish doctor, Ber Kafor.

The Jewish Folksbank played an important role in the economic life of Kovarsk's Jews. It began its activities in 1920 with 31 members: by 1927 the membership had risen to 104, but decreased to 90 members by 1935. In 1939 there were twelve telephone-owners, two of them Jews.

The Lithuanians established consumer cooperatives in 1919 and these began to compete with the Jewish shops. They encouraged a boycott of the Jewish shops.

In the same year, on the Lithuanian army recruitment day, the Lithuanians attacked and robbed Jewish stores. In several homes, shutters, windowpanes and even doors were smashed. Officers of the recruitment committee managed to stop the frenzied crowd and dispersed them, but many Jews were harmed and economically destroyed. The national economic crisis at the beginning of the 1930s affected the town's Jews badly and as a result many emigrated to South Africa and a few to *Eretz-Yisrael.*

Jewish children received their elementary education in the Hebrew school of the religious *Yavneh* network, where Yiddish was the language of instruction in some of the classes. The community had erected the school building, which a former Kovarsk resident generously financed. Forty pupils studied there in 1935. Some of its graduates continued their studies at *Or* (Light), the Hebrew high school in Vilkomir.

The library, with its 500 Hebrew and Yiddish books, had an extensive circle of readers. The town also had a repertory society, which occasionally performed stage shows: its income funded the buying of books for the library.

The rabbis during this period were Duber Shnitser and Dov Sukmansky; both were victims of Lithuanians in the Holocaust.

Many of the local Jews belonged to the Zionist movement and almost all Zionist parties had their subscribers. These included the Sirkin Society (Z. S.) and *Hehalutz-Hatsair*, one of the Zionist youth organizations.

The Beth Midrash

The results of the elections for Zionist Congresses are given below:

Cong No.	Year	Tot Shek	Total Votes	Labor Party Z"S	Z"Z	Rev	Gen Zion A	B	Gros	Miz
16	1929	10	---	---	---	---	---	----	----	1
17	1931	16	6	2	1	---	3	----	----	---
18	1933	----	66	66		---	---	---	---	---
19	1935	----	91	86		---	1	2	1	1

Key: Cong No. = Congress Number, Tot Shek = Total Shekalim, Rev = Revisionists, Gen Zion = General Zionists, Gros = Grosmanists, Miz =Mizrahi

The rabbi (seated in the middle) with the *Gabaim*

The Bath House

The writer Eliezer Heiman (1910-1944) was born in Kovarsk. He published stories in Hebrew and Yiddish in the Jewish press and also published the historic story "Avraham Mapu" (Kovno 1937). He perished in the Kovno ghetto.

During World War II and Afterwards

In June 1940 Lithuania was annexed to the Soviet Union and became a Soviet Republic. Following new rules, the majority of the shops belonging to the Jews of Kovarsk were nationalized and commissars were appointed to manage them. All Zionist parties and youth organizations were disbanded and Hebrew educational institutions were closed. The supply of goods decreased and, as a result, prices soared. The middle class, mostly Jewish, bore the brunt and the standard of living dropped gradually.

After the German army invaded the Soviet Union on the June 22, 1941, Lithuanian nationalists took over Kovarsk. They entered Jewish houses and robbed them of anything they fancied. They broke windows in Jewish houses and set fire to the Jewish homes in Ukmerge Street. They detained thirty Jewish men and women on the pretext that they were supporters of Soviet rule, but the probable reason was a personal grudge. With the entry of German troops into the town on the June 26th, all those detained were shot on the banks of the river, near the village of Pumpuciai, south of Kovarsk. The situation of the remaining Kovarsk Jews, who lived in mortal fear, was unbearable. The Lithuanians humiliated them, maltreated them and robbed them of their property. Later, they led them to Vilkomir (Ukmerge), where they were murdered en masse in Pivonija forest together with other Jews, both from the town itself and from its surroundings. This atrocity apparently occurred on September 5th, 1941 (13th of Av 5701). No Kovarsk Jews survived. The names of the Lithuanian murderers can be seen in the archives in *Yad Vashem*.

The mass grave near Pumpuciai village

At the beginning of the 1990s a monument was erected on the mass graves adjacent to Pumpuciai village and on it the inscription in Yiddish: **"At this site in 1941, Hitler's murderers and their local helpers killed Kovarsk's Jews, men, women and children." "May their memory be sacred."** is written below in Lithuanian.

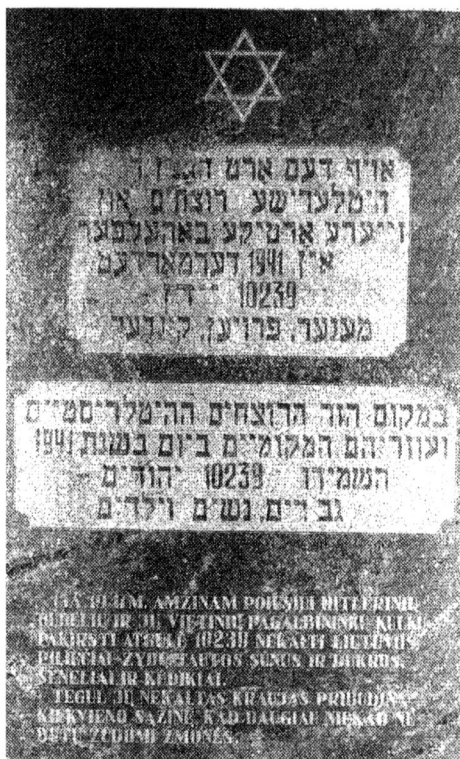

The monument located on the mass grave at Pivonija forest. The inscription in Yiddish, Hebrew and Lithuanian says: "In this place in the days in the year 1941 the Nazi murderers and their local helpers executed 10,239 Jews - men, women, children."

Sources:

Yad Vashem Archives -M-33/978

Dos Vort (The Word, Yiddish), Kovno - 17.12.1934

Di Yiddishe Shtime (The Jewish Voice, Yiddish) Kovno-29.8.1919; 31.5.1922; 23.2.1923; 15.7.1930; 16.6.1936; 14.9.1938

Folksblat (Yiddish) (Popular Newspaper), Kovno - 10.7.1930; 15.7.1935

HaMelitz (Hebrew), St. Petersburg - 5.11.1883; 23.11.1883; 28.12.1883; 13.6.1899; 4.8.1899.

Mažeikiai (Mazheik)

The town of Mazeikiai (Mazheik in Yiddish) lies in northwestern Lithuania, in the Zamut (Zemaitija) region, on the Venta River. Before the second half of the nineteenth century it was a small village with only a few dozen inhabitants. In 1868 a railway was constructed between Romni in Ukraine and Liepaja (Libau) in Latvia, prompting the development of Mazheik into a larger town. In 1872 Mazheik was connected to Riga by a railway, and it became an important junction through which tens of trains passed every day. Mazheik developed rapidly after 1902 when locomotive and wagon repair shops offered services, and a school for railway workers was established. Most of the students at the school were Russian.

The Station Street

During Russian rule (1795-1915) Mazheik was included in the Vilna Province (*Gubernia*) and from 1843 in Kovno Province. On May 1st, 1901, the name of the town was changed to Muravievo, after governor-general (*General Gubernator*) Muraviov who crushed the Polish rebellion of 1863.

During the period of independent Lithuania (1918-1940) the name reverted to Mazeikiai and it became a district administrative center. It retained this status during the Soviet rule (1940-1941), during the Nazi occupation (1941-1944) and after World War II when Mazheik was included in the Soviet Union once more.

Jewish Settlement until World War II

Jewish settlement in Mazheik dates back to the 1870s when the rapid development of transportation services and commerce began. Most of the Jews made their living from peddling and small trade with the surrounding villages. They were also wholesalers: they owned stores and exported some consumer goods. There were a few Jewish factory owners as well.

A street in Mazheik

The "Temporary Regulations" of the Czarist government of 1882 forbade other Jews to settle in Mazheik. This restriction was annulled in 1903, but the prohibition for Jews to purchase property remained unchanged until the end of the Czarist rule. As a result Jewish homes were built on plots registered to non-Jewish names. Many of the Jewish children studied in Russian schools. In 1885 Rabbi Ze'ev Volf Avrekh commenced duties in Mazheik.

According to the all-Russian census of 1897, there were 1,979 residents in Mazheik, 435 (21%) of them Jews.

A Zionist society was formed in town. Lists published in *HaMelitz* in 1898 and 1899 included 33 names of Mazheik donors. The fundraiser for the Odessa Committee for support to Jewish Agrarians in Syria and *Eretz-Yisrael* was Leib-Zalman Epel (see **Appendix 1**). Mosheh Markusevitz was the local correspondent for *Hamelitz*. The religious anti-Zionist *Agudath Yisrael* party was very active and its list of membership for the year 1913 included ten Mazheik Jews (see **Appendix 2**).

Shortly after the outbreak of World War I, in 1915, many Lithuanian, Courland and Mazheik Jews were exiled to Russia by order of the Russian military.

A street with the Central Pharmacy

After the war, following the establishment of the Lithuanian independent state, some of the exiles returned to their hometown, which was almost entirely burnt down by then. Following the law of autonomies for minorities issued by the new Lithuanian government, the Minister for Jewish Affairs Dr. Menachem (Max) Soloveitshik, ordered elections to community committees (*Va'adei Kehilah*) to be held in the summer of 1919. In Mazheik, a community committee with seven members was elected in November 1920. At the first meeting of the committee, on July 12th 1921, Mosheh Tov was elected chairman, J. Rubinshtein secretary with Avraham Getz as the treasurer. The committee worked through structured cultural and social service subcommittees under the chairmanship of Rabbi Josef-Ze'ev MamYafe. The members of the Culture Subcommittee included Benjamin Rier and Yits'hak Avrekh, while Dov Klaf and M. Rubel served on the Social Service Subcommittee. Later, the staff of the committee and its subcommittees changed several times. The committees served until December 1925 when autonomy was annulled.

Most of the Jews integrated well into the life of the town during its period of restoration and economic development. With the active assistance of the Joint Distribution Committee ("The Joint"), retail and wholesale trading in food staples such as eggs and poultry increased, while timber and other agricultural products were exported successfully to Germany and England. Jews took over several light industries: flour mills, flax-processing shops, shingle production, match manufacture, liquor, clothing and others. The weekly market days were held on Monday, Wednesday and Friday, resulting in significant revenue to the Jewish merchants.

According to the first census of the new Lithuanian government in 1923, the population of Mazheik was 4,281; 682 (16%) were Jews. In 1936, 4,960 people were resident in town with 750 (15%) of them being Jewish.

According to a survey performed by the Government in 1931, there were 89 shops in Mazheik, 77 (86%) owned by Jews. The business distribution of these is given in the table below:

Type of Business	Total	Owned by Jews
Grocery store	9	8
Grain and flax	1	1
Butcher shop and Cattle Trade	7	5
Restaurant and Tavern	5	5
Food Products, Eggs	13	13
Beverages	2	2
Dairy Products	2	1
Textile Products and Furs	11	10
Leather and Shoe store	8	8
Haberdashery and House Utensils	7	5
Medicine and Cosmetics	3	2
Watches, Jewels and Optics	2	1
Hardware Products	4	3
Bicycle and electrical equipment	1	1
Timber and Furniture	1	0
Heating Materials	5	5
Machines, Transportation	2	2
Stationery and Books	1	0
Others	5	5

There were 35 types of light industry concerns, 20 (57%) owned by Jews.

Type of Factory	Total	Jewish owned
Machines, Metals, Locksmiths	3	1
Headstones, Glass, Bricks	1	0
Spirit, Soap, Oil	1	1
Textile: Wool, Flax, Knitting	5	5
Sawmills and Furniture	5	2
Flour mills, Bakeries	11	6
Dresses, Footwear	5	2
Leather Industry: Production, Cobbling	2	2
Others	2	1

In 1937, there were 28 Jewish tradesmen in town: seven tailors, four shoemakers, four butchers, two dressmakers, one baker, one printer, one barber, one leather worker, one corset-maker, one tinsmith, one painter, one seamstress and three others.

The booming economic situation in the 1920s resulted in the resettlement to Mazheik of many Jews from the neighboring towns of Latskeve (Leckava), Pikeln (Pikeliai) and Siad.

מאזשייקער איד. פאלקס-באנק.
גער. יולי 1928ר.

The management and workers of the Mazheik Jewish Folksbank

Sitting from left: B. Levit, L. Yezersky, H. Glikman, B. Zarende, M. L. Levit, A.B. Rabinovitz, A. Shtupel, Sh. Landver

Standing from left: D. Hurvitz, Sh. Shakhmundes, Y. Rier, Y. Minster, Y. Lempert, Y. Itzikson, Y. Deletitsky, Y. Rabinovitz

Starting in 1929, the economic situation of Mazheik Jews deteriorated with the economic crisis in Lithuania and rising competition from Lithuanian merchants, who took over many Jewish commercial enterprises. The economic stagnation of the Jewish community was reflected in the budget of the Jewish Popular Bank (*Folksbank*) which decreased from 45 million Litas in 1929 to 17 million in 1934. During that period, the number of clients with term deposits in the bank decreased from 312 to 280 and at the same time emigration to America, South Africa and *Eretz-Yisrael* increased.

In the mid-thirties, there were two Jewish doctors in Mazheik, three dentists and one lawyer. In 1934, three of the twelve members of the Municipal Council were Jews.

The students and teachers of the Hebrew school and pro-gymnasium
(Picture courtesy of Yehoshua Trigor -Trigubov)

A group of Jewish girls. Sitting from left: Pesia Kalner, Sarah Likhtenshtein, Keile Aharonovitz, Henia Klaf, ----, Gita Trigubov

Standing from left: Mrs Paris, Bilhah Rubin, Tirtsah MamYafe, Shoshanah Smole

(Picture courtesy of Yehoshua Trigor-Trigubov)

Mazheik girls, students of the Hebrew gymnasium *Or* in Vilkomir all of them members of *HaShomer HaTsair*

Sitting in the middle-Keile Aharonovitz; third from left-Gita Trigubov;

Standing second from right-Shoshanah Smole, third-Michael Dreznin, fourth-Miriam Halavin

(Picture courtesy of Yehoshua Trigor-Trigubov)

Children at an *OZE* playing ground , 1929

(Picture courtesy of Pesakh Navoth)

In 1939 there were 128 telephone subscribers, of whom 41 (32%) were Jewish. In that year vandalism against Jews was reported – breaking of the windows at the Jewish pharmacy and bakery, tearing the sign off the Jewish bank and other acts.

The community committee established in 1920 worked in various aspects of Jewish life, and in particular in the cultural/educational field. It founded a Hebrew elementary school of the *Tarbuth* network and a Hebrew pro-gymnasium. The first director of the latter was Mr. Yafe. In 1928, Dr. Goldshtiker replaced him, followed by Dr. Heselzon. In 1930, during Dr. Goldshtiker's time, the teachers in the pro-gymnasium were Fania Goldshtein, Mr. Ox, Sonia Nahimovitz, Etl Beker, Aliza Laiptsiger and Mr. Katz. The secretary of the school was a Mr. Verblovsky. 120 students attended the four classes of the elementary school and the six classes of the pro-gymnasium. Later, a kindergarten was established. The *Tarbuth* society organized evening courses and in 1922 thirty people participated in the program.

The *Maccabi* soccer team

With the decrease of the Jewish population in the second half of the 1930s due to emigration, in particular to South Africa, the Hebrew pro-gymnasium was closed and many students continued their studies at the government high school.

There were two Jewish libraries, and the town had several active groups. Among them, the leftist Yiddishist *Kultur Lige* worked in the field of culture, the non-party *Frauen Verein* (Women's Society) worked in the welfare field, and the Zionist *Maccabi*, established in 1924 with 84 members, worked in sports. The local branch of the OZE was very active in the health care of the school children. The local volunteer Fire Brigade, all Jews, excelled in acts of bravery on numerous occasions.

A great number of Mazheik Jewish youth were active in the Zionist youth organizations *HaShomer HaTsair*, *Betar* and *Benei Akiva*. In 1932 the Zionist Socialist party (its official name was "Education Society named after Nakhman Sirkin") was established in town with thirty members. This party supported the local *HeHalutz* branch with its twenty-five members. Most of the Zionist women were organized in *WIZO*. Only a few belonged to the Yiddishist Society of *Libhober fun Visen* and to anti-Zionist leftists. The results of the elections to the Zionist Congresses are given below:

Cong No.	Year	Tot Shek	Total Votes	Labor Party		Rev	Gen Zion		Gros	Miz
				Z"S	Z"Z		A	B		
15	1927	71	58	11	12	8	20	----	---	7
16	1929	195	100	30	38	4	23	----	----	5
17	1931	114	88	23	33	7	22	----	----	3
18	1933	----	253	164		42	38	---	7	2
19	1935	300	256	155		--	25	49	11	16

Key: Cong No. = Congress Number, Tot Shek = Total Shekalim, Rev = Revisionists, Gen Zion = General Zionists, Gros = Grosmanists, Miz =Mizrahi

The Mazheik *Betar* branch 1936

(Picture courtesy of Yehoshua Trigor)

After the death of Rabbi Avrekh in 1922, his son-in-law Rabbi Josef-Ze'ev MamYafe succeeded him, continuing to serve the community until its liquidation at the hands of the Nazis.

Training Kibbutz of *Hehalutz* in Mazheik 1934
(*Picture courtesy of Yehoshua Trigor*)

Between the years 1885-1914 there were forty-five subscribers to rabbinic literature in the town.

Among the personages born in Mazheik were:

> Hayim Kruger (1875-1933), who lived in Canada from 1907, a Yiddish-Hebrew journalist and writer who published articles and stories in the Canadian Jewish press and a book on the life and work of the Rambam
>
> Leib Yudeikin (born 1904), emigrated in 1925 to South Africa: he published stories in Yiddish periodicals on Jewish life in South Africa
>
> Artist Pinhas Abramovitz (born 1909), who emigrated to *Eretz-Yisrael* and served as chairman of the Association of the Artists and Sculptors in Israel (1981-1984): his works are exhibited in museums in Israel and abroad
>
> Yehoshua Trigor (Trigubov), one of the senior staff of the Israeli Foreign Ministry
>
> Brothers Engineer Pesakh Navoth and Professor Yisrael Navoth.

During World War II and After

In 1940 Lithuania was annexed to the Soviet Union and became a Soviet Republic. Following new rules, factories owned by Jews were nationalized. Jewish shops and farms were also nationalized and commissars were appointed to manage them. All Zionist parties and youth organizations were disbanded and the Hebrew school was closed. In its place a Yiddish school was founded. The activities of religious institutions were restricted. Supply of goods decreased and as a result, prices soared. The middle class, mostly Jewish, bore the brunt and the standard of living dropped gradually. Several activists of the leftist camp moved into government and municipal institutions.

At that time, there were about 900 Jews in Mazheik.

With the German invasion of Lithuania on June 22nd, 1941, many Jews, in particular activists working for the Soviet government, attempted an escape to the Soviet Union. Only a few managed to make the journey, as many perished on the way and others returned home. A few became stranded in Latvia on their way to Russia. Among these was the communist activist Leizer Baro, who later worked in the anti-Nazi underground in the Riga ghetto.

On June 25th, 1941 the Germans entered Mazheik, which at that time was under Lithuanian rule established by nationalist circles. The Lithuanians worked in the service of the Germans, rendering them particular support with the liquidation of their Jewish neighbors. Already in July 1941, the Lithuanians had helped the Germans to bring all the Mazheik Jews (except for Dr. A. Krongold) to the *Beth Midrash*, and in a few days transferred them to big barns near the River Venta. Women and children were sent to Psharkasniai farm, near the town of Tirksliai (Tirkshle). Fania Lampe, the dentist and her little son were shot dead before the transfer to the barns, because she refused to leave her house.

The men were detained in the barns for several weeks and were forced into hard labor, all the while being abused and maltreated by their Lithuanian guards. On August 3rd, 1941 (10th of *Av*, 5701) all the men were led to prepared pits near the Jewish cemetery and shot by a Lithuanian firing squad. One of the victims, Kalman Rakhmil, managed to shout to the murderers, "Our blood will not be silent! The revenge will come." Inevitably, the dead victims were looted of their clothes and valuables by their Lithuanian executioners.

Two days later, the women and the children were returned to the barns and kept there for four days under terrible conditions. On August 9th, 1941 (*Shabbat*, 16th of *Av*, 5701) all, including Dr. Krongold, were taken to the same pits where a week earlier the men were murdered, and there they too were killed in the most vile and cruel manner. Women were forced to undress. The children were thrown into a long ditch and many of them were buried under heaps of soil and lime while still alive. In the same place, together with the Mazheik Jews, Jews from the nearby towns of Akmyan (Akmene), Vekshne (Vieksniai), Zhidik (Zidikai), Tirkshle (Tirksliai), Pikeln (Pikeliai), Klikol (Klykouliai) and Siad (Seda) perished.

The mass murder site near the Jewish cemetery

The monument at the entrance of the murder site with the inscription in Yiddish and Lithuanian: "At this site Hitler's murderers and their local helpers executed about 4000 Jews and people of other nationalities".

Remains of the Jewish cemetery of Mazheik

(Picture courtesy of the photographer, Gilda Kurtzman, July 2005)

After the German retreat from the region, the Government Committee for Investigation of the Nazi Crimes was convened in the autumn of 1944 following the re-establishment of Soviet rule. It finally reported on December 7th, 1944 that the site near the Jewish cemetery contained five mass graves and that more than 4,000 bodies were buried there. Nevertheless, nobody maintained these gruesome sites for several years, but thanks to the efforts of several survivors, the site was fenced in and a monument with a black marble plaque was finally built.

After the war some Jews returned to settle in Mazheik. In 1970, there were three Jewish persons living in the town, in 1979 the number increased to twenty and in 1989 to twenty-two, probably Russian.

Sources:

Yad-Vashem Archives, Jerusalem, M-1/Q-1455/279; M1/E-1670/1555, 1771/1637, 03-6692.

Koniukhovsky Collection 0-71, files 21, 165

YIVO, New York, Collection of Lithuanian Communities, files 554-584, 1528,1667

Dos Vort, Kovno, 11.9.1934; 13.11.1934

Di Yiddishe Shtime, Kovno, 18.1.1922; 20.1.1922; 5.8.1929; 17.2.1931; 28.3.1931; 25.8.1931; 20.5.1932; 5.12.1932; 8.3.1933; 6.5.1938; 29.5.1938; 9.8.1939

Di Tsait, Kovno,21.5.1932

HaMelitz, St.Petersburg, 1893, #192; 1894, #54

Folksblat, Kovno, 11.9.1930; 19.11.1940

Tsait, Shavl, 9.5.1924; 29.5 1924; 12.6.1924

Neuzmirsime (We will not forget), on the crimes of the nationalist bourgeois during the Hitler occupation in the Mazheik district, Vilna 1960

Trigor Yehoshua - The Litvak who Survived, Rescued, Went to *Eretz-Yisrael* (Hebrew), Jerusalem 2005

Appendix 1
List of Mazheik Donors for the Settlement of *Eretz Yisrael*
(from Jewishgen.Org.>Databases>compiled by Jeffrey Maynard)

Surname	Given Name	Comments	Source	Year
ABARACH	Eliezer		Hamelitz #42	1899
AHARONOWITZ	Bentzion	visiting Vieksna	Hamelitz #68	1898
ARENOWITZ	Bentzion		Hamelitz #42	1899
EDELSHTEIN	Moshe		Hamelitz #42	1899
EITELSOHN	Tzvi		Hamelitz #42	1899
EIZENMANN	Shlomo		Hamelitz #42	1899
EPEL	Leib Zalman	Official Collector	Hamelitz #171	1893
EPELTZIN	Gimpl		Hamelitz #42	1899
EPELTZIN	Yitzchok		Hamelitz #42	1899
EPPIL	Yehuda		Hamelitz #42	1899
FRIDLANDER	Yehoshua		Hamelitz #42	1899
GLIKK	Yakov		Hamelitz #42	1899

GLIKMAN	Chaim		Hamelitz #42	1899
GROS	Tzvi		Hamelitz #42	1899
GVOS	Mansh		Hamelitz #42	1899
HETZ	Avraham		Hamelitz #42	1899
HETZ	Yitzchok		Hamelitz #42	1899
KAPLAN	Moshe		Hamelitz #42	1899
KOHN	Shmuel Yehuda		Hamelitz #42	1899
KOIFMAN	Avraham Yitzchok		Hamelitz #42	1899
LIWERHAND	Yechezkel		Hamelitz #42	1899
MARKOSWAWITZ	Tzvi Hirsh		Hamelitz #42	1899
METZ	Shraga		Hamelitz #42	1899
NATENZOHN	Yehuda		Hamelitz #42	1899
NEIMAN	Yosef		Hamelitz #42	1899
PORTNOI	Yisroel		Hamelitz #42	1899
PRUSH	Shalom		Hamelitz #42	1899
RABINOWITZ	Tuvia		Hamelitz #192	1893
RABINOWITZ	Tuvia		Hamelitz #42	1899
SHMITMAN	Shlomo		Hamelitz #42	1899
SHUB	Leib	husband of Reitze Kopelowitz, married 1898 in Mazheik	Hamelitz #188	1898
TOW	Yehuda		Hamelitz #42	1899
WIGODER	Yisroel		Hamelitz #42	1899

Appendix 2

List of Mazheik Jews, paid up members of the *Agudath Yisrael* party from 1913

Avrekh Eliezer

Epel Leib

Glikman Hayim

Itelson Tsevi-Ze'ev

Hekst Avraham

Hetz Avraham

Metz Shraga

Portnoi Yisrael

Pun Leib

Tov Ben-Zion-Yeh

Pajuris (Payure)

Pajuris (Payure in Yiddish) lies in western Lithuania, on the east bank of the Jura River, about 40 km. (25 miles) north west of the administrative district center of Taurage (Tavrig). The forested hills around the town attract vacationers in the summer months.

The land and the village that developed nearby are mentioned in documents dating back to the sixteenth century. In the eighteenth century the land and the village were owned privately. Until 1795 Payure was part of the Polish Lithuanian Kingdom. The third division of Poland by the three superpowers of the times, Russia, Prussia and Austria, resulted in most of Lithuania becoming Russian territory until World War I. Between 1915 and 1918 the Germans occupied this zone, until in 1918 it was handed over to the new Lithuanian state.

General view of Payure

It is not known when Jews began to settle in Payure. During the Russian rule about 50 Jewish families lived there. From 1918 until 1940, under the rule of independent Lithuania, the number of the Jews in Payure decreased until just prior to the Holocaust only 30 Jewish families remained. Most of the Jews who departed, emigrated to South Africa.

In the 1900 list of donors in *HaMelitz* #121, the name of Ya'akov-Mordehai Abramson appears. He gave money, probably for the Settlement of *Eretz-Yisrael*.

Jews made their living from trade and crafts. The weekly market days on Mondays and Fridays and the quarterly fairs provided the main source of livelihood for the Jewish residents. Almost every family had an auxiliary farm near its home, where they grew vegetables and fruit trees. Some of the farms formed chicken cooperatives.

According to the first government census conducted in 1923, there were 499 residents in Payure, 280 (58%) being Jews.

The 1931 survey of local stores conducted by the Lithuanian government shows there were three leather shops, two bakeries and a pharmacy owned by Jews. Several wealthy timber merchants lived in town. In nearby villages a few Jewish agrarians lived, who would visit Payure during holidays.

In 1937 Payure had twelve Jewish tradesmen: two tailors, two butchers, two bakers, two painters, a cord twister, a photographer, a bookbinder and a milliner.

The Jewish Folksbank in nearby Shilel (Silale) served the Payure Jews.

In 1939 two non-Jewish families owned telephones.

Jewish children acquired their elementary education at the Hebrew school of the *Tarbuth* network. Some of the children studied in a *Heder* in town. Most of the boys continued their studies at the *Yeshivoth* of Kelm and Telz.

The *Beth Midrash*

The town's repertory society had a library that was open to the public. Most of the Payure Jews were members of the religious Zionist camp. In the elections for the 19th Zionist congress in 1935, 69 voters participated: 67 voted for the *Mizrahi* party, one for the Labor Party and one for the Grosmanists.

In Payure there was a wooden *Beth Midrash* with a splendid *Aron-Kodesh*. The rabbis of Payure included Yisrael-David Rabinovitz from 1850 to 1865, Shalom-Gershon son of Mosheh-Zelig Kav from 1910 to 1925 and Mosheh Kravitz who served from 1925, while the last rabbi was Yehudah Asovsky.

Institutions listed in the area included *Bikur Holim* and *Linath Hatsedek*.

The *Aron HaKodesh* in the *Beth Midrash*

On June 22nd 1941, the German army invaded Lithuania. At that time only about 120 Jews (approximately 30 families) lived in Payure. Some escaped to the village of Tenen (Teneniai), about 6 km. (3 miles) away. Two Jewish farmers lived there, the Feiges and the Zaltsmans: they and their children were murdered by Lithuanians at a site about 5 km. (3 miles) distant from the village on the road to Khveidan (Kvedarna). Those Jews who arrived at the village were imprisoned in a barn where they were kept for several days without food or water. They were brought to Kvedarna and killed, together with the local Jews, in the Tubines forest on June 29th, 1941 (4th of Tamuz 5701).

A mass grave in the Tubines forest, one of two massacre sites

The Jews who remained in Payure were led to Shilel and slain along with the other local Jews in the Tubines forest, 7 km. (4 miles) north of the road from Silale to Tubines on September 16th, 1941 (24th of Elul 5701). There are two mass graves in the forest, 300 meters (330 yards) north of Tubines and 350 meters (380 yards) southwest of Tubines. There were 700 victims, men, women and children, in the two graves.

The inscription on the monument in Lithuanian and Yiddish:

"In 1941, at this site, Hitler's assassins and their local helpers murdered 700 Jews - men, women, children."

Source:

Yad Vashem Archives, Koniuhovsky Collection 0-71, file 12

Plungė (Plungyan)

Plunge (Plungyan in Yiddish) lies in north-western Lithuania, in the Zamut (Zemaitija) region, 28 km. (17 miles) southwest of the district administrative center of Telsiai (Telz) and 50 km. (31 miles) northeast of the seaport city of Klaipeda (Memel). An estate named Plunge is mentioned in historical documents dating back to the fourteenth century. The town developed near the estate and in 1658 became a county administrative center. In 1792 it received the rights of a town and an emblem. In the eighteenth century Plungyan became an important junction on the commercial roads between Zamut, Memel and Liepaja in Latvia. Quarterly fairs were held in the town, the main trade being in cattle and horses. A market was held twice a week.

After the third division of Poland in 1795 by the three superpowers of that time, Russia, Prussia and Austria, part of Lithuania including Plungyan was handed over to Russia. During Russian rule (1795-1915) Plungyan was included in the Vilna *Gubernia* (province) but from 1843 was included in the Kovno *Gubernia*. During the period of independent Lithuania (1918-1940) the town ruled itself: that is, it had its own municipality and was also a county administrative center.

The estate, together with the town Plungyan, became the property of the noble family of Oginsky in 1873: they built a splendid palace with a garden of 50 hectares, which still exist.

The Oginsky Palace

(Picture taken and supplied courtesy of Elkan Gamzu, July 2005)

In 1888, 1894, 1914 and 1931 fires ravaged the town.

A sorry sight after a devastating fire, probably in 1931

The burial of the holy books and Torah scrolls damaged in the fire of 1931

Jewish settlement until after World War I

According to headstones in the Jewish cemetery, Jews settled in Plungyan during the sixteenth century. In the middle of the seventeenth century, during the *Va'ad Medinath Lita* (1623-1764), the Plungyan community was included in the Keidan district (*Galil*). In 1719 its first synagogue was built and Jewish houses were erected in the center of town and in the main streets. In 1769 the bishop of Zamut allowed Plungyan Jews to build a synagogue on church land on condition that it should not be higher than the church. As the Jews did not abide by this, a fine was imposed on them, but it is not known for how long they paid the imposition.

The Bath House Street

In 1765, 816 Jews lived in Plungyan. Their number had increased to 2,917 by 1847.

In 1848 an outbreak of cholera spread to Zamut and Plungyan and several hundred Jews succumbed in the epidemic.

Plungyan was one of the nineteen Jewish communities that objected to the Russian government order of 1843 stating that all Jews who resided less than 50 Viorst (about 50 km. or 31 miles) from the western border of the state should move to other *gubernias* further into Russia.

Local Jews dealt in trade, crafts and agriculture. The merchants in town maintained close commercial connections with the Memel region, then part of Germany, selling cattle, horses, geese, flax and other merchandise to the Germans. Jewish artisans, the tailors, shoemakers, butchers and others made a satisfactory living. In the 1880s there were several Jewish-owned workshops for processing amber, each employing 40 to 50 workers, and their products were sold all over Russia. Many families maintained auxiliary farms near their homes.

During these years hundreds of Plungyan Jews emigrated, mostly to South Africa and a few to America.

In the period 1869 to 1872, when some parts of Lithuania suffered a serious famine, Plungyan Jews sent money to Jewish victims through the aid committee in Memel. The Hebrew newspaper *HaMagid* (1872) published a list of Plungyan Jews who donated money to Jewish victims of the great famine in Persia (see **Appendix 2**). The fundraisers were Ya'akov Margalith and Josef Sol.

A large fire in the summer of 1888 burned down 25 Jewish houses, leaving 48 families without shelter and in great poverty. M. Oginsky, the estate owner, managed to contain the fire with the help of his workers. Later he did what he could to help the victims and this included the building of a hospital for the Plungyan Jews.

On a Fair day in July 1894, another fire destroyed 400 houses, 323 of them owned by Jews. Visitors to the fair escaped from the burning town but blocked the roads, and thus the fire brigade, on its way from the estate, was unable to reach the town. Many public buildings were razed, including the famous beautiful synagogue built in 1814, the great *Beth Midrash* built in 1864 which included two *Yeshivoth* with more than 100 students, the *Kloizim*, the *Talmud Torah* and the *Gemiluth Hesed* houses, and the ritual bath. Only 45 small houses escaped serious damage in the fire but about 2,500 Jews were left destitute. *HaMelitz* (July 20th, 1894) published an appeal to Jewish communities and to former Plungyaners abroad for help. Rabbi Zevulun Leib Barit, a member of the aid committee, signed this appeal. The address for sending donations was that of the chairman of the help committee, the nobleman Michael Oginsky. After the fire he accommodated several hundreds people in buildings on his estate and also fed them. Near the market square, where dozens of Jewish shops had burnt down, Oginsky built 36 permanent shops, making them available to the Jewish merchants at low prices to be repaid in twelve annual payments. For very poor merchants the payments were spread over twenty-four years. In addition, on his own account, he built a ritual bath house for the Jews and also lent the community the money to rebuild the big synagogue, on condition that half the sum would be repaid to him during the building and the balance in two years. Indeed, after two years the synagogue was ready.

Jews also lived in villages around Plungyan. In 1895 several Jews were murdered by neighbors: this prompted the exodus of many Jews.

In 1901 a Society for Supporting the Poor was established in order to stop beggars from knocking on doors for donations.

In that same year a house for the *Talmud Torah* was bought.

Among the rabbis who officiated in Plungyan were:

> Yehudah-Leib Ziv (lived during the eighteenth and at the beginning of the nineteenth centuries), he granted his approval (*Haskamah*) to print the *Vilna Talmud*

Yehiel Heler (1814-1863), who published many books on Judaism. These were printed in Koenisberg. He died in Plungyan.

Hayim-Yits'hak HaCohen Blokh (1867-1948), born in Plungyan, rabbi and head of the local *Yeshivah*. Later he emigrated to New Jersey in the United States, serving as Honorary President of the Association of the American and Canadian Rabbis. He published articles in *HaTsefirah* and in *Pardes*.

Zevulun Barit

Shemuel-Avigdor Faivelson (1859-1929).

The Great Synagogue

The *Beth Midrash*

In a list of yearly membership subscribers to *Agudath Yisrael* published in the party journal *HaDerekh* in Frankfurt, 56 Plungyan Jews were mentioned, headed by Rabbis Avigdor Faivelson and Josef Shakhnovitz (see **Appendix 1**).

Plungyan children studied in *Hadarim* where 20 to 30 youngsters were crowded into a small room. Later a *Talmud Torah* housed in the tailors' *Kloiz* was opened with about 80 children, most of them from poor families, and two *Melamdim*, Yeruham Levinsky being one of them for many years. One of the wealthy men in town donated a building for the *Talmud Torah* and employed *Melamdim* of a higher level, including a teacher for general subjects. Graduates of this *Talmud Torah* were accepted into *Yeshivoth*.

The *Shamash* Mosheh'le Reizes

In 1888 a Society for Teaching Crafts was established to teach poor children and orphans arts and crafts. The children who finished their studies at the *Talmud Torah* but did not continue at *Yeshivoth* were accepted as apprentices to craftsmen and the society paid for their tuition.

In 1891, a learned woman named Lina Odes opened a school for Jewish girls, which was licensed by the government. Russian, German and French languages were taught there.

According to the all-Russian census of 1897 there were 4,498 residents in Plungyan, 2,502 (56%) of them Jews.

In 1906 a Jewish teacher. Gutl, opened a *Heder Metukan* (improved Heder) where all subjects were taught in Hebrew. The students even performed plays in Hebrew. Due to pressure from the orthodox, who called this school a *Heder Mesukan* (dangerous Heder), this institution was closed after two years and only the *Talmud Torah* remained. During the years before the war the children of the wealthy also studied here but in the German occupation (1915-1918) the rulers opened an elementary school where the teaching language was German and all Jewish children studied there.

The *Hibath Zion* movement was quite active and in an 1896 list of Members who supported Jewish Agrarians in Syria and *Eretz-Yisrael*, three Plungyan Jews are mentioned. The Zionist movement influenced Plungyan when the first Zionist congresses were held.

Lists of donors published in *HaMelitz* for the settlement of *Eretz-Yisrael* in 1898, 1899, 1903 and 1909 mention many Plungyan Jews (see **Appendix 3**). Meir and Mosheh-Yits'hak Fleisher were the fund raisers, whereas the correspondents to *HaMelitz* from Plungyan were Ya'akov Mark and David-Mosheh Mitskun.

In 1901 the *Benoth Zion* (Daughters of Zion) society was founded, with 300 members. Most members tried hard to speak only Hebrew amongst themselves. From July 1901 until July 1902, 62 *Shekalim* were sold.

One delegate representing Plungyan, Telz and Salant participated in the conference of Zionist Societies from the provinces of Suwalk and Kovno in 1909.

Emigrants from Plungyan to *Eretz-Yisrael* at this time included Tovah Azulai, who arrived in 1906 and was known as a public worker in Jerusalem (where she established a public kitchen), and Avraham Liberman, who was the first *Shomer* (guard) in Herzliya and later became head of the municipality.

In the cemetery on the Mount of Olives in Jerusalem there are at least six headstones of Plungyan Jews:

> Pinhas, died 1862
>
> Batyah daughter of Yedidyah, died 1868
>
> Josef son of Azriel, died 1870
>
> Ze'ev son of Meir, died 1878
>
> Sarah daughter of Ze'ev, died 1882
>
> Golde wife of Ze'ev, died 1889.

The Period of Independent Lithuania (1918-1940)

At the end of the German occupation, Plungyan Jews retrieved their businesses and resumed their economic life.

In 1918 two Jewish youngsters, Garb and Bunka, voluntarily joined the newly organised Lithuanian army and fought for the independence of the new state. They were awarded medals for outstanding service as well as plots of land, as were given to other volunteers.

According to the government census in 1923, Plungyan had 4,236 residents, and 1,861 (44%) of them (including 46 from neighboring villages) were Jews.

Following the law of autonomy for minorities issued by the new Lithuanian government, the minister for Jewish affairs, Dr. Menakhem (Max) Soloveitshik ordered elections to community committees (*Va'adei Kehilah*) to be held in the summer of 1919. In Plungyan a community committee of fifteen members was elected: eight from *Akhduth (Agudath Yisrael)*, two General Zionists, two *Tseirei-Zion*, two workers and one non-party man. The committee was active in all aspects of Jewish life in the town from 1919 until March 1926.

The municipal elections of 1924 resulted in a council of fifteen members including seven Jews. Together with the elected Progressives they constituted an absolute majority. Two out of three candidates for mayor of the town were Jews. David-Barukh Goldvaser was the mayor for ten years. In the 1931 elections, four Jews, Mordehai Puzin, Avraham Lipman, Shelomoh Levi and Yehezkel Zaks, were among nine council members elected. But the elections of 1934 produced only three Jews (Puzin, Goldvaser and Lipman) in a council of nine. The deputy mayor was a Jew.

By and large, relations with Lithuanians were normal, despite the fact that Jews were often ridiculed or treated with scorn, and on several occasions offences were committed against Jews because of libel or false indictments. In 1935 there were serious anti-Semitic incidents, prompting the mayor to sign a public denunciation bearing the signatures of the priest and the local judge. The situation worsened after the Nazis came to power in neighboring Germany and especially after the annexation of the Memel region to Germany in 1939. On one Sunday, when hundreds of peasants were in town, a pogrom resulting from a blood libel was prevented at the last moment.

During this period the number of Jews decreased through emigration. The number of deaths exceeded the number of births: between 1930 and 1934 there were 94 births and 134 deaths, while 32 weddings took place.

Plungyan Jews made their living from trade, crafts, light industry and agriculture. According to the government survey of 1931 there were 54 shops, 47 (87%) of them owned by Jews.

Corner at the market, a shop and an ice cream seller (on the left)

Type of Business	Total	Owned by Jews
Groceries	4	4
Grains and Flax	3	3
Butchers and Cattle Trade	10	8
Restaurants and Taverns	3	2
Food Products	1	1
Beverages	2	2
Textile Products and Furs	10	10
Leather and Shoes	3	3
Haberdashery and Home Utensils	2	2
Pharmacies	4	3
Radio, Sewing Machines, Electric appliances	1	1
Hardware Products	6	5
Heating Materials	2	2
Miscellaneous	3	1

According to the same survey there were 27 enterprises, 20 (74%) Jewish owned:

Type of Factory	Total	Jewish Owned
Metal Workshops, Power Plants	1	1
Chemical Industry: Spirits, Soaps	1	1
Textile: Wool, Flax, Knitting	4	3
Sawmills, Furniture	1	1
Food Products: Mills, Bakeries	3	3
Dresses, Footwear, Furs, Hats	5	2
Leather Industry: Production, Cobbling	7	6
Hairdressers, Bristles and others	5	3

Because of the economic crisis in Lithuania and the open campaign of the Lithuanian merchants' association (*Verslas*) urging the non-Jews to boycott Jewish shops, the financial status of Jewish concerns deteriorated and in a few years their number declined to almost half. The situation of the Jewish artisans was no better. In 1935 there were about 60 Jewish artisans: thirteen bakers, eight shoemakers, six tailors, five blacksmiths, four tinsmiths, three tanners, three mirror makers, three photographers, three seamstresses, two hatters, two glaziers, two locksmiths, two barbers, two watchmakers, a carpenter and a saddler. Several Jewish families engaged in agriculture in neighboring villages. There were three Jewish doctors and two Jewish lawyers. By 1925 there were two Jewish doctors and a Jewish woman dentist. The Shavl-Memel (Siauliai-Klaipeda) railway, which began to operate in 1932, deprived many Jewish carters of their livelihood.

About 70% of Plungyan Jews received financial support from their relatives in South Africa, America and even *Eretz Yisrael*.

The Jewish Popular Bank (*Folksbank*) played an important role in the economic life of Plungyan Jews. In 1929 it had 321 members, but by 1935 the number had decreased to 220, 15% being Lithuanians.

An extensive fire razed half of the town's houses in March 1931, leaving 250 Jewish families roofless and destitute. Lithuanian Jewry organized help for the victims. In December 1932 a committee established for this purpose reported receiving donations from 200 settlements and institutions to help rehabilitate the victims. Most of the houses, bigger and more beautiful, were rebuilt over several years. Some owners, however, accrued great debts, which they could not settle.

The management and workers of the Folksbank

Education and Culture

In 1919 two schools, one Yiddish and one Hebrew opened in Plungyan: these amalgamated in 1927 under an order of the Ministry of Education. However, the majority of students preferred the Hebrew instruction. At the outset about 200 pupils had studied in both schools, but, due to the decreasing Jewish population, the number dwindled, and in 1935 only 130 to 140 pupils enrolled. For two years a Hebrew kindergarten existed. There was a *Talmud Torah*, at which 60 boys studied in substandard buildings, as well as a *Yeshivah* of about 50 boys.

A Hebrew pro-gymnasium supported by the government was housed in a building donated to the community by nobleman Oginsky before World War I. Its teachers were Yofe, Eidelman, Klibansky (Puzin), Amalsky and others. This building also housed the *Tarbuth* library with 500 books in Hebrew and 500 in Yiddish.

In 1930 the Yiddishist *Libhober fun Visen* (Fans of Knowledge) society established a library containing about 1,000 books in Yiddish, which was named after the writer Y. L. Peretz . Next to it was a reading room where the daily newspapers from Kovno were available. In 1935 there were 60 subscribers to the various Jewish daily newspapers.

Occasionally cultural activities took place. In April 1933 a protest meeting was held against the persecution of the Jews in Germany. The speakers included the well-known Dr.Ya'akov Robinson, the lawyer Hirsh Rolnik and others. On June 5th, 1935 there was a mock public trial on the subject of the attitude of Jewish youth to the nineteenth Zionist congress that had taken place in this year.

Zionist and other activities

Many Plungyan Jews belonged to the Zionist movement. All Zionist parties were represented. The Plungyan Zionists voted for the various parties at seven Zionist Congresses as follows:

Cong. No.	Year	Total Shek.	Total Voter	Labor Party Z"S Z"Z		Rev.	G.Z. A B		Gros.	Miz.
14	1925	27	--	--	--	--	--	--	--	
15	1927	24	17	2	5	---	5	--	--	5
16	1929	109	51	14	6	2	17	--	--	12
17	1931	----	70	25	4	24	11	--	--	6
18	1933	----	156	116		21	6	--	3	10
19	1935	246	212	144		--	5	50	2	11
21	1939	86	64	52		---	5	Nat	Block 7	

Cong. = Congress; Shek. = Shekalim; Rev. = Revisionists; G.Z. = General Zionists;

Gros. = Grosmanists; Miz. = Mizrahi; Nat. Block = National Block

In May 1932 the new Zionist Socialist Party Club opened with a festive ceremony. The *HeHalutz* branch at this time consisted of about 50 members and extensive cultural activities took place here. Among the Zionist youth organizations active in Plungyan were the *HaShomer HaTsair*, *HeHalutz Hatsair* and *Betar*.

In 1933 an urban *Kibbutz* with 22 *Halutsim* and *Halutsoth* existed. Several of them emigrated to *Eretz-Yisrael* and were among the founders of *Kibbutz Ramath HaShofet*. Sports activities took place at the branches of *Maccabi* with its 80 members, also under the auspices of *HaPoel* and Sport, the latter a society connected to the Peretz library.

There was an all Jewish fire brigade whose commander was a man named Rest.

קבוץ,המפלס",פלודזאגין, לפני עליבתם על החברה שלמה רעקב

Kibbutz of *HeHalutz*, *Hamefales* 1934

Jewish members of the volunteer fire brigade

Religion and Welfare

The great synagogue, the new *Beth Midrash* and three *Kloizim* of the orthodox were located in the *Shulhoif*, the center of religious life of Plungyan

Jews. Religious youths were organized in a *Tifereth Bahurim* organization which in 1929 had about forty members. There was also a children's society *Pirhei Shoshanim* (Rose Flowers) whose aim it was to collect religious books for the synagogue. After the *Simhath Torah* holiday these books would be delivered to the synagogue in a festive ceremony while the children were carried on the arms of the adults to this event.

Two rabbis served in Plungyan at this time: Levi Shpitz (1887-1941), one of the most important rabbis in Lithuania, who wrote an essay on the Talmud, but was murdered in the Holocaust, and the last rabbi, Avraham Mordehai Vesler (1892-1941), the spiritual director of the teachers seminar in Telz, and an active member of *Agudath Yisrael*. He was also put to death in the Holocaust, together with his community.

The Hevrah Kadisha

Help and welfare institutions included: *Gemiluth Hesed*, which gave loans without interest or against goods deposited in a pawnshop, a hospital, the *Bikur Holim* society which provided medical help and medicine to the needy, a *Hevrah Kadisha* and others. The OZE organization provided free pediatric treatment and free meals to poor school children and sent the sick to summer camps in Kalniskiai, a village 3 km. (2 miles) from Plungyan. In 1939 this organization also provided free medical help and financial support to refugee children from Memel. OZE also supported Jewish sport clubs and libraries.

The money it received was used for financing its activities came from fundraising events and amateur shows.

When refugees arrived from Memel after the German annexation of their town in March 1939, a committee was established to take care of them. Avraham Puzin left his business and dedicated all his time to collecting money for this task, in which he excelled.

These were some of the personages who were born in Plungyan:

Yits'hak Ze'ev Olshvanger (1825-1896), rabbi in Tavrig and St. Petersburg and active in the *Hovevei Zion* movement.

Josef-Jozel Hurvitz (1848-1920), a pupil of Israel Salanter, who propagated his *Musar* (Ethics) doctrine among thousands of his pupils. He died in Kiev and his coffin was brought to Israel in 1963. He was buried in Jerusalem.

Eliezer-Lazarus Goldshmidt (1871-1950), who translated the *Talmud-Bavli* (the Babalonian Talmud) printed in 1930-1936 and the Koran into German. He died in London.

Mordehai Plungyan-Plungyansky (1814-1883), a Hebrew writer, the secretary and proofreader of the well-known *Rom* printing establishment in Vilna, which published books on Jewish issues.

Luis Rozental (born in 1888), among the greatest sculptors of his time in America.

Adv. Tsevi Rolnik, the director of the Hebrew pro-gymnasium in town.

Meir Rolnik, brother of Tsevi Rolnik (above), a well-known publisher in Jerusalem.

David Shur (1901-1987), emigrated to *Eretz-Yisrael* in 1920 and was among the founders of *Kibbutz Ayeleth HaShahar and Moshav Yarkonah*. He was a specialist in beekeeping, and published books and articles on bee breeding.

Tsevi-Hirsh Brik (Barak) (1905-1995), graduated in law at the University of Kovno; member of the Zionist Socialist Center in Lithuania; imprisoned in the Kovno ghetto for three years; wrote articles in the Kovno newspapers *Di Tsait* and *Dos Vort*; lived in Israel from 1949; one of the editors of *Yahaduth Lita* Vol. 4 (Tel Aviv 1984); father of Aharon Barak, the president of the High Court of Justice in Jerusalem. He died in Jerusalem in the 1990s.

Zalman Levi, born in 1907; studied at Telz Yeshivah, in Johannesburg South Africa from 1927; wrote political articles for the periodical *Proletarishe Shtime* (Johannesburg) and was its editor from 1970. Wrote many articles in the *Afrikaaner Yiddishe Tsaitung*.

During World War II and Afterwards

With the annexation of Lithuania by the Soviet Union in 1940, the factories and also most shops, many Jewish owned, were nationalized, with the owners becoming the managers. All Zionist parties and youth organizations were disbanded and Hebrew educational institutions were closed. The supply of goods decreased and as a result prices soared. The middle class, mostly Jewish, bore the brunt, and the standard of living dropped. At the beginning of June 1941, five Jewish families, who were considered "undesirable elements", comprising fourteen people, including four young children, were exiled to Siberia. However some Jewish youths were happy with the new regime and played an active part in its institutions.

In 1940 Plungyan had about 6,000 residents, about 1,700 (28%) of them Jews.

When the news of the German invasion into the Soviet Union on June 22nd, 1941 became known, Jews fled to villages near the town and to Russia. But only thirty families and some individuals succeeded in their flight. A train that had departed from Plungyan was bombed by the Germans and all its passengers were killed, among them many Jewish families.

The Germans entered Plungyan on June 25th, 1941. Before the Germans arrived, armed Lithuanians identified by white stripes on their arms had already taken over the town. On the second day of their rule the Jews were ordered to leave their houses and to congregate in the synagogue and in the *Beth Midrash*. Armed guards at the doors did not permit the admission or distribution of any food brought by Lithuanian friends or the maids of their former employers. About sixty young men were sent to work on farms in the vicinity while other men and women were assigned to various chores every day. They swept the streets and cleaned latrines manually while being assaulted.

The Lithuanian guards would perform different pranks in order to humiliate the Jews and to delight the masses. For example, they forced five or six respected Jews to carry a wooden beam, over which they poured petrol and which they then set alight. The Jews were compelled to carry the beam until the fire spread onto their garments. One who attempted to escape from the fire was beaten to death.

Guards cut off the beard of the town's rabbi, Avraham-Mordehai Vesler: they then forced him and his wife to walk arm in arm through the streets, carrying a bucket each, to the jeers and laughter of the residents.

One day a fire broke out in the bath house street and the Lithuanians blamed the Jews for starting it. Under this a pretext they spread a rumor in town that the Jews were all dangerous. Thus the Jews were all imprisoned in the synagogue, where crowding, hunger and lack of sanitation made conditions unbearable. The pharmacy owner Efrayim Israelovitz, the pharmacist Hayah

Shlomovitz, the flourmill owner Karabelnik, the blacksmith Shelomoh Gilis and the textile engineer Bishitz who had continued with their jobs until then, were also imprisoned in the synagogue. The young men who worked on the farms did not return to the synagogue. They were murdered en route.

On Sunday, July 13th, 1941 Lithuanian guards transported the Jews in groups to sites where pits had been prepared. The first group of sixty men were led there on foot. As they passed the textile factory, the factory guards, testing their weapons and with the encouragement of the escorts, murdered about forty of the hapless men. The remaining victims, group by group, were transported to the execution site in trucks. There they were forced to undress and to sit on the brim of the pit, where they were shot from behind.

A group of girls was led on foot to the gruesome site. Passing the Catholic church one of the girls, Orela Tsin, said harsh words to the Lithuanians. The murderers poured kerosene over her and set her on fire. Among the victims were sixty girls who had agreed to convert to Christianity in order to be saved. According to the evidence of Josefa Osovsky-Olshvang, a righteous among the nations, a monk named F. Lignogaris who taught religion at the gymnasium and knew the girls, had convinced them to convert to Christianity in order that their lives would be spared. But soon after the massacre they too were killed and buried in a mass grave near that of their families. According to the witness, the monk later lost his mind and was committed to a mental hospital. The killing spree lasted from Sunday morning and all through the night until Monday. In the morning the executioners returned to the town in trucks, singing. Two Germans who were in the town did not interfere. All the "work" was done by Lithuanians, most of them residents of Plungyan and its vicinity. The names of several of these killers are listed in the Yad Vashen archives in Jerusalem.

Only one Jew survived the murder, having married a Lithuanian woman before the war and converted to Christianity: his wife and the local priest saved him. After Soviet rule returned to Plungyan, this man revealed the names of the murderers and helped to find them. Some, who did not escape with the Germans, were caught and sentenced.

According to Soviet sources, 1,800 victims were buried in mass graves near the village of Kausenai, about 4 km. (2.5 miles) northwest of Plungyan, and the bodies of the sixty youngsters who worked on the farms were found in a forest near the village of Milosaiciai, about 6 km. (4 miles) south of Plungyan.

Only 221 Plungyan Jews survived the war. Some were hidden by Lithuanians, some remained in the Shavl ghetto and others settled in the Soviet Union. Twenty-six Plungyan youths fell in battle as soldiers of the Red Army.

After the war a monument was erected on the mass grave in Kausenai. In 1988 another was erected in memory of Plungyan Jews by the Jewish sculptor Ya'akov Bunka and a team of Lithuanian sculptors.

Plungyan born Masha Rolnik was in the Vilna ghetto with her family. She was moved to concentration camps in Germany. Somehow she survived, and wrote her memoirs in Yiddish. Her book (I Have To Tell, Jerusalem 1965) has been translated into many languages, including Hebrew.

After Lithuania was liberated from Nazi rule, about thirty Jewish families returned to Plungyan. They settled in their homes after evicting the Lithuanian tenants. In 1946 armed Lithuanians who were roaming the forests because they refused Soviet rule, murdered a single Jew who had returned from the Soviet Union. In 1953 a blood libel was circulated concerning a war invalid who had allegedly abducted a Lithuanian girl in order to use her blood. The main instigator, a drunkard and criminal, together with the girl's mother, threatened Plungyan Jews. The commander of the local police enlisted soldiers from a nearby camp and when the girl was found to be healthy and unharmed, the situation was defused. The mother was sentenced to fifteen days in jail and the instigator, who had vandalised the windows of Jews and was found with stolen property in his flat, was sentenced to three years in prison.

However, many Plungyan Jews left town. Some moved to larger towns in Lithuania and some emigrated to Israel. In 1970, 41 Jews were resident in Plungyan; in 1979, there were 25; in 1989, only 15.

In the early 1990s, on the site of the old Jewish cemetery, a monument was erected with the inscription in Yiddish and Lithuanian: "The old Jewish cemetery. Let the memory of the deaths be sacred."

The mass graves near the village of Kausenai
(Picture taken and supplied courtesy of Elkan Gamzu, July 2005)

The murder site and the monument

The inscription on the monument: "At this site, the Nazi murderers and their helpers, on 13-15 July 1941, brutally murdered 1800 Jews, children, women, men."

Two of the three memorial wooden sculptures by Ya'akov Bunka

The third sculpture

Sources:

Yad Vashem Archives -M-1/E-1697/1565; M-40/MAP/76; O-2/946; O-33/976, 2349; Koniuhovsky collection 0-71, files 37-39

YIVO - New York, Collection of Lithuanian Communities, files 716-727, 1397, 1398, 1537

Zikhron Meir, Memorial book for Meir Rolnik (1900-1973), Jerusalem 1974

Piker, Yankel - So it was (Yiddish), Tel Aviv 1979

Rolnik, Masha - I have to tell (Hebrew), Jerusalem 1965

Yiddisher Lebn - Kovno-Telz, No.165

Dos Vort - Kovno, 13.11.1934; 27.9.1935

Dos Naie Vort- Kovno, 9.7.1934; 12.6.1934

Di Yiddishe Shtime - Kovno, 3.10.1919; 22.6.1928; 22.7.1930; 1.4.1931; 7.4.1931; 10.4.1931; 14.4.1931; 15.4.1931; 17.6.1931; 26.6.1931; 21.8.1931; 13.10.1931; 23.12.1932; 2.9.1935; 4.11.1935

Di Tsait - Kovno, 21.5.1932

HaMelitz - St. Petersburg, 22.9.1869; 18.9.1878; 25.10.1881; 9.5.1887; 10.1.1888; 22.5.1888; 21.6.1888; 11.2.1891; 27.10.1891; 20.7.1894; 9.3.1895; 13.11.1895; 26.6.1901; 20.5.1902; 12.6.1903

HaNe'eman - Telz, No. 1-2, Teveth, 5689 (1929)

Folksblat - Kovno, 21.7.1930; 29.8.1930; 1.1.1933; 19.4.1933; 5.6.1935; 13.6.1935; 16.6.1935; 25.4.1939; 21.5.1939; 2.7.1939; 12.7.1939

Jerushalayim d'Lita (Yiddish) - Vilna, No. 5(7), May 1990

Pakalniskis A. (Lithuanian) - Plunge, Chicago 1980

Naujienos - Chicago, 11.6.1949

Respublika - Vilnius, 25.6.1992

Appendix 1
List of paid-up members of the *Agudath Yisrael* party

Abramovitz Hayim

Alkanovitz Ben-Zion

Berman Ben-Zion, shohet

Broda Ze'ev

Dimant Yehoshua

Epil Mordehai

Fain Mosheh-Zelig

Faivelzon Shemuel-Avigdor, Rabbi

Gamzu Shimon

Garb Eliezer

Garzansky Shelomoh

Getz Ze'ev

Gibor (Gvor) Yits'hak

Gornzinsky Yedidyah

Hotz Eliezer

Hovsha Sheraga

Israelevitz Yisrael-Eliyahu

Klotz Benjamin

Klotz Sheraga

Kreszol Aizik

Kriger Shaul

Kruskol Mosheh-Leib

Leibovitz Yehoshua

Levinsky Yeruham

Liberman Avraham

Likhtenshtein Meir

Lipman Tsevi

Litvin Mordehai

Luria Aharon-David

Luria Hilel

Metz Ya'akov

Metz Yehoshua-Mordehai

Odes Yits'hak

Orliansky Zalman

Patsun Ya'akov

Pozin Mosheh

Ritov Benjamin

Rostovsky Eliezer

Rubinshtein Tsevi

Segal Yits'hak

Shakhnovitz Josef, rabbi

Shapiro Ben-Zion

Shpitz Barukh

Shlavin Zalman

Shereshevsky David

Sher Yits'ha-Leib

Sher Azriel

Sher Zalman

Sher Joel

Shtutsin Yehezkel

Verzaner Dov

Yaffe Josef

Yafet Tsevi

Zak Yits'hak-Josef

Zinger H.G.

Zusmanovitz Yits'hak

Appendix 2

List of Plungyan Jews donors to the victims of the Persian famine

(From Jewishgen.oOrg.>Databases >*HaMagid* # 15, 1872, by Jeffrey Maynard)

ADEM Leizer	BLANK Michel
EDILMAN Yisroel	ELAZAR Yakov
FEINSHTEIN Michael	FISHEL Leah
FRAINK Yitzchok & son GARB Feitel	GARB Moshe
GARB Yechezkel Leib	GARB Yitzchok Yakov
HATZIN Shimon	KA"TZ Baruch
KA"TZ Meir	KLEWANSKI Eli
KONIGSBERG Abba	KONIGSNERG Aharon
LEIB Yosef	LEWINZOHN Dovid
LEWINZOHN Mendil	LIFSHITZ Hillel Rabbi
MARGOLIOS Dov Ber	MEIR Gershon
MINDA Meir	NATHANZOHN Eidel
NATKIN Chaim Nachman	POTSTERM Dovid
POTSTERM Neta	PRISTOW Dovid
ROSMOWSKI Shlomo ben Yosef	ROSMOWSKI Yitzchok
SENER Levi	SHAPIRO Bentzion
SHAPIRO Shai	SHAPIRO Yitzchok
SHMATZINSKI Uri	SHU"V Zondil
SIL Leib	SIL Meir Zev
TROIB Meir bridegroom	TROIB Michel
YAFFE Yosef	YAMKOWSKI Apamheker (female?) 1872
YEZNER Leizer	ZAK Zelig
ZAKS Heshil	ZATON Shalom
ZIN Hirsh Leib	ZIV Ezriel
ZIV Shaul Yitzchok	Ezriel from Kuliai (Kohl)
Leib ben Pazriel	Levi ben Monash brother of Shmuel
Shmuel ben Monash brother of Levi	Yakov from Birstonas
Yakov Hirsh	Yakov Meir

Appendix 3

List of Plungyan Jews donors to the Settlement of *Eretz Yisrael*

(From Jewishgen.Org.>Databases>Lithuania>Hamelitz. Compiled by Jeffrey Maynard)

Surname	Given Name	Comments	Source in Hamelitz	Year
ABRAMOWITZ	Chaim		#211	1899
AKUM	A		# 225	1903
ALBIN	K		# 225	1903
ALBIN	K		# 225	1903
ALBIN	Kalman		#211	1899
ARINZON	Paula wife of Y Levenshtein	wed lag b'omer	#123	1900
BEINSHTEIN	Sh		#123	1900
BERENSHTEIN	Gedaliah		#142	1898
BERENSHTEIN	H		# 130	1897
BERNSHTEIN	G		#123	1900
BERNSHTEIN	Yosef Zev	from Chotzer Wilmishken near Plungian	#4	1895
BLANK	Sh		# 225	1903
BLANK	Shmuel		#144	1898
BLOCH	Chaim		#211	1899
BRIK	Mina wife of Shmuel Shor of Telz	wed	#215	1893
BRIK	Sh		#142	1898
BRIK	Sh		#211	1899
BRIK	Sh		# 225	1903
BRIK	Shraga		#90	1898
BROIDA	Moshe		#115	1898
COHEN	G		# 225	1903
COHEN	Nachum		#211	1899
DAGISHEWSKI	M		# 225	1903
DIMANT	M		# 225	1903
DRUK	A		#211	1899
DRUK	A		# 225	1903

DRUK	Eli		#44	1899
DRUK	Eliahu		#90	1898
EDELMAN	Chaim		#211	1899
ELKANOWITZ	B		# 225	1903
EMDEN	Y R		# 225	1903
EMDIN	Batia wife of Chaim Dov Lewinzohn	wed in Plungian	#209	1893
FAKTOR	H		# 225	1903
FEIGELMAN	Nesanel Yehuda	wed	#79	1899
FEIN	M Z		# 225	1903
FEIN	Yitzchok		#115	1898
FEIN	Yitzchok		#79	1899
FEIN	Yitzchok fiance of Leah Katzenelenboigen	engaged	#142	1898
FEIN	Yitzchok husband of Leah Katzenellenbogen	wed 1898	# 228	1898
FEINSHTEIN	M		# 225	1903
FIN	Yitzchok		#211	1899
FLEIKS	M A		# 228	1898
FLEISHER	Devorah sister of M A	deceased TRGZ	#115	1898
FLEISHER	M A		#142	1898
FLEISHER	M A		#235	1898
FLEISHER	M A		#90	1898
FLEISHER	M A		#211	1899
FLEISHER	M A		#123	1900
FLEISHER	M A		# 225	1903
FLEISHER	M A brother of Devorah		#115	1898
FREIA	Y		# 225	1903
FREIA	Yisroel		# 228	1898
FREIA	Yisroel		#211	1899
FREINK	B		#123	1900
FRIDENSOHN	R wife of G Kaplan	from Lodz wed 1898	#235	1898
FRIDLAND	Pesach husband	wed	#142	1898

	of Ita Rabinowitz			
FRIDMAN	Y D		# 225	1903
GABOR	Y		# 225	1903
GAMZO	Y		#211	1899
GAMZO	Y		# 225	1903
GARB	A		#211	1899
GARB	A		# 225	1903
GARB	M		# 225	1903
GARB	M		# 225	1903
GARB	Y		#211	1899
GARB	Y R		# 225	1903
GARB	Yakov Dov		#211	1899
GARB	Yitzchok		#211	1899
GESELOWITZ	Shmuel		#144	1898
GETZ	A		#228	1898
GETZ	A		#211	1899
GETZ	A		# 225	1903
GETZ	Aharon		#144	1898
GETZ	Z		#211	1899
GLEZER	Tz		# 225	1903
GLIKMANTZ	Shifra		# 228	1898
GRAF	Z		#123	1900
GRAF	Z		# 225	1903
GRINMAN	A B		# 225	1903
GURWITZ	R		#144	1898
GUTMAN	Avraham Yosef		#160	1897
HAGAR	Yitzchok husband of Leah Knopfing from Libau		#4	1895
HESHELOWITZ	Sh		#211	1899
HESHELOWITZ	Sh		# 225	1903
HIRSH	M		# 225	1903
HIRSHOWITZ	Peretz	in Africa	#44	1899
HOWSHA	Sh		# 225	1903
IZRAELEWITZ	Ephraim		#211	1899
IZRAELEWITZ	Ephraim		#272	1900

IZRAELOWITZ	Y		# 225	1903
KALZIN	Tz		#123	1900
KANTOR	Hillel		#211	1899
KANTOWITZ	Aizik		#211	1899
KAPLAN	A Ch father of G		#235	1898
KAPLAN	Eliezer Leib		#206	1895
KAPLAN	G son of A Ch husband of R Fridensohn	wed 1898	#235	1898
KAPLAN	Sh Ch		# 225	1903
KARG	B		# 225	1903
KATZENELENB OIGEN	Leah fiancee of Yitzchok Fein	engaged	#142	1898
KATZENELLEN BOGEN	Leah wife of Yitzchok Fein	wed 1898	# 228	1898
KATZIN	B		# 228	1898
KATZIN	B A		#79	1899
KATZIN	Tzvi		#144	1898
KATZIN	Y T		# 228	1898
KENIGSBERG	Kalman		#90	1898
KENIGSBERG	Kalman		#79	1899
KESEL	Chaim		#211	1899
KESSEL	Chaim		#44	1899
KIRSH	M		#44	1899
KIRSH	Tz		# 225	1903
KLOIZNIN	Sh	from Salant	# 228	1898
KLOTZ	Sh		#44	1899
KLOTZ	Sh		#79	1899
KLOTZ	Sh		# 225	1903
LASKAS?	B		#123	1900
LASSER	Izidor husband of Regina Lewinzohn	wed in Chicago	#229	1895
LEIBOWITZ	A		# 228	1898
LEIBOWITZ	D B		# 228	1898
LEIBOWITZ	Y		# 228	1898
LEIBOWITZ	Y		# 225	1903

LENMAN	Avraham		#235	1898
LENTIN	A		#123	1900
LENTIN	A		# 225	1903
LENTIN	Avraham		#156	1895
LENTIN	Avraham		# 228	1898
LENTIN	Avraham		#115	1898
LENTIN	Avraham		#142	1898
LENTIN	Avraham		#144	1898
LENTIN	Avraham		#90	1898
LENTIN	Ephraim		#211	1899
LESHEM	Boris		#90	1898
LESHEM	Boruch		#211	1899
LESHEM	H		# 225	1903
LESHEM	Sh		# 225	1903
LEVENSHTEIN	Y husband of Paula Arinzon	Doctor - wed lag b'omer	#123	1900
LEWI	Aba		#211	1899
LEWIMZOHN	L father of Yosef Chaim		#123	1900
LEWIN	A		# 225	1903
LEWINZOHN	Chaim Dov husband of Batia Emdin	wed in Plungian	#209	1893
LEWINZOHN	D		# 225	1903
LEWINZOHN	Dovid		#144	1898
LEWINZOHN	Dovid father of Regina		#229	1895
LEWINZOHN	Eliezer		#90	1898
LEWINZOHN	L		# 225	1903
LEWINZOHN	Leib		#142	1898
LEWINZOHN	Leib		#144	1898
LEWINZOHN	M A		# 228	1898
LEWINZOHN	M L		# 225	1903
LEWINZOHN	Regina bas Dovid wife of Izidor Lasser	wed in Chicago	#229	1895
LEWINZOHN	Yosef Chaim ben L	born 1899	#123	1900

LEWINZON	Dovid	#90	1898
LEWINZON	Dovid	#211	1899
LEWINZON	Leib	#211	1899
LEWIT	M L	#82	1899
LEWIT	M L	#123	1900
LEWIT	Moshe Leib	#144	1898
LEWIT	Moshe Leib	#235	1898
LEWIT	P Y	# 225	1903
LEWIT	Shraga	#90	1898
LEWITT	Moshe Leib	#115	1898
LEWITT	Sh	# 228	1898
LIPSKI	Sh	# 225	1903
MARK	N	# 225	1903
MARKUS	M	#123	1900
MERE	B	#211	1899
MESHI	Avraham	#44	1899
METZ	Yakov	#90	1898
MIRWISH	M Ch	# 225	1903
MIRWISH	Moshe Chaim	# 228	1898
MIRWISH	Moshe Chaim	#44	1899
MOTZ	Ch M	# 225	1903
NATANZON	Eidel father of Miriam	#90	1898
NATANZON	Miriam bas Eidel	#90	1898
NEIMAN	Tz	# 225	1903
NEIMAN	Z	# 225	1903
NURWITZ	Tz R	#123	1900
OLSHWANG	M	# 225	1903
OLSHWANG	P	# 225	1903
PLUNGIANSKI	A	#211	1899
PLUNGIANSKI	A	#123	1900
PLUNGIANSKI	A	# 225	1903
PLUNGIANSKI	Eliahu father of Ezriel	#144	1898
PLUNGIANSKI	Ezriel	#211	1899
PLUNGIANSKI	Ezriel ben Eliahu wed LG B'Omer	#142	1898

PLUNGIANSKI	Linie	widow	#144	1898
PLUNGIANSKI	Tz		#123	1900
PLUNGIANSKI	Y		# 225	1903
POPIN	P M wife of Dovid Rachmal	wed	#79	1899
POZEN	Yakov		#201	1895
POZIN	Avraham		#90	1898
POZIN	Avraham		#44	1899
POZIN	Moshe		#211	1899
POZIN	Sh Y		#90	1898
POZIN	Sh Y		#79	1899
POZIN	Y		#123	1900
POZIN	Y		# 225	1903
POZIN	Yakov		#144	1898
POZIN	Yakov		#90	1898
POZIN	Yakov		#211	1899
RM	Rabbi Zelig		#144	1898
RABINOWITZ	A		#211	1899
RABINOWITZ	A		#79	1899
RABINOWITZ	A		#123	1900
RABINOWITZ	A		# 225	1903
RABINOWITZ	A Sh		#123	1900
RABINOWITZ	Aharon Sh		#82	1899
RABINOWITZ	Eli		# 228	1898
RABINOWITZ	Eliahu		#144	1898
RABINOWITZ	Eliahu		#90	1898
RABINOWITZ	Ita wife of Pesach Fridland	wed	#142	1898
RABINOWITZ	Sh L		# 225	1903
RABINOWITZ	Yoel Eli		#201	1895
RACHMAL	Dovid husband of P M Pozin	wed	#79	1899
REIT	Yermiahu	engaged	#144	1898
REST	Yermiahu		# 228	1898
REST	Yermiahu		#211	1899
ROCHMAL	Yona		#211	1899
ROLNIK	Aba		#44	1899

ROSHTOWSKI	N		# 225	1903
ROSHTOWSKI	Y		# 225	1903
ROSTOWSKI	A		#211	1899
ROSTOWSKI	A		#123	1900
ROSTOWSKI	A Y		# 225	1903
ROSTOWSKI	Aharon		#144	1898
ROSTOWSKI	Aharon father of Shmuel Leib		#90	1898
ROSTOWSKI	Shmuel Leib ben Aharon		#90	1898
ROZIN	Avraham		#79	1899
SEGAL	B		# 228	1898
SEGAL	B		#211	1899
SEGAL	Bendet brother of Yakov Heshil		#68	1898
SEGAL	Shalom Yosef		#115	1898
SEGAL	Yakov		#115	1898
SEGAL	Yakov		#144	1898
SEGAL	Yakov		#90	1898
SEGAL	Yakov		#211	1899
SEGAL	Yakov Heshil brother of Bendet husband of Eitil Zaks	wed	#68	1898
SHAPIRO	Malka	wed	#144	1898
SHAPIRO	Yosef		# 228	1898
SHAPIRO	Yosef		#79	1899
SHER	B		# 225	1903
SHER	Sh		# 225	1903
SHEREKOWSKI	D		# 225	1903
SHIR			#211	1899
SHLEZ	Sh		# 225	1903
SHMUEL			#211	1899
SHOCHAT	Tzvi		#144	1898
SHOR	M		#123	1900
SHOR	Moshe		#142	1898
SHOR	Sh		# 225	1903

SHOR	Shmuel		#144	1898
SHPITZ	B		# 225	1903
SHPITZ	Boruch		#144	1898
SHPITZ	Boruch		#211	1899
SHTOTZIN	A		#211	1899
SHTOTZIN	Y		# 225	1903
SHULMAN	Yosef		#211	1899
TROIB	Aizik		#44	1899
TZIN	Shmuel		#144	1898
TZIN	Zalman		#115	1898
TZINKOWSKI		widow from Vilna	#90	1898
TZIRA	Dovid		# 225	1903
WISTOW	A		# 225	1903
WOLPERT	Y		# 225	1903
YAFE	Ephraim		#211	1899
YAFE	Ephraim		#211	1899
YAFE	Ephraim		# 225	1903
YAFE	P		#123	1900
YAFE	Tz		#123	1900
YAFE	Tz		# 225	1903
YAME	Y		# 225	1903
YAVETZ	Yakov		#144	1898
YUDELMAN	Ch		# 225	1903
YUDELMAN	Sh		# 225	1903
YUDELMAN	Y		#123	1900
YUDELOWITZ	M		# 225	1903
ZAK	H		# 225	1903
ZAK	Zelig		#79	1899
ZAKS	A		# 225	1903
ZAKS	Eitel wife of Yakov Heshil Segal	wed	#68	1898
ZALIS	Y		#211	1899
ZELIG	A		# 225	1903
ZELIG	Shlomo		# 225	1903

ZIW	Yitzchol		#211	1899
	Shmuel Tzvi		# 228	1898
SHER	Avraham	in Weinberg, suburb of Capetown, SA	#131	1900

Raguva (Rogeve)

Raguva (Rogeve in Yiddish) lies on the Panevezys-Ukmerge highway, on the west bank of the Nevezis River, about 28 km. (17.5 miles) southeast of the district administrative center of Panevezys. An estate and a county by the name of Raguva were mentioned in documents dating back to 1501. In 1610 Raguva was mentioned as a town. In the seventeenth century, the town belonged to the noble family of the Oginskys. Until 1795, Rogeve was part of the Polish Lithuanian Kingdom. At the third division of Poland by the three superpowers of those times, Russia, Prussia and Austria, most of Lithuania became Russian territory until World War I. The town began to grow in the nineteenth century and became a county administrative center.

During World War I, in 1915 to 1918, Germany occupied this zone. In 1918 it became part of the new Lithuanian state. Starting in January 1919, the Soviets ruled the town for four months. During the period of independent Lithuania (1918-1940), Rogeve kept its status as a county administrative center. For many years there was no road or railway connecting Rogeve to nearby towns. There was no electricity in town, and in winter it was almost cut off from the world. In the 1930s a bus route to Panevezys was finally opened.

Jewish Settlement of Rogeve until World War I and Thereafter

Jews started settling in Rogeve, most likely in the seventeenth century. This conclusion is drawn from the very old Jewish tombstones in the Rogeve cemetery. Among them one can find tombstones of Panevezys Jews, who didn't have their own cemetery at that time and would bring their dead to be buried in this cemetery. In the seventeenth century several Karaite families are known to have lived in Rogeve as well.

In 1766 there were 1,187 Jewish poll-tax payers in Rogeve.

Until World War I, the economic situation of Rogeve Jews was quite good. They traded goods with the estate owners in the vicinity and made a decent living.

There was a leather factory owned by Faivel Pram, and a brush manufacturer who used processed pig bristles for his trade. Both businesses belonged to Jews and employed a total of about 100 workers. There were also tradesmen and peddlers who would stay in other villages during the week and return home for the *Shabbat*. The Jewish workers influenced the local orthodox community life in town. This was felt mainly in 1905 when revolutionary activity began in Russia. On one *Shabbat* in 1905, a member of the *Bund* organization stepped up to the *Bimah* at the synagogue, took out a pistol and burst into a ferocious verbal attack against the Czar. However with the rise of

Zionism, public opinion moved in support of this movement. Jews from Rogeve emigrated to *Eretz-Yisrael* long before the *Hibath Zion* movement was born. At the old cemetery in Jerusalem there are at least two tombstones of Rogeve Jews who died there in 1864 and in 1881:

> Eliezer Mordehai Jafe son of Shelomoh Zalman died in 1864
>
> Mordehai Jafe son of Yisrael died in 1881.

The old wooden synagogue was built in the eighteenth century. The solid building of the *Beth Midrash* with its artistically carved *Aron Kodesh*, built in the nineteenth century, was the center of Jewish life in Rogeve.

The Synagogue

Among the rabbis who officiated during this period in Rogeve were Benjamin Rabinovitz (1859–1861), who became famous for his struggle against the *Haskalah*, in particular against Mosheh-Leib Lilienblum; Shneur-Zalman Hirshovitz (died in 1904), a student and friend of Rabbi Yisrael Salanter, and Mordehai Rabinovitz who officiated between the years 1864-1885.

According to the all-Russian census of 1897, 1,762 residents lived in town, 1,223 (69%) of them Jews.

During the years 1839 and 1908 there were 21 subscribers to rabbinic literature in town.

The list of contributors for the victims of the Persian famine in 1872 includes the names of 41 Rogeve Jews (see **Appendix 1**). The fund raiser was Yehudah Gen.

The *Beth Midrash*

At the end of the nineteenth century and at the beginning of the twentieth century, two large fires destroyed almost half the homes in town. The fire of 1905 destroyed 100 houses.

At the beginning of World War I, in 1915, on the eve of *Shavuoth*, the Russian military ruler ordered Rogeve Jews to leave their homes in twenty-four hours and they were exiled deep into Russia. After the war only half of the exiled returned to their hometown.

During the Period of Independent Lithuania

Following the institution of the Law of Autonomy for Minorities issued by the new Lithuanian government, the minister of Jewish affairs Dr. Menachem (Max) Soloveitshik ordered elections for community committees (*Va'adei Kehilah*) to be held in the summer of 1919. In 1919 the elections to the community committee of Rogeve took place, and nine members were elected.

The committee worked until the end of 1925 when autonomy was annulled. The committee collected taxes as required by law and was in charge of all aspects of community life.

According to the first census performed by the Lithuanian government in 1923 Rogeve had 1,015 residents including 593 (58%) Jews.

The Nevezys River flowing through Rogeve

During this period Rogeve Jews made their living from trade, peddling and crafts. Several other families worked in agriculture. The weekly market days and three annual fairs provided an important source of livelihood for the local Jews.

In 1937, there were eighteen Jewish tradesmen in town: six shoemakers, three barbers, two glaziers, two tinsmiths, two blacksmiths, an oven builder, a tailor and a dressmaker.

The Folksbank, opened in 1924 and boasted 98 members in 1927, played an important role in the economic life of Rogeve Jews. In 1939, there were sixteen telephone owners, including 2 –Jews, a merchant and a doctor.

According to the 1931 government survey there were twelve shops in Rogeve, of which eleven were Jewish owned.

Type of Business	Owned by Jews
Groceries and Dairy products	2
Textile Products and Furs	5
Leather and Shoes	2
Sewing Machines, Electric Equipment	1
Medicine and Cosmetics	1

According to the same survey there were two flourmills in town, both owned by Jews.

In the mid-1930s the number of Jews decreased, because of the economic crisis in Lithuania. Also, the openly anti-Semitic propaganda of the

Lithuanian merchant association *Verslas* led to a boycott of Jewish shops, which caused enormous hardship to Jewish merchants. Cases of physical abuse were also recorded. In 1927 and 1939 there were pogroms in Rogeve; Jews were attacked in the streets and in their homes. The guards of the fire brigade, which was entirely Jewish, provided resistance to the murderers. The Jewish youth looked for a solution and many emigrated to *Eretz-Yisrael*, America and South Africa.

A Hebrew school of the *Tarbuth* network, established in 1925, provided some education for about 100 children.

Until the beginning of the 1930s, two libraries operated in town - one supported by the Zionist Socialist party and the other by the *Yiddiist* Fans of Knowledge (*Libhober fun Visen*) society. For some reason the Yiddish library was closed and only the Zionist Socialist library with about 600 Hebrew and Yiddish books remained open. From time to time lectures, Public Judgments and amateur productions were staged.

As always, the old synagogue and the *Beth Midrash* were the center of religious life in Rogeve. The synagogue was an attraction for tourists, Jewish and non-Jewish, who came to admire the artistic carvings inside.

Societies for studying the *Talmud, Mishnah, Ein Ya'akov* and more were active in town. There were many scholars of Judaism. Among the rabbis who officiated in this period in Rogeve were Mosheh-Mishel-Shemuel Shapira (in Rogeve from 1887 till his death in 1933), who published many books on religious issues, and Yisrael Mel, the last rabbi, who was murdered by Lithuanians during the Holocaust.

The welfare institutions *Ezrah, Gemiluth Hesed* and *Linath Hatsedek* offered their services to Rogeve Jews.

Many Rogeve Jews belonged to the Zionist camp. The number of *Shekel* purchasers increased during the years. The Zionist Socialist party was the most active and it was the initiator of almost all the cultural activities. There were also branches of the *Mizrahi*, the General Zionist parties and others. Many voted in the elections for the Zionist Congresses. The table below shows the division of votes for each party:

Cong No.	Year	Tot Shek	Total Votes	Labor Party Z"S	Z"Z	Rev	Gen Zion A	B	Gros	Miz
15	1927	44	41	9	23	---	2	----	----	7
16	1929	107	62	20	34	---	1	----	----	7
17	1931	47	42	16	18	---	1	----	----	7
18	1933	---	85	83		---	2	----	---	---
19	1935	160	160	107		---	---	1	12	40

Key: Cong No. = Congress Number, Tot Shek = Total Shkalim, Rev = Revisionists, Gen Zion = General Zionists, Gros = Grosmanists, Miz = Mizrakhi

Zionist youth organizations included *Gordonia* with forty members, *Deror* with fifty members, *HaShomer HaTsair-N.Z.H* and *Hehalutz HaTsair*.

Jews of note whose roots can be traced back to Rogeve include Yehoshua Palovitz (1875-1937), an author who wrote the *Shevuah* (Oath) that became the anthem of the *Poalei Zion* party. He emigrated to the USA in 1906 and published many poems and articles.

Michael Higer (1898-1952), researcher in Judaica, published books with critical views on Talmudic literature. Yehezkel Yofe (1858-1910), an important public worker in Kovno. A. Lazarov, a public worker, and a founder of the Folksbank network in Lithuania. Henakh Shtein (born in 1910), who emigrated to the USA and from 1929 in Baltimore, Maryland published Yiddish stories and poems.

During World War II and Afterwards

In June 1940, Lithuania was annexed to the Soviet Union and became a Soviet Republic. Following new rules, the flour mills owned by Jews were nationalized. A number of Jewish shops were also nationalized and commissars were appointed to manage them. Supply of goods decreased and prices soared. The middle class, mostly Jewish, bore the brunt but the standard of living dropped gradually. All the Zionist parties and youth organizations were disbanded and the Hebrew school was closed.

On June 22nd, 1941 war was declared between Germany and the Soviet Union. On June 26th the German army entered Rogeve. Immediately a local Lithuanian organization, active in the killing of the local Jews, offered itself to the service of the Nazis. .

At this time there were about 500 Jews in town.

The first to be detained and murdered were Jewish youngsters, followed by those who were in some way connected to Soviet rule.

In the middle of August, all the Jews, men, women and children were transferred to Panevezys, the district administrative center, and brought into the existing ghetto. On August 24th and 25th, 1941 (1st –and 2nd of Elul 5701), Rogeve Jews together with Panevys Jews were led to the Pajuoste forest, about 8 km (5 miles) east of the town, where they were ruthlessly massacred.

After the war the Soviets unearthed the mass grave: 7,000 victims were found there.

In the 1990s a new monument was added at the site.

The monument on the mass graves in Pajuoste forest

The inscription in Yiddish and Russian says: "Monument to the four mass graves of Jews of Panevys and surrounding area murdered by the German-Lithuanian Fascists in 1941." (Erected during the Soviet rule)

The inscription in Lithuanian: "At this site the Nazis and their helpers in August 1941 murdered about 8000 Jews men, women and children."

Sources:

Yad Vashem Archives M-9/15(6); M-1/E-1357/1308; M-1/Q-1219/71;
1407/181

YIVO - Collection of Lithuanian Communities, files 75-1080, 1544, 1560,
1678

Di Yiddishe Shtime (The Jewish Voice) Kovno, 10.1.1922; 8.1.1928;
24.8.1932; 3.4.1933

Der Yiddisher Cooperator - Kovno, No. 8-9, 1929

Folksblat - Kovno, 9.7.1935

Kovner Tog, 9.7.1926

Appendix 1
A list of donors for the famine victims in Persia in 1872
(Jewishgen.Org - Databases *HaMagid* - compiled by Jeffrey Maynard)

Surname	Given Name	Comment	Source in HaMagid	Year
BERGER	Zalman		#10	1872
DAYAN	Yehuda		#10	1872
DRUKER	Tuvia		#2	1872
DRUKER	Tuvia		#10	1872
GEN	Yehuda		#2	1872
GEN	Michel		#2	1872
HALEVI	Shabasai		#10	1872
HALEVI	Shabasai		#2	1872
HURWITZ	Shimon		#10	1872
KA"TZ	Leib Gershon		#10	1872
KATZ	A Y		#2	1872
KATZ	Avraham Yitzchok		#10	1872
KATZ	Ephraim		#10	1872
KATZ	Leib Gershon		#2	1872
KOPELOWITZ	Menachem Mendl		#10	1872
LURIA	Moshe		#10	1872
MEIAREIK	Henich		#2	1872
MELTZER	Yuda		#10	1872
S"TZ	Ephraim		#2	1872
SHMIT	Bentzion		#2	1872
SHMIT	Binyomin		#10	1872
SHMIT	Moshe	Kelme	#10	1872
SHOR	Eliezer		#10	1872
SHOR	Eliezer		#2	1872
SHOR	Moshe	Kelme	#10	1872
WAINER	Chaim		#2	1872
WEIN	Kopil		#10	1872
WEINER	Chaim		#10	1872
ZAIANTZIG	Dovid		#10	1872
ZAIANTZIG	Menachem		#10	1872
ZAIANTZIK	Dovid		#2	1872
ZAIANTZIK	Menachem		#2	1872

Avraham	#10	1872
Dovid Yisroel	#2	1872
Shalom ben A	#10	1872
Shlomo ben Abba	#2	1872
Uri Zelig ben A	#10	1872
Yakov Yitzchok	#2	1872
Yehuda ben G	#2	1872
Yehuda ben Tzvi	#2	1872
Yuda ben G	#10	1872

Salakas (Salok)

Salakas (Salok in Yiddish) lies in northeastern Lithuania. Forests and lakes surround the town. One of the lakes, the Luodis, is about 1 km. (0.6 miles) from the town.

An estate named Salakas was mentioned in historical documents dating back to 1586. From the sixteenth to the nineteenth century the town was owned by the Bishop of Vilna. At the beginning of the eighteenth century, during the Northern War with the Swedes, Salok was completely burned down.

Local fighting units were involved in the rebellion against the Czarist rule of 1863.

In 1731 the town boasted a flourmill, a beer brewery and a cheese factory.

In the second half of the nineteenth century large markets and annual fairs were organized in Salok. At that time, there were more than thirty stores and small pubs in town, most of them owned by Jews. Salok was known for its pottery production. There were a Catholic church, an elementary school and three Jewish prayer houses in the town.

At the end of the nineteenth century and in the first half of the twentieth century, Salok was a county administrative center with its own police.

In 1862 significant tension developed between the Jewish and gentile populations and there was a warning of a pogrom, but the timely intervention of the *gubernator* (governor) helped to avert a disaster.

In the middle of August 1886 a raging fire broke out in Salok and seventy Jewish houses burned to the ground, devastating their owners. The three prayer houses were also lost and the community was left without a place of worship. The Hebrew newspaper *HaMelitz* published an appeal for help, signed by several respected men of Salok; Asher son of Shneur Zalman and David Mosheh, Naftali Hertz and Dov Aryeh Rom. Another fire broke out in July 1901, destroying about 300 houses and affecting hundreds of people.

Elhanan Rapoport, a student, and M. J. Yafit sent reports of the fire to *HaMelitz*, while Matityahu Bravo reported it in *HaYom*.

In 1902 yet another fire erased the entire town but due to its proximity to the St. Petersburg - Warsaw railway, the town was rebuilt and its population grew. However, six years later, on July 27th, 1908 fire again destroyed hundreds of homes.

At the end of 1918 a revolutionary Bolshevik committee started its activities. Consequently Soviet rule was enforced in the town. Its power lasted only until early 1919, when fighting broke out with the newly organized Lithuanian army, and the Bolsheviks were forced to retreat from the town.

General view of Salok

During the period of independent Lithuania, a plan was proposed to reconstruct Salok into a scenic vacation town, since the soil was not particularly suitable for agriculture.

The Jewish settlement in Salok was one of the first in Lithuania. The Jews earned their living by trading in agricultural products, timber and fishing. Their economic situation before World War I was relatively good.

In 1879, the local philanthropist Eliezer Matityahu Bravo built a fine new shelter for the poor, to replace the old one. The Bravo family was known to have been the first literate family in Salok.

The population census of 1897 revealed 2,386 residents in Salok, 1,582 (66%) of them Jews.

In Salok, between the years 1875 and 1899, there were 32 subscribers to rabbinic literature.

After World War I, the situation in Salok changed considerably. The new borders, redrawn as a result of the Polish army's occupation of the Vilna region, cut Salok off from the railway station of Duksht and from Vilna. In fact, Salok was left without any economic resources and many Jews left, emigrating to South Africa, Cuba and *Eretz-Yisrael*. The Jewish population was thus markedly depleted. Many young people enrolled in training *kibbutzim*, hoping to emigrate to *Eretz-Yisrael*. The remaining Jews scraped together a living, mainly by trading and peddling in the surrounding villages or working in small workshops as sock machinists, shoemakers and tailors.

Following the law of autonomies for minorities issued by the new Lithuanian government, the minister for Jewish affairs, Dr. Menahem (Max) Soloveitshik, ordered elections for community committees (*Va'adei Kehilah*) to be held in the summer of 1919. At the beginning of 1920, elections took place and seven members were elected, three from *Akhduth* (*Agudath Yisrael*) and four non-party men.

The first population census conducted by the Lithuanian government in 1923 showed that there were 1,918 residents in Salok, 917 (48%) of them Jews.

According to the government survey of 1931, there were eleven shops in Salok, all of them Jewish: three textile shops, three hardware stores, two restaurants, one grocery, one shop selling sewing machines and one butcher shop. There were nine small workshops, all Jewish: four weaving, three wool combing and two bakeries.

By 1937, there were 56 Jewish tradesmen in Salok: fourteen needle workers, thirteen shoemakers, six butchers, seven metal workers, four carpenters, a baker, a watchmaker and ten tradesmen working in other occupations. A few Jews were fishermen in the nearby lakes and many others were peddlers.

In 1939, there were eighteen telephones, six of them in Jewish homes.

In 1939, after Vilna and its region were annexed to Lithuania once again, Salok experienced some recovery. When the city of Vilna became affected by severe shortages of food and heating fuel, Salok Jews supplied it with timber and agricultural products, as well as exporting a variety of goods to Russia. But this prosperity was short-lived and ended on June 15th, 1940, when Lithuania was occupied by the Red Army and annexed by the Soviet Union as one of its republics.

The *Kloiz*

At this time the Kletsk *Yeshiva* (Polish) was moved to Salok from Janeve (Jonava). According to one source, thirty-three students of the *Yeshiva*, together with their teacher, managed to escape to Russia.

Many of the Salok Jews were affiliated with the Zionist camp. The Zionist Socialist (Z. S.) party was very active in Salok. Zionist youth organizations *HaShomer HaTsa'ir* and *Betar* had branches in Salok while the *Maccabi* sports organization had just twelve members.

Salok Zionists bought *Shekalim* and voted at elections to the Zionist congresses. The division of votes for each party is presented below:

Cong No.	Year	Tot Shek	Total Votes	Labor Party Z"S	Z"Z	Rev	Gen Zion A	B	Gros	Miz
14	1925	20	----	----	----	--	----	----	----	----
15	1927	24	22	9	3	---	5	----	----	5
16	1929	41	13	4	3	---	2	----	----	4
17	1931	14	12	6	1	---	2	----	----	3
18	1933	---	100	69		21	4	----	- ---	6
19	1935	---	284	187		---	---	1	---	96
21	1939	35	30	17		---	---	Na	Block	
	1939								13	

Key: Cong No. = Congress Number, Tot Shek = Total Shekalim, Rev = Revisionists, **Gen Zion = General Zionists, Gros = Grosmanists, Miz = Mizrakhi, Na block = National Block**

About 25 Jewish children received their elementary education at a *Heder*, while the Hebrew *Tarbuth* school had about 110 students. The town had a fine library with many Yiddish books. From time to time an actor or a theater group would visit Salok and perform a show or an operetta in Yiddish, ignoring objections by *Betar* members, who preferred shows in Hebrew.

Religious life was concentrated around the *Beth Midrash*, the *Kloiz* and the *Hasidic Shtibl* (Prayer room). Among the Jewish organizations of Salok, the welfare society *Linath Hatsedek* was well known. There were two Jewish cemeteries, the old and the new.

Rabbis who served Salok included the noted Rabbi Yehudah-Leib Mohliver, who died in Salok. His son, Rabbi Shemuel Mohliver (1824-1898), was a leader of the *Hibath Zion* movement, and later became active in the religious Zionist party. The kibbutz *Gan-Shemuel* in Israel is named after him.

Ya'akov Kelmes (1880-1952) was the rabbi during the years 1910-1914. Between 1926 and 1933 he was the Chief Rabbi in Moscow, subsequently emigrating to *Eretz-Yisrael* where he became a member of the Chief Rabbinate. He died in Jerusalem.

The *Hasidic Shtibl*

Eliyahu Mordehai, son of Tsevi Yehiel HaLevi Valkovsky (1874-1962), was Rabbi for a short period in Salok, emigrating to Eretz Yisrael 1934. There he too became a member of the Chief Rabbinate. He published eleven volumes of his research on the *Talmud*, and died in Jerusalem.

The last rabbi, Ya'akov Ralbe, was murdered by the Lithuanians in 1941, together with his community.

Notable Jews born in Salok include Dr. Aryeh Behm (1877-1941), delegate to the fourth Zionist Congress and an ardent campaigner for a Jewish State in *Eretz-Yisrael*. In 1914 he moved to *Eretz-Yisrael* where he established the first Pasteur Institute in Jerusalem and became a founder of the Medical Council there. He published brochures on medical and health issues. Dr. Behm died in Tel-Aviv.

Ya'akov Kronitz was one of the leaders of the Revisionist party in Lithuania and a delegate to Zionist congresses. He died in 1939 in Kovno.

In June 1940, Lithuania was annexed to the Soviet Union and became a Soviet Republic. Following new laws, light industry enterprises owned by Jews were nationalized. A number of Jewish shops were nationalized as well, and commissars were appointed to manage them. Supply of goods decreased and prices soared. The mostly Jewish middle class bore the brunt and the standard of living dropped. All community institutions, Zionist parties and youth groups were disbanded; the Hebrew school was closed.

On June 22nd, 1941 the German army invaded the Soviet Union. At that time about three hundred Jewish families lived in Salok.

A group of Salok children

(Picture courtesy of the Archives of the Association of Lithuanian Jews in Israel)

The Germans entered Salok on June 29th, 1941. The first week after the invasion, Jews were subjected to a virulent range of anti-Semitic acts by their Lithuanian neighbors. Heavy decrees were imposed on them: they were forbidden to leave town, they were ordered to stitch the letter "J" or a yellow *Magen David* on their outer garments, and on their homes the word "Jude" was scribbled in paint. The market was strictly out of bounds and to approach a German was forbidden. They were forced into labor on the farms of the Lithuanians, and in addition, the Lithuanians extorted money from the Jews on every possible occasion. Lithuanian auxiliary policemen fulfilled German orders with enthusiasm even when there were no Germans in town. This occurred incessantly. Under the orders of the Lithuanians, a *Judenrat* was established, its members being Rabbi Ya'akov Ralbe, Faivush Gilinsky and Avraham Bakh.

The first casualty was Berl Krupnik, a shoemaker, who was accused of being the director of the cooperative grocery shop during the Soviet rule. Another Jew was murdered because his children were members of the *Comsomol* (The Communist youth organization).

On August 2nd, 1941 (13th of Av 5701) all Salok Jews were ordered to gather in one place, and from there they were led to the Sungardas forest, about ten km. (6 miles) southeast of the town. They were not permitted to take anything with them except a small parcel of food. About one hundred and fifty people in all, the educated and the public workers, including their wives and children, were selected from the crowd, and led to the village Pa'ezere. On the Sabbath, *Shabbat Nahamu*, on or about August 9th, 1941, all were shot and buried in the forest, a short distance outside the village of Rakenai. The remaining Jews in the Sungardas forest were brought back to Salok, but not to their homes. Instead, they were placed in a makeshift ghetto on Planova Street in apartments left vacant by Lithuanians. Before the Lithuanians abandoned their apartments, they took with them everything, including doors and windows. Before the Jews were allowed to enter their new living quarters, Lithuanian policemen searched them thoroughly and robbed them of all the valuables and money they could lay their hands on.

The mass grave and the monument situated in the Sungardas forest, about 10 km. (6 miles) from Salok

On August 26th, 1941, all the remaining Jews were ordered to gather at the market place and to bring their equipment and tools. They were told they were going to work on a government farm in Rakishok. The Lithuanian Chief of Police promised that no evil would happen to them and that they need not take anything with them except their tools and some food for the trip, as everything would be supplied at the new workplace. To gain more credibility he gave the three committee-members special certificates stating that Salok Jews were decent people.

The monument with the inscription in Yiddish and Lithuanian: "Here in this place the Nazi murderers and their local collaborators cruelly murdered Jews - children, women, and men. Blessed is the memorial of the innocent victims."

The people believed him. Maybe they were content to move away from their Lithuanian torturers. Women, children and the elderly were loaded on carts brought by the Germans from other villages, and the others went on foot surrounded by armed Lithuanians. The convoy moved in the direction of Dusiat and Antaliept, but ten km (6 miles) from Salok it left the road and preceded to a plot surrounded by barbed wire. On the fence there was a sign warning that anyone entering the area without permission would be shot. The carts and the cart owners were not permitted to return home lest it became known that the Jews were not led, as promised, to Rakishok.

Among the Jews in that group were men, women and children from the neighboring communities of Zarasai, Dusetos, Antaliepte, Dukstas and other communities. All the non-Jewish residents who lived within three to five kilometers away from this place were ordered to leave their homes for three days.

The unfortunate Jews spent the night outside in the open air, and in the morning the murders began. Group by group, the victims were led to the nearby Pazemis forest, about 500 meters (1600 feet) off the road from Deguciai to Dusetos directly to freshly dug, long, deep pits. There they were ordered to undress. The men obeyed but the women refused. Screaming, they tried to protect their children. The Lithuanians beat them with rifles and whips and pushed them all into the pits. A firing squad shot the victims with rifles and machine guns, sparing no one. Two of the cart owners went mad hearing the terrible screams. The murderers were Lithuanians, drunk on vodka freely supplied by the Germans. On a nearby hill two SS men stood and watched, barking orders. The cart owners were warned not to speak about what they had witnessed. The victims numbered 2,569 men, women and children. According to a Lithuanian source, a Lithuanian named Radzevitz and three family members were among the dead, murdered by Germans because they harbored Jews.

After the war a few survivors from Salok returned to their town. They found the two mass graves had been desecrated and were neglected. The pits were still uncovered and human remains were scattered around, left so by grave-looters who took what valuables and gold teeth they could find. The returned survivors covered the graves with earth, and a monument with an inscription in Yiddish and Russian was erected. In the 1990s a new monument was built with inscriptions in Yiddish and Lithuanian: see photos in the Antaliepte article.

Sources:

Yad Vashem Archives-M-1/E-1613/1497; M-1/Q-1952/453; 0-3/1890; 319/210 (testimony of Yerakhmiel Korb)

Bakaltchuk-Felin, Melakh*; Yizkor Bukh fun Rakishok un Umgegnt* (Yiddish), Johannesburg 1952, pages 424-428

HaMelitz (St. Petersburg) (Hebrew) January 8, 1879; May 14, 1883; July 1901

Dos Vort, Kovno (Yiddish) 8.10.1934

Folksblat, Kovno (Yiddish) 3.8.1936

Yerushalayim D'Lita, Vilna (Yiddish) No. 7-8, September-October 1993

Naujienos, Chicago, (Lithuanian), 10.6.1949.

Saločiai (Salat)

Salociai (Salat in Yiddish) is located in northern Lithuania, on the shores of the Musa (Musha) River, about 23 km (14 miles) west of the district administrative center of Birzai (Birzh). It was mentioned for the first time in historical documents in 1514. A commercial route connected Posvol (Pasvalys) to Bauska in Latvia through Salat. As early as 1525, several shops and pubs could be found in Salat. During the wars with the Swedes (1700-1721) the town was burned down. During the Russian rule (1795-1915) Salat was first included in the Vilna Province and from 1843 onwards was in the Kovno Province (*Gubernia*). From 1915 to 1918 the town was under the German military rule and during the period of Independent Lithuania (1918-1940), it was considered a county administrative center.

Jewish Settlement before World War II

Jews began to settle in Salat in the nineteenth century. A community of Karaites lived in the area from the seventeenth century until the middle of the nineteenth century. In the 1880s approximately eighty Jewish families lived in the villages around Salat. They barely survived, working as craftsmen and trading agricultural products in neighboring villages. The catholic priest of Salat preached to the village peasants not to rent their houses to Jews, threatening them with refusals to hear their confessions. The rabbi of Posvol tried to convince the priest to stop inciting the peasants against the Jews. Eventually he succeeded, and the priest became a sympathizer of the Jews.

A Loans and Savings fund was established in Salat before World War I.

In spring of 1915, the Russian military exiled Salat Jews deep into Russia. After the war only a fraction of the exiled residents returned to their town.

Following the law of autonomies for minorities issued by the new Lithuanian government, the minister for Jewish affairs Dr. Menahem (Max) Soloveitshik ordered elections to community committees (*Va'adei Kehilah*) to be held in the summer of 1919. A community committee of five members was elected in Salat. The committee worked from 1920 until the end of 1925 and covered all aspects of Jewish life.

The first census performed by the Lithuanian government in 1923 showed 621 residents in Salat, including 174 (28%) Jews. Salat Jews worked in trade and agriculture. Their main source of income was weekly market days (Tuesdays) and the annual fairs.

According to the government survey of 1931, in Salat there were seven shops, all Jewish owned; a grocery, a textile, two haberdashery and domestic tools, one cosmetic store and two others. In addition to these stores, there were five other small Jewish shops.

The market square in Salat

According to the same survey, there were five Jewish-owned light industry enterprises; one for shoes, one dye and two candy factories and one bakery.

In 1939, there were fifteen telephones in town, only one belonging to a Jew.

Salat had a synagogue and a Jewish school. Among the rabbis who served in Salat was Josef, son of Mosheh Yafe,(1846-1893), who died in Manchester, England. In 1910 Hayim-Shaul Levitan became the official rabbi and he was replaced by the last rabbi of Salat, Rabbi Mosheh-Yonah Vainer, who was murdered in the Holocaust .

Many Salat Jews belonged to the Zionist camp. Most of the Zionist parties had supporters in the town. In 1934, an Urban Training Kibbutz of *HeHalutz* was formed. At the elections for the Zionist congresses Salat Jews voted as shown:

Cong No.	Year	Tot Shek	Total Votes	Labor Party Z"S	Z"Z	Rev	Gen Zion A	B	Gros	Miz
18	1933	---	31	17	---	7	5	----	1	1
19	1935	---	25	21	---	---	---	4	---	---
21	1939	30	15	5		---	4	Nat.	Block	
	1939								4	

Key: Cong No. = Congress Number, Tot Shek = Total Shkalim,   Rev = Revisionists, Gen Zion = General Zionists, Gros = Grosmanists, Miz = Mizrakhi Nat. Block= National Block (General Zionists B+Grosmanists+Mizrahi)

Yisahar Ber Falkenson was born in Salat in 1764, and qualified as a Doctor of Medicine in Berlin. Falkenson was a friend of the philosopher Mosheh Mendelson. He published poems in German: the German poet Goethe wrote a review on Falkenson's book entitled _Gedichte eines polnischen Juden_ (Poems of a Polish Jew).

During World War II and Afterwards

In June 1940, Lithuania was annexed to the Soviet Union and became a Soviet Republic. Following new rules, the majority of the factories and shops belonging to the Jews of Salat were nationalized and commissars were appointed to manage them. All Zionist parties and youth organizations were dismantled and Hebrew educational institutions were closed. At this time about 25 Jewish families lived in Salat.

The Germans arrived in Salat a few days after the German army invaded the Soviet Union on June 22nd, 1941. The Lithuanian nationalists, who by then were well organized, immediately murdered thirteen Jews and six Lithuanians, looting everything they could get their hands on. In August 1941, the Lithuanians transferred the remaining Salat Jews to Posvol (Pasvalys). There they were kept together with local Jews and others who were brought from towns and villages in the area. On the morning of August 26th, 1941 (3rd of Elul, 5701) many large trucks arrived in the town. The Jews were forced onto them and transported to Zadeikiai forest, about 4.5 km. from Posvol, near the Pyvesa River. There all were shot and buried in the freshly dug pits prepared in advance. In these pits 1,358 men, women and children were buried.

The mass grave in Zadeikiai forest

The monument on the mass grave with the inscription in Yiddish and
Lithuanian: "In this place on the 26th of August 1941 Hitler's murderers
and their local helpers murdered 1358 Jews, men, women, children."

Sources:

Yad Vashem Archives - Koniuhovsky Collection-0-71, files 70,71

YIVO - New York, Lithuanian Communities Collection, files 659-669

HaMelitz - St, Petersburg, 29.2.1881; 12.4.1881; 29.6.1882; 10.8.1882

Širvintos (Shirvint)

Sirvintos (Shirvint in Yiddish) lies in eastern Lithuania, on the shores of the Sirvinta Stream, about 28 km. (17 miles) southeast of Ukmerge (Vilkomir), the district administrative center.

The town is mentioned in historical documents from the end of the fourteenth century. In 1580 it became the property of the Great Prince of Lithuania, but at the beginning of the eighteenth century, in the Northern War, the Swedes robbed the town.

After the third division of Poland in 1795 by the three superpowers of that time, Russia, Prussia and Austria, Russia annexed this section of Lithuania, including Shirvint. During Russian rule (1795 to 1915) the town was part of the province (*gubernia*) of Vilna.

In 1879 a station for mail carriages was established in Shirvint, as it lay on the road from Vikomir to Vilna.

After World War I ended and the independent Lithuanian state was established in 1918, fighting continued in Shirvint and its surroundings until 1922 between the Lithuanian army and the Bolsheviks, and later with the Polish army and Polish partisans. Only in the spring of 1923 was the border finally fixed between Poland and Lithuania, about 3 km. (2 miles) from Shirvint. This border was closed until 1938.

From the end of the nineteenth century and during the period of independent Lithuania, Shirvint was a county administrative center.

Jewish Settlement until after World War II

Jews probably settled in Shirvint at the beginning of the eighteenth century. Some rented land from the estate owner, Pesitsky, while others opened inns and pubs along the road between Vilkomir and Vilna, and the town grew and developed. Later, when Pesitsky evicted his Jewish tenants, their main livelihood came from keeping inns, pubs and shops.

In 1847 there were 216 Jews in the town. Fifty years later, the government census revealed that 1,864 residents resided in Shirvint, 1,413 (76%) of them being Jews.

Due to the worsening economic situation, the *Lehem Aniyim* (Bread for the Poor) society was established in 1881, as was a society named *Ma'ahal Kasher* (Kosher Meals) which supplied kosher food for Jewish soldiers serving in the local garrison. The number of Jewish soldiers increased from five to twenty-five by 1887. In 1903 the *Refuah Shleimah* (Complete Recovery) society was established to aid the sick in the town.

A street in Shirvint

Shirvint welfare committee elected by the Chicago committee

Before the war there was a Loan and Savings Bank in town.

Shirvint's social and economic connections were primarily with Vilna. Students and apprentices went there to study and to work, returning home for holidays and vacations bringing with them the big city atmosphere and news of its political and cultural happenings. Some Shirvint Jews became advocates of the *Haskalah* and also of the *Hibath Zion* and Zionist movements, with which they were very impressed. In the *Hibath Zion* receipt books there are names of Shirvint Jews; the receipts of the *Hovevei Zion* organization in Vilna for the years 1885-1888 also show donations from Shirvint Jews. Fifty *Shekalim* were sold locally in 1902.

A single Shirvint donor, probably to *Eretz-Yisrael*, Leah Bernshtein fiancée of Yitzchok Rodin of Panevezys, was listed in *Hamelitz* #125 of 1893.

After the 1905 revolution in Russia, fears that pogroms against the Jews could occur caused Shirvint Jewish youth to organize a self-defense group.

Rabbis who officiated in Shirvint during this period include:

> Yits'hak Grodzensky (1801-1867), served in Shirvint for seven years
>
> Yits'hak-Eliezer-Lipa Shereshevsky (1840-1920)
>
> Menahem-Mendel HaLevi-Lifshitz, served in the 1890s, died in 1912.

Between the years 1834-1895 there were 44 subscribers to rabbinic literature.

In an 1869-1878 list of immigrants to the United States eight Shirvint Jews are mentioned; E. Segal, J.B. Openheim, E. Palemboim, B. and M. Kabaker, S. Orzhalkovsky, T. Bubtelsky, M. Manheim.

During World War I, in the summer of 1915, the Russian military ordered Shirvint Jews exiled far into Russia. During the German occupation (1915-1918) Jews from Vilna settled in Shirvint. After the war only two-thirds of the exiles returned, and had to be helped by *YeKoPo* (Jewish Aid Committee).

During the period of independent Lithuania, Shirvint Jews made their living from trade, crafts and peddling. Several families dealt with agriculture, their main income being earned on market days.

According to the government survey of 1931 there were 37 shops in Shirvint, of which 34 (92%) were Jewish owned. The distribution is given in the table below:

Type of business	Total	Owned by Jews
Groceries	3	2
Butcher's shops and Cattle Trade	4	4
Restaurants and Taverns	2	2
Grains and Flax	1	1
Textile Products and Furs	6	6
Leather and Shoes	4	4
Pharmacy	2	1
Timber and Heating Material	12	1
Hardware Products	1	12
Bicycles, electrical appliances, sewing machines	1	1
Other	1	0

According to the same survey there were three wool-combing workshops and one flourmill in Jewish hands.

A Jewish peddler in Shirvint

In 1937, 49 Jewish artisans worked there: nine tailors, nine shoemakers, six oven builders, five bakers, five butchers, three hatters, three barbers, two tinsmiths, two watchmakers, two dressmakers, one carpenter and two others.

The Jewish Popular Bank (*Folksbank*) was established in Shirvint in 1924 and was accepted into the Union of Popular Banks in Lithuania in 1928. At this time it had 191 members, and local Jews were greatly assisted by this institution in their struggle for daily existence.

In 1939 there were thirty telephone subscribers, two of them Jewish.

The *Talmud-Torah* (1938)

Slowly the number of Jews in Shirvint decreased. Being cut off from Vilna and its region as well having to compete with Lithuanian merchants, caused the liquidation of many Jewish businesses. This, and the effects of the Lithuanian economic crisis of the 1930s, resulted in the emigration of many Shirvint Jews to South Africa, America, Cuba, Mexico and *Eretz-Yisrael*.

About 100 Jewish children from Shirvint studied at the Hebrew school of the *Tarbuth* network. Some graduates continued their studies at the *Or* (Light) Hebrew gymnasium in Vilkomir. There were also a Yiddish school and two *Talmud Torah* schools with about fifty pupils, that were established by a former Shirvinter in Chicago.

Shirvint's youth divided into two groups, Zionist and anti-Zionist, which meant that there was a split in the town's cultural life; thus two different large libraries were active locally, one Hebrew and one Yiddish.

The stamp of the Hebrew library

Many Shirvint Jews were members of the Zionist movement. A society named after Nakhman Sirkin (Zionist Social Party) and the committee for *Keren Kayemeth LeYisrael* (The Jewish National Fund) functioned here, and initiated numerous cultural activities. The table below shows how Shirvint Zionists voted for four Zionist congresses:

Cong No.	Year	Tot Shek	Total Votes	Labor Party Z"S Z"Z		Rev	Gen Zion A	B	Gros	Miz
16	1929	44	16	9	2	3	2	---	----	---
17	1931	29	21	6	3	7	5	---	----	---
18	1933	---	145	82		10	3	---	43	5
19	1935	---	344	181		---	1	5	132	64

Key: **Cong No. = Congress Number, Tot Shek = Total Shkalim, Rev = Revisionists, Gen Zion = General Zionists, Gros = Grosmanists, Miz = Mizrakhi**

HaShomer HaTsair, *Betar* and *Benei Akiva* were among the Zionist youth organizations. Sport activities were carried out in the local *Maccabi* branch.

Many *Yeshiva* graduates lived in Shirvint and a daily *Gemara* page was studied in all three prayer houses and in the *Shtibl*.

The *Beth Midrash*

The *Shtibl* of the *Hasidim*

The *Shamash* of the *Beth Midrash* waking people for the morning prayer (*Shaharith*)

Rabbi Avraham Aryeh Leib Grosbard (1870-1941), served in Shirvint from 1913, together with his son-in-law Zundl Kruk who eventually took over from him. Both were murdered in the Holocaust.

Bikur Holim and *Linath HaTsedek* were the local welfare institutions.

Personalities born in Shirvint included:

> Eliyahu-Eliezer Grodzensky (1831-1887), the son-in-law of rabbi Israel Salanter, who was one of the three members of the religious high court in Vilna.

> Leon Hazanovitz (his real name was Katriel Shub 1882-1925), one of the leaders of the *Poalei Zion* party, writer and editor of his party's periodicals.

> Avner Tenenboim (1848-1913), reporter and writer published hundreds of articles and books on nature, history and geography in America. He translated books from world literature into Yiddish, which were sought after by Yiddish readers.

> Tsevi Bernshtein, arrived in *Eretz-Yisrael* in 1935, an executive member of *Hapoel HaMizrahi.*

During World War II and Afterwards

In June 1940, Lithuania was annexed by the Soviet Union and became a Soviet Republic. Following new rules, light industrial enterprises owned by Jews were nationalized. A number of Jewish shops were nationalized and commissars were appointed to manage them. Supply of goods decreased and, as a result, prices soared. The middle class, mostly Jewish, bore the brunt, and their standard of living dropped. All Zionist parties and youth organizations were disbanded and the Hebrew school was closed. At least three Jewish families from Shirvint were exiled to Siberia by the Soviet authorities.

A few days after the German invasion into the Soviet Union on June 22nd, 1941, German soldiers arrived in Shirvint. They set fire to the three prayer houses and spread the Torah scrolls in the streets so that people would trample on them. A Jewish woman and her son who lived in the building of the *Beth Midrash* were burned alive.

Several days later, after the German soldiers left the town and moved eastwards, Lithuanian nationalists took over the rule of the town. Many people who had had some connections with Soviet authorities were detained, both Jews and non-Jews. All were sent to prison in Vilkomir; the non-Jews received 25 lashes and were released. The Jews were executed.

In the middle of July 1941 young men and women up to the age of eighteen were selected for agricultural work on the Sheshulki farm, about 10 km. (6 miles) from Shirvint. From time to time groups of 20 to 25 people were taken and sent to so-called labor elsewhere. Later it became clear they had been imprisoned in Vilkomir.

On August 10th, 1941 all Jews who owned a horse and a cart were ordered to present themselves on the morrow, ready for a journey. Lithuanian police pulled men off the streets and put them on the carts, and many Jews who resisted were sentenced on the spot to die by fire. In fact, fuel was spilled over them and they were burned alive.

At the end of August all Jews were ordered to leave their houses and move to about twenty ramshackle buildings in the old part of town, the area around the bath house and the *Mikveh*. The rulers called this place the Ghetto. According to one source, the old rabbi Avraham-Leib Grosbard and his son-in-law Zundl Kruk tried to organize life a little, but did not succeed, because Lithuanian auxiliary police would come and demand that the Jews hand over their money and property.

At dawn on September 18th, 1941 (26th of Elul, 5701) the ghetto was surrounded by Germans and Lithuanians. All Jews were forced into trucks and transferred to Vilkomir. From there they were taken to Pivonija forest near the town where pits had already been prepared. They were forced to undress and were then pushed into the pits and murdered. A few resisted.

Little children were thrown into the air and the Lithuanians shot at them for live target practice. On the same day a sign was erected at the entrance of Shirvint stating that the town was *Judenrein* (Clean of Jews).

The entrance gate to the murder site at Pivonija forest

The mass graves at Pivonija forest

The monument at Pivonija forest

The tablet on the monument

The inscription in Yiddish, Hebrew and Lithuanian: "At this site in the year 1941 Hitler's murderers and their local helpers murdered 10,239 Jews, men, women and children."

After the war two Jews returned. In 1989 only two Jews lived in Shirvint.

At the beginning of the 1990s, on the site of the Jewish cemetery which had become a housing estate, a memorial was erected with an inscription in Yiddish and Lithuanian: "The Jewish cemetery was at this site until 1961".

Sources:

Yad Vashem Archives, file 22/54

Erd un Arbeit (Yiddish) - The *Poalei Zion* party's journal, Kovno, 22.7.1922

Der Yiddisher Cooperator (Yiddish), Kovno, #7-8, 1.8.1928

Folksblat - Kovno, 28.11.1938

Jewishgen Org.>Databases>Lithuania. Compiled by Jeffrey Maynard

Šaukėnai (Shukyan)

Saukenai (Shukyan in Yiddish) lies in northwestern Lithuania, about 33 km. (20 miles) north of Siauliai (Shavl), the district administrative center, with dusty unpaved roads connecting it to Kelme and Kursenai. Shukyan was mentioned in historical documents from the end of the fifteenth century. In the sixteenth and seventeenth centuries merchants and artisans resided there. In 1760 the king granted the people of Shukyan permission to maintain a weekly market and hold three fairs annually.

Shukyan was part of the Polish Lithuanian Kingdom until 1795, when the third division of Poland by the three superpowers of the times, Russia, Prussia and Austria, resulted in most of Lithuania becoming Russian territory until World War I. During the Russian rule (1795-1915) Shukyan was included in the province (*Gubernia*) of Vilna and from 1843 in the province of Kovno, the town developing in particular during the nineteenth century. Until 1896 and during independent Lithuania (1918-1940) Shukyan was a county administrative center.

Jewish Settlement until after World War I

Jews apparently settled in Shukyan at the beginning of the eighteenth century. In 1766 there were 177 Jewish poll tax payers, who made their living from minor trading with surrounding villages. Market days and fairs were their main source of income.

In 1812 the nearby estate of Zhelataria owned ten taverns in the surrounding villages, nine of which were managed by Jews. 569 Jews lived in Shukyan in 1847, and according to the all-Russian census of 1897 this had increased to 624 (63%) Jews out of a total population of 992.

The Hebrew newspaper *HaMagid* #18 (1872) published a list of 64 Shukyan Jews who donated money to alleviate the Persian famine (see **Appendix 1**).

A serious fire in 1891 reduced the living standard of Shukyan's Jews.

The wooden synagogue built in the eighteenth century was famous for its beautiful carved *bimah* and *aron kodesh*.

Rabbis who officiated in Shukyan during this period include: Yits'hak-Ya'akov Reines (1840-1915) who lived in Shukyan between the years 1867-1869 and was one of the founders of the *Mizrahi* party, and also published many books on Judaism; Nahum-Mihal Kahana (from 1872); Josef-Eliyahu Frid (between the years 1875-1891), immigrated to America; Ya'akov Pralgever (from 1891).

There were 48 subscribers to rabbinic literature between the years 1898 and 1928.

The Famous Wooden Synagogue of Shukyan

During the Period of Independent Lithuania (1918-1940)

Following the Law of Autonomy for Minorities being instituted by the new Lithuanian government, the minister of Jewish affairs Dr. Menakhem (Max) Soloveitshik, ordered elections to community committees (*Va'adei Kehilah*) to be held in the summer of 1919. In Shukyan a *Va'ad Kehilah* with seven members was elected: two from the General Zionists party, one from *Tseirei Zion* and four non-party men. The *Va'ad* (committee) was active in most aspects of Jewish life until the end of 1925.

According to the first census performed by the government in 1923, there were 791 residents in Shukyan, 324 (41%) of them Jews.

During this period, the Shukyan Jews made their living from trade, crafts and light industry while in the surrounds of nearby villages there were several Jewish farmers.

The government survey of 1931 revealed that the town had four Jewish shops: three textile shops and an agency for Singer sewing machines. According to the same survey there were six Jewish-owned factories: one shoe manufacturer, two sawmills, one flourmill, one leather factory and one millinery.

The economic crisis of the 1930s and the blatant anti-Semitic propaganda of the Association of Lithuanian Merchants (*Verslas*) led to a boycott of Jewish shops, causing many people to seek their future elsewhere. Shukyan Jews emigrated mainly to South Africa, to America, and *Eretz-Yisrael*.

In 1937 there were still ten Jewish artisans in Shukyan: three shoemakers, two tailors, two butchers, a baker, a hatter and a knitter.

In 1939 the town had seventeen telephones, one of them Jewish-owned.

An average of forty-five Jewish children studied at the Hebrew school, which was part of the religious *Yavneh* network.

The religious life of Shukyan centered around the old synagogue (burnt down in 1944 when there were no Jews resident in the town) and the *Beth Midrash*. The last rabbis who officiated in Shukyan were Yisrael-Benjamin Faivelson (who died in 1938) and his son Barukh.

Many Shukyan Jews were Zionists and were members of almost all the Zionist parties. The results of the elections for the Zionist congresses are given in the table below:

Cong No.	Year	Total Shek	Total Votes	Labor Party Z"S	Z"Z	Rev	Gen Zion A	B	Gros	Miz
15	1927	11	7	---	2	----	---	----	----	5
16	1929	12	3	---	2	---	---	----	----	1
17	1931	---	7	1	2	---	---	----	----	4
18	1933	---	17	14		---	2	----	---	1
19	1935	86	82	43		---	37	--- -	---	2

Key: Cong No. = Congress Number, Total Shek = Total Shkalim, Rev = Revisionists, Gen Zion = General Zionists, Gros = Grosmanists, Miz = Mizrakhi

During World War II and After

In June 1940 Lithuania was annexed by the Soviet Union and became a Soviet Republic. Under new laws, the majority of the factories and shops belonging to the Jews of Saukenai were nationalized and commissars were appointed to manage them. All Zionist parties and youth organizations were disbanded and Hebrew educational institutions were closed.

At this time, some 700 residents lived in the town, including about 300 (43%) Jews.

The war between Germany and the Soviet Union broke out on June 22nd, 1941. Several days later, on June 26th, the German army occupied Shukyan. During the first days of the occupation, armed Lithuanians burst into the synagogue during prayers, driving out the men who were wrapped in their *Talith* and *Tefilin* and led them off to labor units. They were forced to remove Russian vehicles from the roads and were abused while doing so.

On July 25th, 1941 the Lithuanians demanded 50,000 rubles from the Jews, threatening them with expulsion from Shukyan if this sum was not forthcoming on their terms. The local priest, to whom a few Jews appealed for help, told them that "this is retribution for what you did to Jesus." The money was collected and handed over to the Lithuanian auxiliary police, the Jews hoping in vain that the situation would now improve.

At dawn on July 28th, 1941, the Lithuanians forced all Shukyan Jews from their homes, confining them to the old synagogue. There they were robbed of their money and valuables. Subsequently they were led, guarded, to the farm of a Jewish family, Rozental, near the village of Shukishok (Sukiskis). Ten Jewish families from the surrounding villages had already been banished there. The Lithuanian guards imprisoned them all in the stables and the barn. robbing them of their shoes and their suits. No Germans were seen in the town.

On July 30th, 1941 the Lithuanians selected 128 children, girls and women plus four men from a list of more than 330 Jews present in the barn; they were all transferred to the farmhouse. The balance, about two hundred, were taken from the barn dressed only in their underclothes and led to the Dulkiskis forest, 5 km. (3 miles) from the town and 500 meters (1500 feet) to the left of the Shukyan-Shavl road. A big pit had already been prepared by local peasants. The Jews were shot in groups at the side of the pit and buried in this mass grave. The families who remained on the farm were told that they had been taken to work.

The remaining Jews in Shukishok were dispersed over five farms in the area. Fifty children and fifteen mothers and girls, who were supposed to care for the children, were imprisoned in a flourmill in Shvila. This mill was owned by a Jew named Tchesler from Kelm, and was 5 km. (3 miles) from Shukyan.

Eight youngsters, who had managed to escape from the Zhager massacre, sought asylum with the priest of Shukyan. He proposed that they become Christians, to which they agreed, but this did not rescue them. They too were shot and buried in the Catholic cemetery where a cross marks their grave.

Early in the 1990's the director of the Jewish Cultural Center in Shavl (Siauliai) asked the local authorities and the local priest for permission to erect a tablet on their graves, with the following inscription: *"Here eight Jewish youngsters are buried, the eldest among them being twenty-four years old. They were murdered on November 1, 1941, All Saints Day. All were led to the ghetto of Zhager, but survived by escaping from there, after which they found asylum in the church of Saukenai. At the end of September 1941 they received the Holy Cross. Priest Jonas Stasevicius baptized and adopted them, but this was not enough for the murderers and their leaders. These youngsters died because they were born Jews. Rest in peace."*

Of the sixteen Jews who escaped from Zhager and returned to Shukyan, only two survived. The others were caught in their refuges and exterminated.

After the war the Soviet authorities located the mass grave in the forest, where they found about four hundred victims.

The mass grave in the Dulkiskis forest

On August 29th, 1941 all Jews from the farms were gathered together and led on carts to Zhager (Zagare). Many Jews from the nearby towns had already been confined there. The fate of Shukyan's Jews was the same as those from Zhager. All were murdered on October 2nd, 1941 (11th of Tishrei 5702).

Sources:

Yad Vashem Archives M-915(6); Koniukhovsky collection 0-71, files 102, 112

YIVO, New York - Collection of Lithuanian Communities, files 1291-1295, 1551

Di Yiddishe Shtime, Kovno 21.5.1937; 25.5.1937

Lituanus, Chicago 27.3.1981

Siauliu Krastas, Siauliai 14.5.1991

The monument on the mass grave in Zagare is where many Shukyan
Jews were among the slain.

Appendix 1

A list of Shukyan donors, published in *HaMagid* # 18 (1872), for victims of the Persian Famine 1872:

(From: JewishGen.org.-Databases-Lithuania-HaMagid-compiled by Jeffrey Maynard)

Surname	Given Name	Comments	Source	Year
ABRAMZOHN	Zusman		Hamaggid #18	1872
AHARON	Boruch		Hamaggid #18	1872
CHANOCH	Leib Meir		Hamaggid #18	1872
FEINBERG	Shlomo		Hamaggid #18	1872
FRIDMAN	Yisroel		Hamaggid #18	1872
HALEVI	Zev		Hamaggid #18	1872
HOTZ	Yisroel Meir		Hamaggid #18	1872
KAHANA	Nachum Michel		Hamaggid #18	1872
KATZ	Moshe Eliezer		Hamaggid #18	1872
KLEIN	Nechamiah		Hamaggid #18	1872
LAZAR	Aharon		Hamaggid #18	1872
LAZAR	Bentzion		Hamaggid #18	1872
LAZAR	Micha		Hamaggid #18	1872
LEWINSHTEIN	Hirsh		Hamaggid #18	1872
LEWITAN	Abraham		Hamaggid #18	1872
LIPSHITZ	Mordechai		Hamaggid #18	1872
LONG	Abab		Hamaggid #18	1872
MALKIN	Yehuram		Hamaggid #18	1872
MALTZ	Ber		Hamaggid #18	1872
MALTZ	Hirsh		Hamaggid #18	1872
MALTZ	yehuda		Hamaggid #18	1872
MANICH	Abba		Hamaggid #18	1872
MAPSMAWSH	Shmuel		Hamaggid #18	1872
NEIHOIZ	Nisan		Hamaggid #18	1872
NOLK	Yitzchok		Hamaggid #18	1872
PAKLIBIK	Yechezkel		Hamaggid #18	1872
PREIS	Yakov		Hamaggid #18	1872
PREIS	Yisroel		Hamaggid #18	1872

REZ	Menachem		Hamaggid #18	1872
REZ	Yitzchok		Hamaggid #18	1872
RUBIN	Abba		Hamaggid #18	1872
RUBINSHTEIN	Chava		Hamaggid #18	1872
SERSMAN	Chaim	from (Haliwian)	Hamaggid #18	1872
SHAPIRO	Yitzchok		Hamaggid #18	1872
SHATZ	Chaim		Hamaggid #18	1872
SHEMESH	Avraham		Hamaggid #18	1872
SHNITKIN	Mendil		Hamaggid #18	1872
SHTEIN	Yechezkel Mordechai		Hamaggid #18	1872
SHU"B	Moshe		Hamaggid #18	1872
SHULDIGER	Feivish		Hamaggid #18	1872
SHULDIGER	Zisel		Hamaggid #18	1872
SHWAB	Avraham		Hamaggid #18	1872
TOIB	Feivish		Hamaggid #18	1872
TORTZIN	Eli		Hamaggid #18	1872
WEINER	Yosef		Hamaggid #18	1872
WEIS	Moshe Aharon		Hamaggid #18	1872
YAKOBZOHN	Helman		Hamaggid #18	1872
ZAK	Ber		Hamaggid #18	1872
ZAKS	Kopil		Hamaggid #18	1872
ZAKS	Yehoshua ben Zev	son of the Rabbi	Hamaggid #18	1872
ZAKS	Zev	Muflag, Nifla	Hamaggid #18	1872
ZIV	Leibtzig		Hamaggid #18	1872
ZUSMAN	Yitzchok		Hamaggid #18	1872
	Boruch Michel		Hamaggid #18	1872
	Eliezer Ephraim		Hamaggid #18	1872
	Leib Hirsh	boy	Hamaggid #18	1872

Užpaliai (Ushpol)

The Sventoji River bisects the town of Uzpaliai (Ushpol in Yiddish). Surrounded by green hills and cold water springs, it lies about 15 km. (9 miles) from Utena (Utyan), the district administrative center.

Dating back to 1453, the town of Huspole appears as a reference in the treaty of Brest-Litowsk. In 1792 the town was granted Magdeburg rights of self-rule. Until then the town and the estate, of the same name, were owned by the noble families of Sapiega, Radzivil and others.

Prior to 1795 Ushpol was in the Polish-Lithuanian Kingdom. However, the third division of Poland by the three superpowers of those times, Russia, Prussia and Austria, resulted in Lithuania becoming partly Russian and partly Prussian. That section of Lithuania, which included Ushpol fell under the rule of Czarist Russia. In 1802 it was in Vilna province (*Gubernia*) and after 1843 it was included in Kovno province (*Gubernia*).

In the nineteenth century the town developed considerably, attracting merchants to settle in the area. Markets and fairs were held regularly. In the period of independent Lithuania (1918-1940) Ushpol was a county administrative center. In 1932 the engineer Lupiansky built a reinforced concrete bridge over the river. This facilitated communication between the two parts of the town. Unfortunately, World War II saw the destruction of the center core of Ushpol.

Jewish Settlement until World War II

In all probability Jews started settling in Ushpol in the eighteenth century. In 1765 there were 109 taxpayers, and it is known that in 1847, 515 Jews lived in Ushpol. Their prayer house was built by 1859. The 1897 Russian census revealed that there were 740 residents in Ushpol. Of these 691 (93%) were Jews.

The Polish unrest in 1863 brought considerable suffering to the Ushpol Jews. A local Jew, Shnaiderman, complained to the Russian authorities about robberies instigated by the rebels in the area, whom the Russians later punished.

One night in the fall of 1888, a fire destroyed most of the Jewish homes and shops and all the three prayer houses. The hapless occupants escaped almost naked and barefoot from their burning homes and were rendered destitute. The Utyan community assisted them by providing garments and money. A desperate appeal for help, signed by the local rabbi Shemuel HaLevi Levin, was published in the Hebrew newspaper *HaMelitz* on October 10th, 1888.

Following the law of Autonomy for Minorities promulgated by the new Lithuanian government, the Minister of Jewish Affairs Dr. Menachem (Max)

Soloveitshik, ordered elections to community committees (*Va'adei Kehilah*) to be held in the summer of 1919. In 1920, elections to this community committee of Ushpol were held, five members being elected. The committee operated in all aspects of Jewish life until 1925, when the autonomy was annulled.

A Jewish Inn in Ushpol

In 1920 there were 58 Jewish families (283 people) in Ushpol: these included 66 children younger than twelve years old. Almost every family had a cow; some had two and a total of 60 cows belonged to Jews.

In the elections to the county council in 1923, three Ushpol Jews were elected. As members of the council, they provided significant help to their fellow Jews.

Ushpol Jews made their living in small trade, crafts and agriculture. In 1931 Ushpol had a total of 22 shops, 15 among them owned by Jews, one trading in flax, another ran a leather shop and two had pubs. In addition there were grain and timber merchants, two of the latter. Among the 23 Jewish tradesmen there were six needle workers, five butchers, four bakers, two shoemakers, one wood-carver, one blacksmith, one wool-comber, one barber, one dressmaker and one photographer. There were also several carters.

The Jewish Popular Bank (*Folksbank*) with 123 members in 1927 played an important role in the economic life of Ushpol Jews.

In 1932, another fire broke out in Ushpol. This time, the greater part of the town including prayer houses and the library were all razed to the ground.

Ushpol Jewish youth in the 1930s

(From the book It was - It wasn't by Y.L. Kopelansky)

Anti-Semitism was rife in the 1920s and 1930s, but after the Nazis took over in Germany, it became much worse. There were attacks on Jews and their homes and the breaking of windows was a regular occurrence.

In 1936, there was a serious threat of a pogrom in Ushpol. The incitement against Jews by some Lithuanians became intense and caused constant fear to all of Jewish descent. On *Shabbath Rosh HaShanah* the local rabbi Aharon-Naftali Kamraz sent a Jew on horseback to Utyan with an appeal to the Chief District Priest for aid in restoring calm to the area. The priest intervened and the planned pogrom was averted.

Jewish children studied at the *Heder* or at the elementary school where the teacher was David Anteshvilsky. The town had two prayer houses, a library with many books in Yiddish, a very good bathhouse and a sauna.

Among those who served in Ushpol were the following rabbis:

> Naftali-Hertz Klatskin (1823-1894)
>
> Yisrael-Mosheh Halbershtam (he died in Ushpol in 1871)
>
> Shemuel Levin (from 1888)
>
> Aharon-Naftali Kamraz (from 1934). In 1939, before World War II, he was paralyzed and succeeded by his son Leib Kamraz. Both were murdered along with many others in 1941.

Many Ushpol Jews were Zionists. Almost all Zionist parties had sympathisers. The results of the elections for the Zionist Congresses are given in the table below:

Cong No.	Year	Total Shek	Total Votes	Labor Party Z"S	Z"Z	Rev	Gen Zion A	B	Gros	Miz
14	1925	30	----	----	----	--	----	----	----	----
15	1927	16	16	12	---	----	---	----	----	4
16	1929	41	23	14	4	1	1	----	----	3
17	1931	14	10	7	1	2	---	----	----	---
18	1933	---	47	43		3	---	----	---	1
19	1935	---	94	82		---	9	1	---	2

Key: Cong No. = Congress Number, Total Shek = Total Shekalim, Rev = Revisionists, Gen Zion = General Zionists, Gros = Grosmanists, Miz = Mizrahi

Among the Zionist youth organizations active in Ushpol was *HaShomer HaTsair* headed by David Even. Sports activities included about thirty athletes in training at the local *Maccabi* branch. Aba Shlosberg and Eidelman were among the outstanding athletes.

The *Maccabi* branch in Ushpol

(From the book It was - It wasn't by Y.L. Kopelansky)

Famous people born in Ushpol included the following:

> Eliyahu Klatzkin, grandson of Rabbi Naftali-Hertz and father of the philosopher Dr. Ya'akov Klatzkin. Eliyahu published many books on Judaism. He died in Jerusalem in 1932.

> Moshe-Mordehai Bloshtein (1894-1964) who lived in Canada from 1919; he studied medicine and psychology and published articles on education and psychology in *Dos Yiddishe Vort*, a periodical in Winnipeg and in other journals.

In 1939 there were twelve telephone lines in town, two of them in Jewish homes.

During World War II and Afterwards

In the summer of 1940, Lithuania was annexed by the Soviet Union and became a Soviet Republic. The new government nationalized several Jewish shops and disbanded the Zionist parties and youth organizations. The Hebrew educational institutions were closed.

A short time after the German invasion into the Soviet Union on June 22nd, 1941, local Lithuanian nationalists took over the control of Ushpol. With the arrival of the Germans in Ushpol on June 26th, 1941, Jews were ordered to move to a ghetto on two narrow streets near the *Beth Midrash* and the bathhouse.

Killing and looting began immediately. Groups of five to ten healthy and strong Jewish men were dragged to the deep swamps at the outskirts of the town, where they were submerged by force until they slowly and cruelly drowned. Jewish families were massacred beside the cemetery and thrown into a lime pit. The remaining Jews, the poor and the wealthy, were taken to so-called "work" and put to death near the Butiskis village and flung into pits prepared in advance. Murders occurred in other places as well — near the Russian cemetery, near the bathhouse, on the road to Utyan near a blacksmith, on the road to Yuzhint near the Bajorai village and at many other places.

There were ruthless rapes and attacks on young Jewish girls. The daughter of the young rabbi Leib Kamraz was raped in the presence of her father. He was held in detention for several days without food or water then marched to the Utyan Road to dig a grave for himself. The rabbi attacked one of the Lithuanians, attempting to strangle the roughneck. The latter was treated in hospital and barely survived, but Leib Kamraz was shot on the spot by another Lithuanian.

Life in the ghetto became increasingly difficult. Fewer and fewer young men remained alive and women, especially the younger ones, were subject to horribly demeaning persecution.

Digging up the remains of Ushpol victims for transfer to graves in the Rashe forest (see Vizhun)

(Both images from the book It was - It wasn't by Y.L. Kopelansky)

The remains were put in coffins and transferred by truck to the mass graves in Rashe forest

On August 29th, 1941 (6th of Elul, 5701) all remaining Ushpol Jews were ordered out of the ghetto, led to Utyan and murdered in the Rase (Rashe) forest, about 2 km. (1.5 miles) from the town, along with Jews from Utyan and surrounding area. The names of these murderers are kept in the Archives of Yad Vashem in Jerusalem.

All the Jews, except for one solitary soul who tried to hide in Lithuanian homes, were caught and perished. Only one Jewish woman, married to a Lithuanian man, survived. With great effort her husband managed to keep her in hiding.

After the war when the few survivors returned, the graves for their fellow townsmen were fenced in and a monument in the memory of those who perished was built.

The sculpture *Skausmas* (Pain) near the road to the mass graves at Rashe forest. Sculptor: V. Simonelis

The mass graves and the monument at Rashe forest

Sources:

YIVO - New York, Lithuanian Communities Collection, files 57-61

HaMelitz - St. Petersburg, 10.10.1888

Yankel-Leib Kopelansky - It was , It wasn't (Yiddish),

Nes Tsiyonah – 1998

Vyžuonos (Vizhun)

Vyzuonos (Vizhun in Yiddish) is located in northeastern Lithuania, about 12 km. (7 miles) north west of the district administrative center Utyan (Utena). The town is surrounded by hills, forests and lakes. Vizhun, both the estate and the town, was first mentioned in historical documents as early as the fifteenth century. In the sixteenth and eighteenth centuries Vizhun was the property of the estate owners Radzivils, Tishkevitzs, Postolskys and others.

The town was totally destroyed in the wars with Sweden at the turn of the seventeenth century.

Until 1795 the rebuilt town of Vizhun was part of the Polish-Lithuanian Kingdom, but the third division of Poland by the three superpowers of those times, Russia, Prussia and Austria, forced Lithuania to become partly Russian and partly Prussian. That part which included Vizhun fell under Czarist Russia. From 1802 it was considered to be in the Vilna province (*gubernia*) and then in 1843 it fell under the jurisdiction of the Kovno *gubernia*, Vilkomir District.

Market days and fairs were held in the town, which then boasted several stores and pubs.

After the outbreak of World War I control of the town's governing body changed hands several times, transferring from the Russian army to that of the Germans and back again. The Germans ruled Vizhun from 1915 until the establishment of the independent Lithuanian state in 1918. For a short while the Bolsheviks were in control of the town. After 1861 and through the period of independent Lithuanian rule (1918-1940), Vizhun was a county center in the Utyan district.

Jewish Settlement before World War I

The Jewish settlement in Vizhun was one of the oldest in Lithuania and its beginning could probably be traced back to the first quarter of the seventeenth century. From 1623 until 1764, when the autonomous institution of the Jews of Lithuania (*Va'ad Medinath Lita*) was in operation, the *Galil Vizhun* (district) in Zhamut (Zemaitija) was one of three administrations of the *Va'ad*. A part of the Lifland region was included in *Galil Vizhun* and the towns of Braslav, Druya, Kreslava and also Utyan and Aniksht fell under its jurisdiction. The Vizhun community was mentioned in the scripts of the *Va'ad Arba haAratsoth* (the autonomous institution of the Jews of the four main districts of Poland) and after 1760 it was mentioned in the scripts of the *Va'ad Medinath Lita*. In 1720, according to a resolution of the *Va'ad*, Vizhun and its *Galil* paid out 1680 golden rubles for a total of 60,000 people - the Head Tax imposed on Polish and Lithuanian Jews.

According to an archival document, Jewish artisans obtained permits to work in Vizhun in 1646. In a Jewish Brisk Community letter to the Karaites in Zamut dated 1667, the Karaites were summoned to pay a debt to Heshl, son of Elyakum of Vizhun without delay.

The story of Menakhem ben Aryeh Man or Mani, the Martyr of Vizhun was passed from generation to generation. In the middle of the eighteenth century, on the eve of *Hoshana Raba*, a convert brought a crucifix into the synagogue and hid it under the ark (*Aron Kodesh*). He then spread a malicious fabrication stating that the Jews were beating and striking the crucified on the crucifix with a sallow (willow, or *aravah* in Hebrew). Policemen entered the synagogue, saw Jews striking with a sallow and uncovered the cross. All the men were handcuffed and walked to Vilna. They were sentenced death by hanging. One of the prisoners who was about to be sentenced, Menakhem Mani, took the blame upon himself. On the 17th of Tamuz 5509 (1749) he was duly hanged, while the remainder of the Jews were freed. This event was recorded in the *Pinkas haKahal* and from then on it was a quarterly custom in Vizhun to remember the soul of Menakhem Mani, "the Martyr," who sacrificed himself to preserve the lives of his fellow Jews.

In 1766 there were 103 Jews in Vizhun. In 1859 there were 150 Jews (23%) in a population of 647. However, by 1897 the Jewish population had grown to 445 (79%) in a total population of 561.

In 1915, by the order of the Russian army, the Vizhun Jews, like most of the other Kovno *Gubernia* Jews, were exiled far into Russia. After the war a considerable number of them managed to return home.

Vizhun in Independent Lithuania

Following the law of autonomies for minorities issued by the new Lithuanian government, the minister for Jewish affairs Dr. Menahem (Max) Soloveitshik, ordered elections to community committees (*Va'adei Kehilah*) to be held in the summer of 1919. In Vizhun a *Va'ad Kehilah* was elected and was active in all spheres of Jewish activity through the years 1920 to 1924.

Vizhun Jews made their living in small trades, dealing with grains, poultry, flax and working in crafts. The 1931 government survey of stores and factories in the area, listed seven stores owned by Jews in Vizhun: grain, grocery, textile and leather shops, a pharmacy, a restaurant and a photo studio. There were also three factories, a power station, a flourmill and an alcohol factory owned by Hayim-Hanokh Polovin.

In 1937, there were 22 Jewish tradesmen in town: five butchers, four needle trade workers, two glass workers, two carpenters, two blacksmiths, two barbers, one oven builder, one knitter, one shoemaker, one potter and one dressmaker. The twice-yearly fairs provided an important source of livelihood for Vizhun Jews.

In 1939 there were five telephone lines in town, two of them in Jewish homes.

A street in Vizhun

Another street in Vizhun

The Jewish *Folksbank,* with its 114 members, provided some relief for the local Jews and helped them overcome daily financial difficulties. The bank services extended to the nearby towns of Dabeik (Dabeikiai), Ushpol (Uzpaliai) and others.

When the Lithuanian consumer cooperative was created in 1923, strong propaganda was spread to boycott the Jewish stores. To prove the point a stereotype was created of Jews cheating the customers on weight, adding sand to sugar and water to salt, etc. Consequently, following a tumultuous period in the Jewish community, the Jews, through their community committee appealed to the Ministry for Jewish Affairs asking for advice and help. Unfortunately there is no evidence available of the success or failure of this appeal.

The economic crisis that began in Lithuania in the 1930s added to the deterioration of life for Vizhun Jews. Many families received help from relatives in America and South Africa.

Jewish children studied in the Hebrew school established in 1918 by local initiative and with the help of the local branch of the *Tseirei-Zion* party. The community also supported a library with mainly Yiddish books. In 1922, the *Tarbuth* organization organized evening classes in town with the participation of about fifteen people.

A Purim party at school – *how many Queen Esthers?*

Many Vizhun Jews were Zionists: several were included in the 1872 list of contributors to the settlement of *Eretz-Yisrael*. The fund-raiser was Ben-Zion Neimark. There is also a list of Vizhun contributors headed by Yisrael-Gershon Kulviansky dated 1910. There were many supporters of various parties, including *Agudath-Yisrael* and the Z"S (Zionist Socialists). The youth leaned mostly towards the latter party and the *HaShomer HaTsair* youth organization. The table below demonstrates how Vizhun Zionists voted for the different parties at six Zionist Congresses:

Cong. No.	Year	Total Shek	Total Voter	Labor Party		Revis.	Gen.Zionists		Gro	Miz.
				Z"S	Z"Z		A	B		
14	1925	15	--	--	--	--	--	--	--	--
15	1927	9	8	4	3	--	1	--	--	--
16	1929	21	11	5	--	--	1	--	--	5
17	1931	9	6	1	3	--	2	--	--	--
18	1933	---	34	31		--	2	--	--	1
19	1935	---	80	50		--	21	--	--	9

Cong.=Congress;   Shek.=Shekalim;   Revis.=Revisionists;   Gro=Grosmanists;
Miz.=Mizrahi

The old synagogue

The wooden synagogue was built in the middle of the eighteenth century. Its *Aron Kodesh* was known for its artistic carvings. The *Eliyahu* Room was where babies were circumcised. The wall of the synagogue had a ring (*Kune*) to which offenders were bound. In addition, the town had a *Beth Midrash* and a *Mikveh*.

One of the Batei Midrash in Vizhun

The famous carved Aron Kodesh

Front: the brothers Ishe-Leib and David Even, Iser Kopelansky

Seated second from left: Leizer Shteiman

(Picture from the book by Y.L. Kopelansky)

Among the Rabbis who served in Vizhun were the following:

> Tsevi-Hirsh Halevi Hurvitz, the Rabbi of the three *Geliloth* of Zhamut Vizhun, Keidan and Birzh. He died in 1649.

> Asher Ginzburg, who served from 1701, head of the religious court (Av Beth Din) of Vizhun and its *Galil.*

> Asher was followed by the two sons of his brother, Meir and David who were each also *Av Beth Din* of *Galil Vizhun.*

> Eliezer Don-Yikhya, an ardent *Hovev-Zion* (served 1864-1876).

> Meir-Eliyahu Vainer (served from 1890).

> Avraham Katz (from 1903)

> Aharon Shmidt, born in Vizhun in 1866, served from 1922 until the mid-1930s. He died in Tel-Aviv in 1965 at the age of 99

> The last Rabbi was Zalman Meltser, murdered in 1941.

Among the well known personages born in Vizhun were:

> Aryeh-Leib Ginzburg, son of Asher, born in 1695, a known scholar of the Torah in the 18th century

> Ben-Zion Don-Yikhya, son of Eliezer, (1871-1941) Rabbi for fifteen

years in Lutsin (Kurland) but murdered in the Holocaust

Yehudah-Leib Don-Yikhya, who lived in *Eretz-Yisrael* the last years of his life and was one of the founders of *Nes-Tsiyonah*

Zelda Kaniznik, born in 1869, who wrote hundreds of poems in Yiddish

Yosef Maizel, born in 1850, became a writer and publisher in England.

A group of Vizhun people in front of the ruined old *Chorshul*

From left: Rabbi Zalman Meltser (with a daughter), Velvel Yofe (shopkeeper and agrarian), Benjamin (the oldest inhabitant), Yosl-Reuven Zakshtein (a peddler), Eliyahu Kovalsky (a blacksmith for 60 years), Itsik Zilber (once an oven builder), Rachel-Mine Rokhman (with the rabbi's twin daughters)

(Picture from the book by Y.L. Kopelansky)

Vizhun in World War II

In June 1940 Lithuania was annexed to the Soviet Union becoming a Soviet Republic. As a consequence, under the new rules, the farms of Josl and Shimon Berkail, Mosheh Lifshitz and Polovin were nationalized as were the large leather shop of the Berkail brothers and the textile shop of Hasia Berkail. All the Zionist parties and youth organizations were disbanded and the Hebrew educational institutions were closed. The Hebrew school was changed to a Yiddish school. Yet, on the occasion of the October celebrations of 1940, the drama circle of the *Folkshilf* organized a play entitled "Death Sentence" performed in Yiddish.

The supply of goods decreased, and as a result, prices soared. The middle class, mostly Jewish, again bore the brunt, and the standard of living dropped gradually. Early in June, the family of Tsalel Korb was exiled to Siberia.

In 1940, there were about 50 Jewish families among 1,400 residents of Vizhun.

On the first day of the war between Germany and the Soviet Union, June 22nd, 1941, local Lithuanian nationalists arrested Kopl Lefshtein, a Jew, whom they intended to kill under allegations that he supported Communists. A unit of Soviet soldiers arrived in Vizhun to lead the fight against the Lithuanians. They freed the Jew who consequently escaped together with his liberators. Another Jew, Moshe Rom, was killed during the shootout. A few Jews who had access to transportation took advantage of a temporary truce to escape to Russia.

With the invasion of the German army a few days later, the Lithuanian nationalists increased their ruthless persecution. Jews were forced into hard labor and were maltreated by the guards. Two Jewish women, Esther-Rachel Gurvitz and Sarah Gurvitz, who were taking food to their husbands and a brother working in the Garguzhina forest, were murdered en route and their bodies thrown into a lake.

On June 26th, 1941 all Jews were ordered to leave their homes and gather in two small alleyways.

The next day several Jewish families were taken out and led to a forest on the road to Svadushch (Svedasai) and there, near a small stream, they were abused and executed.

The ruthlessness of the murderers was unbelievable. Yankele (Ya'akov) Polovin was thrown by his so-called friends into a burning oven and his tormentors delighted in his battle with the fire until his merciful release in his death. One of the most beautiful girls in town, Shimon Berkail's daughter Malkah, was assaulted by two Lithuanian hooligans, Paseluk and Kuntchinas, then taken out into the yard, tied by her hair to a tree and raped. Kuntchinas then hit her on her head with a bottle and she lay bleeding until she too mercifully died. After the war Paseluk was shot while hiding in the forest but Kuntchinas managed to escape to Canada.

On June 29th, armed Lithuanians force-marched another group of Jews, among them many young people, to a forest in Shventupe, near Gargozhina farm. There they were kept for several days without food. The women were raped and others were abused before they were all shot and buried under the trees and the bushes. The remaining Vizhun Jews were led to Utyan where they too were put to death on August 7th, 1941 (14th of Av, 5701) in the Rase forest, 2 km. (1 mile) north of Utyan. One Jew, Avraham Fainshtein, who managed to escape from the murder site, hid in the town until a Lithuanian woman handed him over to the police. He too was shot.

The mass graves and the monument at the Rashe forest

The inscription on the monument in Yiddish and Lithuanian:

"At this site Hitler's fiends and their local helpers murdered about 8,000 Jews - men, women, children - in July and August, 1941"

After all the Jews were murdered the hooligans collected the Torah scrolls, prayer books and Talmud books and burned them all.

The Jewish cemetery was totally destroyed. Headstones were smashed and were used as bricks to build houses.

Of all the Vizhun Jews, excluding those who escaped to Russia, only two survived. They were Rivkah Blumberg, a young woman rescued by Baziene, a Lithuanian flourmill owner who provided her with a document stating that she was of Tatar origin, and a Jewish man who worked as a worker for Masanish, a Lithuanian farmer.

A group of Vizhun survivors at the grave in Rashe forest where the remains of Vizhun victims were re-interred.

Among the few Vizhun Jews who managed to escape to the Soviet Union at the beginning of the war were young men who fought against the Germans in the front lines of the Red Army and fell in battle. Others were recognized and decorated for their heroism (See **Appendix 1**)..

Among the few murderers caught after the war and sentenced in Soviet courts were the former county chairman Kevlis (he died in prison); a teacher, Stasys Slapsis; another teacher, Marcinkevicius, who was sentenced to life imprisonment but was freed under Krushchev's amnesty; the two brothers Morkunai who were shot in the forest; Masiunas who lived in New York; Kutkus Albinas also shot in the forest; Rashimuk Kestutis who died in prison and Geidamavicius who also received a sentence of life imprisonment.

Sources:

Yad Vashem Archives - M-1/E-1655/1539; 0-3/2582; M-33/971;
Koniuhovsky Collection - 0-71, files 42. 52, 53
Yankel-Leib Kopelansky - *It Was...It Wasn't* (Yiddish), Nes Tsiyonah,
August 1998
Di Yiddishe Shtime - Kovno, 25.4.1938
Fun Letsten Hurbn - Muenchen, No. 10, December 1948
Naujienos - Chicago, 11.6.1949

Appendix 1

Vizhun soldiers who fell in battle (from the book by Y.L. Kopelansky)

Yudele Elisberg	Khone Finkel, Officer
Hayim Elisberg	Leibke Berkail
Shimon Lefshtein, Sgt.	Eli Bunke Kopelansky

Vizhun soldiers who were decorated for heroism (from the book by Y.L. Kopelansky)

Leizer Ainbinder	Mikhael Segal
Peretz Ulim	Kopl Lefshtein
Yankel-Leib Kopelansky	Mosheh Zilber

List of Vizhun Jews in Hamelitz, donors for the settlement of Eretz-Yisrael
(from Jewishgen. rg.> Databases> Lithuania. Hamelitz Compiled by Jeffrey
Maynard)

Surname	Name	Comments	Source	Year
SEGAL	Chaim Zev	gabai	#121	1900
WEINER	Meir Eli	rabbi gaon ABD	#121	1900
ZILBER	Eliezer	Chassidic Minyan	#121	1900

Varniai (Vorne)

Varniai (Vorne in Yiddish) lies in the western part of Lithuania, in the Zamut (Zemaitija) region, on the west bank of the small stream Varnele, about 30 km. (18 miles) south of the district administrative center, Telz (Telsiai). The large Lake Lukstas is situated to the south of the town while there are two other small lakes on the north side.

Vorne youngsters rowing in Lake Lukstas

The settlement dates back to the sixteenth century. At that time, a settlement called Medininkai, on the east bank of the stream, included the residence of the Bishop of Zamut. Later this settlement was renamed Varniai. In 1635, the town was granted the Magdeburg rights of self-rule. The emblem of the town is highlighted by a Latin inscription: *Sigillium Civitatis Vornensis Ducatus Samogit* (Vorne is subordinate to the Bishop of Zamut).

In 1740 a school of higher education for priests was moved to Vorne. The town fairs brought 20,000 visitors, with many from Vilna and Riga. The Northern Wars with Sweden, the rebellions against the Russian rule, and the fires and epidemics wrought havoc on the people of Vorne. In 1863, as a result of the Polish rebellion, the residence of the bishop and the school for the priests were both moved from Vorne. Nevertheless, with the construction of barracks for the local Russian garrison, the town developed economically and culturally. The number of the residents increased, and the number of professionals and artisans among them increased as well; thus at the end of the nineteenth century about 60 shops and taverns and some 30 light industry workshops were in operation in the town.

Throughout Russian rule (1795-1915), German military rule (1915-1918) and that of independent Lithuania (1918-1940), Vorne was a county administrative center of the Telz district. At the outskirts of the town the Lithuanian government established a detention camp for about 150 political prisoners, mostly with communist leanings. There were quite a few Jews among these prisoners.

The Jewish Settlement until after World War I

The first Jews probably settled in Vorne in the second half of the seventeenth century. The bishop granted rights to a few Jews to run taverns, sell liquor and collect taxes during the fairs. Later, peddlers, merchants and artisans arrived in town. Jews, provided the majority of tradesmen, including tailors.

Jewish homes in an alleyway

Their workshops were small and run by families.

The tradesmen of the time numbered twenty-two tailors, ten carters, sixteen shoemakers, six blacksmiths, three carpenters, three hatters, two builders, one book binder, one painter and one mould-maker. There were also well known timber tradesmen: one of these, Aharon Raskin, was a very prominent member of the community. The timber was loaded on to rafts and sent to Memel (Klaipeda) en route to Germany. The local flourmill was owned by Rafael Zax. Liquor distillation plants were also run by Jews. Several families kept stores, and they would travel to the large regional town of Shavl (Siauliai) to stock up on goods.

As the population grew, a cemetery and prayer houses were built - the *Kloiz* and the *Shtiblekh* on two of the sides of the *Shul*, a building with a high dome for prayers in the summer.

One of the prayer houses in Vorne

Later, welfare associations were established. *Linath HaTsedek*, *Bikur Holim*, *Gemiluth Hesed*, *Hakhnasath Kalah* and *Hakhnasath Orkhim* were among these. Social assistance was mostly provided by generous women with initiative. One such was Ida-Pesia, the wife of Aharon Raskin the timber merchant. He was also the *Gabai* of the local *Yeshivah* with its 60 students. This *Yeshivah* was established and directed by Nahum-Lipa Hananyah, and it existed for 35 years until his death in 1910. Many of the young people in the town studied in the Telz Yeshivah and in other *Yeshivoth* in the area. Quite a few acquired a general education as well.

In 1874, a blood libel was initiated by a local priest who gave money to a Christian boy to disappear from the town. Then he announced that the Jews had murdered the boy for his blood. The priest, together with a group of peasants armed with knifes and sticks, went out in the streets and attacked every Jew they met. A few were injured and taken to hospital. The uproar stopped when the boy returned home.

In 1847, 1,084 Jews lived in the town. Half a century later, according to the government census of 1897, there were 3,121 residents in Varniai, including 1,226 (39%) Jews.

Jewish agrarians were Motl Sheifer, the owner of a water-powered flourmill; David Karklaner; Hirsh Krengl; Velve Shnaider; Mosheh the *Yanepoler* and Shelomoh Katz the *Vidmanter*. They lived in the villages around Vorne.

Jewish children aged three years and older studied at the traditional *Heder*. A more modern school, called *Heder Metukan* (improved *Heder*) was opened several years before World War I. Most of the students came from the more affluent families. One of them, Ya'akov-David Kamzon, became famous as a writer and poet in *Eretz-Yisrael*. In addition to religious subjects, the school taught Hebrew grammar, mathematics and other secular subjects. There was considerable objection to this method of learning from the more conservative circles in town. As a result, the initiator and director of this institution, Yeshayah Ben Zion Fridman was questioned. He was known as a strictly religious and educated man who combined intellectuality with Zionism. Loyal to his views, he changed his surname to the Hebrew *Ish-Shalom* (Man of Peace). Years later, one of his sons, Mordehai Ish-Shalom, became the mayor of Jerusalem.

The *Hibath Zion* movement was very active in Vorne. In 1898, it had 100 members. The list of donors to the settlement of *Eretz-Yisrael* published in *HaMelitz* in 1898, 1899, 1900 and 1903 contained 127 names of Vorne Jews (see **Appendix 1**). The fund-raisers were as follows: in 1898, Hayim Gutman, Zalkind Likht; in 1899, Hayim Levin; in 1903, Hayim Leshem.

The cemetery on the Mount of Olives in Jerusalem has at least five headstones of Vorne Jews:

> Rabbi Simhah son of Eliyahu, died 1865
>
> Rivkah-Leah daughter of Yehezkel-Pinhas, died 1867
>
> Peshe daughter of Yehudah, died 1869
>
> Dusha wife of Faivel, died 1869
>
> Yehezkel-Pinhas son of Mordehai, died 1871

With the outbreak of World War I in August 1914, the Germans bombed Vorne. Most of the Jews ran for shelter, but several days later, after the German army occupied the town, they returned home. Throughout that war, Vorne residents were under strict German rule and, among other orders, endured the forced labor imposed on many of them. However, Jews gained permanent representation in public affairs on behalf of the community, which had established a good rapport with the local German commander. Nevertheless, a local group of Jewish youths still found it necessary to find secure hiding places for the forced laborers, and helped many to escape.

A local Rabbi reported to German authorities in 1918 that seven Jews died in the first quarter of that year: five women, one man and one child.

After World War I, there was still no peace for Vorne and the surrounding areas. Sporadic fights among the Lithuanians and other nations continued and the Jews feared that the unrest would result in pogroms. To be ready for this potential evil, a self-defence group of Jewish youths armed themselves with pistols. They were trained by German deserters hired by the community. These Germans together with the Jewish youngsters stood guard over the community until stability was restored to the region.

The Rabbis who served in Vorne during this period were:

> Shemuel Shmelke Itinga (died in 1902)
>
> Benjamin Verber (also died in 1902)
>
> Josef-Leib Blokh, (1849-1930) served in Vorne between the years 1902-1904 and later became the director of Telz *Yeshivah*
>
> Shalom-Yits'hak Levitan (1878-1941) served in Vorne 1908-1909, published several books on Judaism. He was murdered in the Holocaust
>
> Yisrael Yehoshua Segal, son of Shemuel-Aryeh, born in 1864 (in Vorne from 1898).

Between 1839-1934, there were 21 subscribers to rabbinic literature in Vorne.

The Period of Independent Lithuania (1918-1940)

With the establishment of the independent Lithuanian State in 1918, most Vorne Jews were old town residents who had lived there before World War I. They continued to make their living in the trades, small commerce and crafts.

Following the Law of Autonomies for Minorities issued by the new Lithuanian government, the minister of Jewish affairs, Dr. Menachem (Max) Soloveitshik ordered elections to community committees (*Va'adei Kehilah*) to be held in the summer of 1919. In July 1920 the elections to the community committee of Vorne were held and nine members were elected: three General Zionists, three non-party men, two tradesmen and one affiliated to the *Mizrahi* party. The committee served in most fields of Jewish life until the law was annulled in the spring of 1926. Jewish representatives were elected to the municipal council of Vorne.

The survey conducted by the community committee in 1920 revealed that there were approximately 800 Jewish residents in town, 54% of them women. Those under 18 years of age comprised 43% of the population, the age group of 19 to 50 was 37% and those between the ages of 51 and 85 the balance (20%). 70% of the Jews were born in Vorne. Among the 132 gainfully employed persons, 34 were shopkeepers, 22 were small traders and peddlers, 14 were shoemakers, eight tailors, eight bakers, eight butchers, four carters and drivers, four *melamdim* (teachers), three hat-makers, three pharmacists, three tinsmiths, two builders, two carpenters, two cantors, one doctor, one watchmaker, one porter, one *Klizemer* (musician at Jewish weddings), one bath attendant, one tanning worker, one hostel owner and one dental assistant.

The Government survey of 1931 listed 23 shops in Vorne, 21 (91%) Jewish owned. The distribution according to the type of business is presented in the table below:

Type of business	Total	Owned by Jews
Groceries	4	3
Butcher shops and Cattle Trade	4	3
Restaurants and Taverns	1	1
Food Products	1	1
Textile Products and Furs	5	5
Leather and Shoes	2	2
Haberdashery and house utensils	1	1
Watches, Jewels and Optics	1	1
Hardware Products	2	2
Bicycles, electrical equipment, sewing machines	1	1
Transportation, Machines	1	1

Also listed in the same survey, were three barbershops, a power station, a workshop for wool combing and a flour mill, all owned by Jews of Vorne.

With the decrease in Vorne's Jewish population, Jewish trade decreased proportionately. In 1937, only 40 tradesmen remained in the town: ten shoemakers, six tailors, four carpenters, three butchers, three watchmakers, three tinsmiths, two hat-makers, two oven builders, two blacksmiths, one binder, one barber and three others.

In 1939, of the 24 telephone lines in Vorne, four were in Jewish homes.

In the 1920s, a Hebrew school with *Tarbuth* affiliation, a library, a drama group and the *Folksbank* (Popular Bank) were established in Vorne. The *Folksbank* had 107 members in 1927, and by 1929 the number had decreased to 92. Although the bank provided great assistance, the condition of the Jewish shopkeepers and tradesmen deteriorated from year to year. The systematic anti-Semitic propaganda of various Lithuanian associations contributed to these difficulties.

The Market Square in Vorne

There were verbal and physical attacks against the Jews and their language on numerous occasions. On October 9th, 1923 all Jewish signs in the town were smeared with tar. October 15th, 1935 saw a blood libel initiated against the Jews. As a result, two were injured and thirty-nine windows in Jewish homes were broken. On November 11th, 1936 one Jew was murdered and thirty-three sustained injuries at the hands of Lithuanian neighbors and peasants at the town fair.

These events and the worsening economic situation resulted in many Vorne Jews emigrating to South Africa, South America and Australia. Some chose *Eretz-Yisrael*: these were the youngsters of the Zionist camp. One such Zionist was Mordecai Ish-Shalom (the son of the founder of *Heder Metukan*): he organized the *Hehalutz* branch in Vorne. He was one of the first stonecutters in *Eretz-Yisrael* and later became the mayor of Jerusalem.

Several young Jewish people joined the Communist party: a few of these were arrested for their subversive activities and were imprisoned in the detention camp outside the town.

Going to the synagogue

Besides the *HeHalutz* branch, there were also many other Zionist youth organizations, including *HaShomer HaTsair*. Zionist and sports activities were also organized by the local *Maccabi* branch. Almost all the Zionist parties had supporters. In the table below we can see how Vorne Zionists voted during five Zionist congresses:

Cong No.	Year	Tot Shek	Total Votes	Labor Party		Rev	Gen Zion		Gros	Miz
				Z"S	Z"Z		A	B		
15	1927	38	29	5	10	1	6	----	----	7
16	1929	45	27	2	6	---	12	----	----	7
17	1931	62	49	7	13	7	9	----	----	13
18	1933	---	77	59		4	9	----	----	5
19	1935	---	249	127		---	58	---	----	64

Key: Cong No. = Congress Number, Tot Shek = Total Shekalim, Rev = Revisionists, Gen Zion = General Zionists, Gros = Grosmanists, Miz = Mizrakhi

Rabbis who served during this period in Vorne included;

Ya'akov son of Zevulun Abramovitz (1880-1937), from 1925-1937,

Aba Shur (1909-1941), the last rabbi of Vorne, who was murdered in the Holocaust.

Among the personages born in Vorne were:

> Boris-Zalman-Dov Shatz (1866-1932) emigrated to *Eretz-Yisrael* in 1906. He was an artist - a painter and a sculptor - and founded the *Betsalel* School of Arts in Jerusalem. He died in Colorado, in the USA.

> Mosheh Dov Magid, born in 1901: from 1934 he lived in *Eretz-Yisrael* and was a member of the *Mizrahi* center and of the Municipal Council of Tel Aviv.

> Zalman-Pinhas Nathans (1893- ?), arrived in America as a young man, graduated at New York University and was a teacher of mathematics and physics in New York high schools. He published "Nathan's Popular Explanation of Einstein's Theory of Relativity" (NY, 1931) in Yiddish. In the 1930s he lived in New Rochelle, New York.

> Ya'akov-David Kamzon (1900-1980), lived in Jerusalem from 1926. A writer and poet in Yiddish and Hebrew, he published his book *Jerusalem* and many children's books; in 1959 published the book *Yahaduth Lita* with many photos of Jewish communities in Lithuania (Publisher *Mosad HaRav Kook*, Jerusalem).

During World War II

In June 1940, Lithuania was annexed to the Soviet Union and became a Soviet Republic. Significant changes in social, economic, cultural and educational life affected the Vorne Jews. Following the new rules, the larger shops and enterprises were nationalized. All the Zionist parties and youth organizations were disbanded and the Hebrew educational institutions were closed. The supply of goods decreased and, as a result, prices soared. The middle class, mostly Jewish, bore the brunt and the standard of living dropped gradually.

On June 25th, 1941, three days after the outbreak of war between the Soviet Union and Germany, the German army entered Vorne. Before the soldiers of the Red Army in Vorne retreated, they set the arms warehouses on fire. As a result the synagogue and most of the homes in town burned down. Some of the Jews found temporary quarters in Jewish homes in neighboring towns. When they returned, they found the town destroyed by fire and under the rule of local nationalist Lithuanians, who were conducting a witch-hunt against Soviet activists. In particular, they focused their evil intentions on their former Jewish neighbors and abused and eventually murdered those whom they suspected of pro-Soviet activity. Among the first victims was a veteran teacher, Tsevi Leibovitz. The remaining Jews were forced into hard labor, cleaning debris, sweeping the streets and more.

At the beginning of July, all Jews were ordered to go to the village of Viesvenai, about 25 km. (15 miles) from Vorne. The adults walked, the aged and the children rode in carts. In Viesvenai, the Vorne Jews together with others from surrounding areas were herded into barns, stables and cowsheds. They were supervised by armed Lithuanians. After several days of maltreatment, on July 16th, 1941, the men were shot and buried in a mass grave. The women and children were sent to Geruliai village near Telz. There, they were murdered on August 30th (7th of Elul, 5701). On December 24th, 1941 (4th of Teveth, 5702) several girls who had been temporarily employed by farmers of the area and in Telz, were put to death.

Only a few managed to escape and survive.

In 1989 only 6 Jews lived in Vorne.

The mass grave near Viesvenai

The mass grave and the monument near Geruliai

Sources:

Yad Vashem Archives, Koniukhovsky Collection 0-71, files 36, 37

YIVO, New York, Lithuanian Communities Collection, files 179-191

Ish-Shalom M., *BeSod Hotzvim Ubonim* (Hebrew), Jerusalem, 5741 (1981)

Elitsur Sarah, *Biyeri UBamistarim* (Hebrew), Jerusalem, 5746 (1986)

Milner M., *Me'Eiver LaKav HaHayim* (Hebrew), Tel Aviv 1981

Fridman Sh.Z., *BeDarhei HaRuakh*, Jerusalem, 1980

Di Tsait (Yiddish), Kovno, 6.5.1924

Masines Zudynes Lietuvoje (Lithuanian) (Mass Murder in Lithuania), Vol. II, page 41

Naujienos (Lithuanian) Chicago, 11.6.1949

Appendix 1

List of 127 Vorne Jewish donors to The Settlement of *Eretz-Yisrael*

(From Jewishgen.org.> Databases>Lithuania> *HaMelitz* Compiled by Jeffrey Maynard).

Surname	Given Name	Comments	Source In Hamelitz	Year
AIZIKMAN	Aizik		#108	1900
ARONOWITZ	Shmuel Meir		#108	1900
BALNIK	Yitzchok		#132	1898
BALNIK	Yitzchok		#108	1900
BALNIK	Yitzchok		#23	1901
BATZFON	Leib		#23	1901
BATZFON	Lev		#204	1895
BATZFON	Yehuda Leib		#132	1898
BERMAN	Tzvi		#132	1898
BORSHTEIN	Moshe		#132	1898
BROIDA	Zev		#132	1898
BROIDA	Zev		#23	1901
CHAIMOWITZ	Ezriel		#151	1898
CHAIMOWITZ	Ezriel Yitzchok		#132	1898
CHAIMOWITZ	Gershon related to Nochum Shlomo Chaimowitz from Taurage		#247	1895
CHAMERDIL	Shaul Yehuda		#108	1900
CHANANIE	Beile Rochel bas Nochum		#23	1901
CHANANIE	Beinish		#23	1901
CHANANIE	Nochum Lipman		#23	1901
DIMANT	Yitzchok		#108	1900
DIMANT	Yitzchok		#23	1901
DOGILEWITZ	Hersh		#23	1901
DOGILEWITZ	Yehoshua		#108	1900
DOMBE	Zelig Leib		#132	1898

EPHRIN	Yisroel		#132	1898
FRIDMAN	Bentzion		#108	1900
FRIDMAN	Bentzion b-i-l of Leah Reitzkin husband of Reitze		#23	1901
FRIDMAN	Reitze wife of Bentzion		#23	1901
GODON	Yeshiyahu		#23	1901
GOLDING	Chaim		#23	1901
GOLDSHTEIN	Dovid husband of Leah Reitzkin	wed 5 Kislev in Manchester, UK	#23	1901
GOLDSHTEIN	Meir		#108	1900
GOLEMBA	Yisroel		#23	1901
GOLUMBA	Yisroel		#185	1895
GRAF	Meir		#132	1898
GRIN	Meir	Shub	#132	1898
GRIN	Meir	Shub	#108	1900
GROF	Meir		#23	1901
GROZ	Yitzchok		#132	1898
GUTMAN	Chaim ben Tzvi Eliahu		#132	1898
HAGNI	Beila		#108	1900
HAGNI	Binyomin Beinish		#108	1900
HAGNI	Moshe		#108	1900
HILLEL	Yakov		#132	1898
KATZ	Raphel Shabasai		#108	1900
KATZ	Yakov Hillel		#108	1900
KATZ	Yisroel		#108	1900
KATZ	Zalman Yitzchok		#132	1898
KAMZOHN	Meir		#132	1898
KATZ	Zalman Yakov		#108	1900
KLOP	Yakov		#108	1900
KOZNITZKI	Yakov		#108	1900
KWEINGIL	Meir		#23	1901

LEIK	Ephraim Eliezer		#108	1900
LEW	Yehuda Leib		#108	1900
LEWI	Yakov Elchanan	Shatz	#108	1900
LEWIN	Yakov Elchanan	Shatz	#132	1898
LEWITAN	Chaim Meir		#132	1898
LIBZOHN	Don Arieh		#23	1901
LICHT	Binyomin		#132	1898
LICHT	Ephraim Eliezer		#132	1898
LICHT	Zalkind		#132	1898
LICHT	Zalkind		#108	1900
LIN	Tzvi		#23	1901
LURIA	Dovid		#132	1898
LURIA	Nachum		#132	1898
LURIA	Nachum		#108	1900
LURIA	Nochum		#23	1901
LURIA	Yakov		#108	1900
MAGID	Beinish		#23	1901
MAGID	Binyomin Beinish		#108	1900
MARIK	Dovid		#132	1898
MARIK	Yosef		#23	1901
MELAMED	Shimon Yehuda		#108	1900
NADIL	Tzemach Dovid		#108	1900
NAWAITZ	Mordechai Eliezer		#108	1900
NOWITZ	Mordechai		#132	1898
OLSHWANGER	Aharon		#108	1900
OLSHWANGER	Eli		#132	1898
OLSHWANGER	Ezriel		#132	1898
OLSHWANGER	Ezriel		#108	1900
OLSHWANGER	Ezriel		#23	1901
OSHROWITZ	Peretz		#132	1898
PIL	Ephraim		#132	1898

POHINSKI	Menucha		#108	1900
POLINSKI	Chaim		#108	1900
POSHINSKI	Chaim		#23	1901
POSHINSKI	Miriam		#23	1901
PRINGEL	Tzvi		#108	1900
PUSHANSKI	Chaim		#23	1901
PUSHINSKI	Chaim		#132	1898
RADALIE	Avraham Dov		#132	1898
REINES	Shneur		#132	1898
REITZKIN	Eliezer brother of Leah & Sheine Feige		#23	1901
REITZKIN	Leah sister of Eliezer & Sheine wife of Dovid Goldshtein	wed 5 Kislev in Manchester, UK	#23	1901
REITZKIN	Sheine Feige sister of Eliezer & Leah		#23	1901
ROSTENBERG	Dovid		#108	1900
ROSTOWSKI	Gitl wife of Chaim Gutman from Kelme	wed in Varna	#123	1897
ROT	Aharon Leib		#108	1900
ROTTENBERG	Dovid		#132	1898
ROZ	Dov Moshe		#132	1898
ROZENTHAL	Tzvi Yehuda		#132	1898
ROZINSHTEIN	Zev		#108	1900
SEGAL	Dov		#132	1898
SEGAL	Aizik		#23	1901
SEGAL	Dovid		#108	1900
SEGAL	Dovid		#23	1901
SHAIBET	Yakov		#23	1901
SHEFTIL	Yehoshua		#108	1900
SHER	Aharon		#132	1898
SHER	Tzvi Menachem		#132	1898
SHER	Yitzchok		#108	1900

SHMIDT	Dovid	#132	1898
SHNITZ	Moshe	#108	1900
SHNITZ	Moshe	#23	1901
SHOCHAT	Shimon	#132	1898
SROL	Yakov Zev	#108	1900
TALPIOT	Avraham uncle of Leah Reitzkin	#23	1901
TZIN	Aharon	#132	1898
TZIN	Eli	#108	1900
TZIN	Eli	#23	1901
TZIN	Eliahu	#132	1898
ZAK	Dov Ari	#108	1900
ZAZINSHTEIN	Zev	#23	1901
	Shaul Yehuda	#132	1898
	Yosef ben Zelig	#132	1898
	Yosef Zev	#108	1900

Zarasai (Ezhereni)

Between the two World Wars Zarasai (Ezhereni in Yiddish), a town in northeastern Lithuania was situated near the borders with Latvia and Poland. The main road from Kaunas (Kovno) to Daugavpils (Dvinsk) in Latvia passed through Ezhereni which is 24 km. (15 miles) from Dvinsk. The town is surrounded by woods and lakes and because of its beauty was known as the "Lithuanian Switzerland".

Originally the town was a village named Yazrusi, where, in the fifteenth century, there existed a Carmelite monastery. In 1481 the army of the Prince of Moscow, Ivan the Third, invaded this area, and in the seventeenth century there was fighting in the vicinity between the Swedes and the Polish-Lithuanian armies.

Until 1795 Ezhereni was part of the Polish-Lithuanian kingdom, when, with the third division of Poland by the three superpowers of those times, Russia, Prussia and Austria, Lithuania became partly Russian and partly Prussian. The part of Lithuania that included Ezhereni fell under Czarist Russian rule and from 1836 until 1915 was included in the Kovno province (*Gubernia*) as a district center.

In 1812 fighting erupted between the Russians and Napoleon's French army near the town, while during the Polish rebellion in 1831 groups of rebels were active in the vicinity of Ezhereni.

Czar Nikolai the First (who ruled from 1825-1855) was so impressed by the beauty of the town during his visit to Ezhereni in 1836, that he ordered it to be turned into a district administrative center, naming it Novo Alexandrovsk. It was built in a similar style to other towns in Russia and became the first town in Lithuania to develop from a plan. In 1839 it was declared a district administrative center and remained so until 1915.

Under independent Lithuania rule the Russian name of the town was rendered invalid and it reverted to its previous title of Ezhereni. However in 1929 it was decided to restore the old Lithuanian name of Zarasai, and so it has remained to this day.

By 1857 there were 163 houses, and in the second half of the nineteenth century Ezhereni boasted a district school established in 1868, a two-class Jewish school, a hospital, a Catholic church, two Pravoslavic churches and six Jewish prayer houses. Many Jewish children attended the government school.

In the nineteenth century there were many workshops, including a printing press. The main Warsaw to St. Petersburg road that passed through Ezhereni was constructed between 1832 and 1836 and as a result the town flourished. At the end of the nineteenth century a brick factory and two water-powered flourmills functioned in the town. In addition to the bi-weekly markets there were also two annual fairs, one in summer and one in winter, attended by merchants from Riga, St. Petersburg, Kazan and Kiev.

In World War I the town suffered badly. It was partly ruined and lost two thirds of its residents, many of them leaving because of the Soviet-Bolshevik rule which lasted from December 1918 until August 25th, 1919. Because of its distance from the center of Lithuania, restoration of the town after the war was slow and the economic situation deteriorated. In 1932 Ezhereni was proclaimed a vacation town.

During World War II 60% of the town's houses were ruined.

Jewish Settlement until World War I

Jewish settlement in Ezhereni started at the beginning of the nineteenth century. In 1847 there were 453 Jews residents; by 1857 this increased to 909 Jews who constituted 26% of the total population. By 1866 the Jews were the majority in town, numbering 3,562 (54%) of a total population of 6,547. The Jews traded in grain and flax, raw hide and pig bristles and dealt in shop keeping, peddling and transportation. Jewish merchants dealt commercially with the Poles of the surrounding estates and also with Vilna, Riga and Dvinsk where agricultural products were sold.

There were also many artisans: tailors, shoemakers and felt boot makers. In 1841 there were five Jewish shoemakers and six tailors. Some Ezherenis made their living from fishing in the nearby lakes. In the 1890s 1,037 Jews earned their living from seven farms on land granted by the Russian government.

The weekly markets took place on Tuesdays and Fridays, but there was also trading on Sundays. Peasants who came to town to attend church would take the opportunity to buy the goods they required.

This was a difficult economic period because of competition from Dvinsk in the grain and flax trade. The drought prevented the peasants from buying in local shops because of lack of money, while on the other hand, when there was a heavy rainfall with the resultant glut of grain, prices dropped and the merchants continued to suffer.

In 1910 the Lithuanians established cooperatives which compounded the dire problems of the Jewish economy.

A report published in *HaMelitz* in 1891 showed that there were many poor Jews who had little food. The fact that about 500 Jews appealed to *Maoth Hitim* before Pesakh was proof of the difficult situation.

There were also sanitation and health problems. There was only one doctor to care for about 8,000 people in their homes and in the town's hospital. This doctor was Yehiel-Aharon son of Mosheh Zandberg (1831-1893). He served there for about 25 years and was respected by all, Jews and Christians alike.

To the credit of the local rabbi, Mordecai Fainshtein, the number of members of *Hovevei Zion* in Ezhereni increased and in 1890 reached 200. Many residents donated money to the settlement of *Eretz-Yisrael*. 162 Ezhereni Jews were listed as donors in *HaMelitz* for the years 1893, 1895, 1897, 1898 and 1900 (see **Appendix 1**). The fund-raisers were Yehudah Shtein and Yerahmiel Berman. The correspondents to *HaMelitz* were Y. Fainshtein (known also as Y. Even-Yafe), Ts. Poliakov, Mosheh-Ozer Levin, Josef Frenkel and Tsevi-Ya'akov Oppenheim.

Among Ezhereni Jews who emigrated to *Eretz-Yisrael* were Sarah Pliner (born in 1870) who died in a fire in *Ein Zeitim* during the Arab riots in 1929. Sarah Azaryahu (a Hebraicized surname) was born in 1873 in Dvinsk, lived in Ezhereni from 1881 and from 1905 in *Eretz-Yisrael* in Yaffo, Jerusalem and finally on Kibbutz Afikim where she died in 1962. She published her memoirs in Hebrew "*Pirkei Hayim*" on Jewish life in Ezhereni.

Ezhereni had excellent Jewish institutions and societies. There were a *Talmud Torah*, a Hebrew elementary school, a library and six prayer houses: the great synagogue (the *Shul*) was built in 1858; the *Beth Midrash* erected on the plot of Itsele Hashem, who had duly received the visiting Czar; the *Shtibl* of the *Hasidim* called the Red *Minyan*; the *Hasidic* green building; the *Beth Hamidrash* at the Foot of the Mountain and the *Kloiz* of the tailors which was built in 1895. The community had a rabbi and two *Shokhtim*.

In the 1880s a controversy broke out in the *Beth Midrash* (*Kloiz*) of the tailors on the issue of appointing a new *shamash* to succeed the deceased beadle. The Jewish community broke up into factions and each supported its own candidate. There were eight contestants for the job and so eight factions.

In 1902 the local rabbi, Gliternik, resigned because of Orthodox intrigues, preferring to teach at the Hebrew elementary school. The official rabbi also left for similar reasons and Ezhereni Jews were unable to decide whom to appoint as a rabbi.

There was a society for supporting the Jewish poor and sick. In 1901 its income derived from its 86 members. Each paid three rubles per annum and this was augmented from any special donations, including 500 rubles from Klonimus Ze'ev Wissotzky, the founder of the Russian tea of that name. In 1901 the society's total income was 1,455 rubles. This covered the fees of doctors, the medic and a midwife. It paid for medicines, instruments, hospitalization, food and heating. Some unfortunates benefited from money grants.

In the 1870s and 1880s there were quite a few local Jewish government officials, which was a rarity in Lithuanian towns at that time. However, in 1884, a circular issued by the deputy of the Kovno Gubernator informed the people that all Jewish officials were dismissed.

In 1886 the authorities called for tenders for activating the government flourmill, but prohibited Jews on the pretext that the mill was situated outside the town. Originally an official dealing with this issue had actually allowed the Jews to participate in the tender, but due to envy, rivals informed on this official to his superiors and the authorities forbade Jewish involvement.

During the period of independent Lithuania (1918-1940)

With the establishment of independent Lithuania in 1918 Ezhereni was cut off from its natural hinterland. Areas in the east were occupied and annexed to Poland, whereas in the north a new border with the recently established state of Latvia was delineated. As a result communications with many settlements whose economic and commercial center had been Ezhereni were also cut off. The worst economic setback to the town was being detached from the railway line now in the Polish occupied area and from Dvinsk. Ezhereni became isolated and its total population (Gentile and Jewish) decreased from 7,128 in 1913 to 3,785 in 1923. The Jewish population concurrently decreased from about 2,500 in 1913 to 1,329 in 1923. A disproportionate number of professional people left the town.

General view of Ezhereni

Following the law of autonomies for minorities issued by the new Lithuanian government, the minister for Jewish affairs Dr. Menachem (Max) Soloveitshik ordered elections to community committees (*Va'adei Kehilah*) to be held in the summer of 1919. In 1921 the elections for the community committee of Ezhereni took place and eleven members were elected, two from *Akhduth*, six non-party men and three independent members. The committee was supported administratively and financially by the Ministry for Jewish Affairs in Kovno. It dealt, amongst other items, with a complaint presented to the Ministry about Jews being assaulted by Lithuanians.

In 1924, the last year of the existence of the committee, its annual budget was 5,720 litas as detailed below:

Income		Expenses	
Taxes	4,800	Culture	1,020
Fees for services	360	*Bikur Holim*	1,000
The Bath House	360	Rent for the rabbi	1,300
Undefined	200	*Lekhem Aniyim*	300
		Office expenses	1,620
		Tax for the Jewish National Committee	480
Total Income	**5,720**	**Total Expenses**	**5,720**

According to the first census in independent Lithuania in 1923, the number of Jews in Ezhereni was 35% of the population (1,329 Jews out of a total of 3,785 residents), the other residents being Lithuanians, Poles and Russians.

Five of twelve members elected to the Town Council in 1924 were Jews. In the elections of 1931 four Jews were successful, Avraham Mushelevitz, Zalman Levitas, Yisrael Traub and Hayim Melnik. The balance of the council comprised four Lithuanians and one Russian. Yisrael Traub was appointed deputy Council Chairman. In the 1934 elections three Jews and six Lithuanians were elected to the Council.

Most Jews lived in flats and houses in the main streets close to their shops. Many made their living trading in agricultural products such as furs, pig bristles, seeds. The more affluent owned shops selling home utensils and liquor. It is worth mentioning the widow Broiman who, together with her sons and daughters, owned several shops —selling galoshes (overshoes) and home utensils, as well as a bar and a restaurant.

The other Jews were peddlers, carters and artisans - blacksmiths, carpenters, shoemakers, tailors, felt shoemakers and so on. Many manufactured clothes. There were also Jewish fishermen and fish merchants. One of the latter, Yonah Zisel, leased a farm and a lake. But sources of livelihood diminished very much during this period. Many merchants were impoverished and the poor became poorer while the numbers of these unfortunates increased.

The Jewish Popular Bank *(Folksbank)*, established in 1920, played an important role in the economic life of Ezhereni Jews. In 1923 its members numbered 345, in 1927, 335 and in 1929, 343, almost unchanged over a seven-year period. This says much for the value of the bank to the community, in light of the worldwide depression at that time.

According to the government survey of 1931, 50 shops, 41 (82%) of them Jewish owned, could be found in Ezhereni. The following table shows the type of business, its number and how many were owned by Jews:

Type of business	Total	Owned by Jews
Groceries	7	7
Grain and flax	2	2
Butchers shops and Cattle Trade	6	6
Restaurants and Taverns	9	2
Food Products	3	3
Paper, Books and Stationary	2	1
Textile Products and Furs	6	6
Leather and Shoes	3	3
Haberdashery and house utensils	2	2
Medicine and Cosmetics	2	1
Heating materials	2	2
Hardware Products	4	4
Bicycles and electrical equipment	1	1
Undefined	1	1

The same survey showed the distribution of 25 light industries, 16 of them (64%) Jewish owned, as shown:

Type of Factory	Total	Jewish owned
Metal, Machines	2	0
Concrete products, Headstones	1	1
Textile: Wool, Flax, Knitting	3	3
Sawmills and Furniture	1	0
Flour mills, Bakeries, Beverages, Candies	6	4
Dresses, Footwear	11	8
Chemical products: Spirit, Soap, Oil	1	0

In 1935 a fire razed several Jewish houses as well as the school.

In 1937 there were 87 Jewish artisans: twenty-five needle workers, twelve shoemakers, eleven butchers, eight metal workers, six bakers, three hatters, three watchmakers, one oven builder, one carpenter, one goldsmith and sixteen others. Four families dealt in agriculture and the others were tradesmen.

There was also a match factory owned by After, a brewery owned by Hurvitz and two flour mills.

In 1939 there were 71 telephone subscribers, only five of whom were Jews.

The community in the 1930s had only three prayer houses. While before World War I the Ezherenis maintained eight *Hadarim* and a *Yeshivah,* at this time there was a Hebrew school of the *Tarbuth* network, whose teachers were Ya'akov Mushel, Yusman and Vilimovsky. Many of the Jewish children continued their studies in the Lithuanian high school. Their parents could not afford the extra financial burden of sending them to Hebrew high schools in the larger towns. There was also a Hebrew library and a drama society.

The following institutions and societies were active locally: a hospital, *Linath HaTsedek, Gemiluth Hesed*, societies for studying *Mishna, Ein Ya'akov* and others. The municipality maintained a home for aged Jews and Russians.

Hehalutz HaMizrahi **branch 1934**

Almost all Zionist parties and youth organizations were represented in Ezhereni. *HeHalutz HaMizrahi, HaShomer HaTsair, Betar*, and the religious *Benei Akiva* were particularly active. *Maccabi* with 128 members controlled local sports.

The results of the elections for the Zionist Congresses are given in the table below. (In 1931 the elections took place at the Jewish *Folksbank*.)

Cong No.	Year	Shek	Total Voter	Labor Party Z"S	Z'Z	Rev.	Gen. Zion		Gros	Miz
15	1927	52	52	---	19	8	24	----	----	1
16	1929	140	57	8	17	---	29	----	----	3
17	1931	100	96	10	21	13	45	----	----	7
18	1933	---	185	120		---	41	----	---	24
19	1935	---	486	239		---	15	78	---	154

Key: Cong No. = Congress Number, Tot Shek = Total Shekalim, Rev = Revisionists, Gen Zion = General Zionists, Gros = Grosmanists, Miz = Mizrakhi

HaShomer HaTsair branch in Ezhereni 1935 – an impressive number

Rabbis who officiated in Zarasai during these years included:

> Shimon Berman - in the 1870s
>
> Leib Shapira - died in 1880
>
> His brother, Rafael Shapira (1837-1921), in Novo Alexandrovsk in 1886
>
> Mordecai Fainshtein (1836-1903)
>
> Meir-Shalom HaCohen, who signed a Zionist appeal in 1900, died at the age of 30
>
> The last rabbi of the community, Eliyahu Reznik, was murdered in the Holocaust.

During the years 1845-1911 there were 81 subscribers to rabbinic literature.

Among the personalities born in Ezhereni were:

> Eliyahu Naividel (1821-1886) published two textbooks on the Hebrew language (in Warsaw, 1874 and 1882). He died in Warsaw.
>
> Menahem Glikman (1870-1945), graduate of the St.Petersburg Academy of Arts in 1903, died of hunger in 1945 in Leningrad.
>
> Yuri Pen, born in the 1870s, a famous Jewish-Russian artist, a graduate of the St. Petersburg Academy of Arts, he died in Vitebsk, Russia.

Heads of the illegal communist party of Lithuania were imprisoned in the town prison, among them Miriam Hodosh and R. Ger.

HaShomer HaTsair at a march – standing still

During World War II

In June 1940 Lithuania was annexed to the Soviet Union and became a Soviet Republic. The majority of shops belonging to the Jews of Ezhereni were nationalized and commissars were appointed to manage them. All Zionist parties and youth organizations were disbanded and most community institutions were closed. The supply of goods decreased and, as a result, prices soared. The middle class, mostly Jewish, bore the brunt and the standard of living dropped.

When war broke out between Germany and the Soviet Union on June 22nd, 1941, Ezherni Jews were at first not concerned, thinking that they were far removed from the front. In fact, the German army entered the town later than in many other towns in Lithuania, so that when the Red Army retreated through the town and masses of refugees arrived, the Jews panicked. Many attempted escaping to Russia, but groups of armed Lithuanians ambushed and shot them on the roads. Not many succeeded in reaching Russia. However, more than twenty escapees served in the Lithuanian division of the Red Army.

Even before the Germans entered the town, Lithuanian nationalists took over and inevitably started their abuse of the hapless Jews. Stories of the atrocities of the local Lithuanians are plentiful. The local gang of rioters was headed by a Russian named Kazanov and his helpers, the teacher Shakys and the former police commandant Bruzikaitis. A Jew, Leib Banke (or Benke), was buried alive in the center of the town. A Pole, Pashkevitz, forced the octogenarian Jewish flourmill owner Ber Novik to run through the streets with a picture of Stalin displayed on his back.

On August 26th, 1941 the now doomed Ezhereni Jews were gathered together and then ordered onto carts brought to the town. They were informed that they were going to Rakishok (Rokiskis) to work and instructed to take some food and clothing with them. They were promised a speedy return. The naive Jews, who had recently witnessed worse events, believed what they were told. The Lithuanian mayor provided the rabbi and two respected community men with letters of recommendation which stated that "these are virtuous people, good Jews", asking to accept and treat them well. And he was believed! The convoy left on the road to Utyan (Utena) guarded by armed Lithuanians.

In the evening, after traveling about 15 km. (9 miles), not far from the town of Antaliepte, the convoy left the road and entered the Deguciai forest. The people were ordered to get off the carts and to undress. Seeing the pits awaiting them, a terrible outcry arose. The women refused to undress and began to scatter, but the guards unleashed their machine guns and soon all the Jews were dead. The infamous, inhuman Pole, Pashkevitz, now one of the guards, dragged an invalid, Yerakhmiel Shtulper, who had no feet, to the murder site and threw him into the pit alive. Other Jews who were murdered there were from Antalept (Antaliepte), Dusyat (Dusetos), Salok (Salakas), Turmont (Turmantas), Rimshani (Rimse) and Duksht (Dukstas). Only two men survived the massacre. For some time they wandered around in the vicinity. They were still alive in 1943, but later one of them, Hayim Shulman was shot and the other, whose first name was Aharon, committed suicide when he realized that there was no hope of survival.

A German source believes that 2,569 Jews, including 687 children, were murdered on that day, but other information gives the number as about 5,000. The mass grave lies in the Krakynes forest, 500 meters (550 yards) from the Deguciai - Dusetos road.

Two Jews were left in the town. One of them, Yisrael Traub, about 60 years old, was accepted by the Lithuanians (during the 1930s he was a member of the Municipal Council and a deputy Mayor). He was appointed to sweep the streets, but this favor did not last long. Yisrael too became a victim of the shooting. The second Jew, Yerakhmiel Shnaider, was married to a Russian woman. He hid in his house and probably became tired of sitting at home or, perhaps his wife insisted he go to work. One Sunday Shnaider went to church with his wife and her family. In the house of prayer, the Russian Kazanov recognized him, took him out during the service and despite the pleading of his wife and her mother, led him to the forest, forced him to take off his Sunday clothes and killed him.

The marker pointing to the massacre site carries the inscription "Let us make sure that this tragedy is never again repeated."

One of the ditches filled with the remains of the thousands of innocent Jewish people

The monument on the mass graves

According to a Lithuanian source a Lithuanian named Karolis Mikutevicius hid a Jew named Berka (?) with his four family members.

Ezhereni was liberated by the Red Army at the end of 1944. After the war the survivors of Ezhereni and the surrounding towns erected a monument on the mass graves on which was written in Yiddish and Lithuanian: "Here at this site the Nazi murderers and their local helpers cruelly murdered 8,000 Jews children, women, men of Zarasai and the vicinity on the 26th of August 1941."

Sources:

Yad Vashem Archives, Jerusalem-M-1/319/210; M-9/15(6); M-33/981; M-35/80; TR-2 report 88; 0-3/4128, 5993, 6836; 0-53/320; Lithuanian communities collection 0-57, file A; Koniukhovsky collection 0-71, file 73

YIVO New York-Files 55/1701, 55/1788, 13/15/131, Z-4/2548

Bakaltchuk-Felin, M. (editor) *Yizkor* Book Rakishok (Yiddish), Johannesburg 1952, pages 306-323

Rafi Julius - Ezhereni (Zarasai) (Hebrew), *Pinkas Hakehiloth-Lita, Yad Vashem* Jerusalem, 1996

Dos Vort, Kovno (Yiddish) 11.11.1934

Di Yiddishe Shtime, Kovno (Yiddish) 29.10.1924; 19.6.1931

Folksblat, Kovno (Yiddish) 4.1.1934; 28.4.1935; 9.8.1935

HaMelitz, St. Petersburg, (Hebrew) 17.10.1873; 21.11.1872; 17.12.1886; 20.5.1893; 2.7.1893; 28.11.1903; 15.9.1903

Indrasius Vytautas - Zarasieciai Didziojo Tevynes Karo Frontuose, (Zarasai People at the Fronts of the Great Homeland War) Zarasai 1984

Naujienos, Chicago 1949

Appendix 1

A list of 162 Ezhereni donors to the Settlement of *Eretz-Yisrael*

(From JewishGen.Org/Databases/*HaMelitz*. Compiled by Jeffrey Maynard)

Surname	Given Name	Comments	Source in Hamelitz	Year
AHUN	Asher		#173	1898
ALBER	Ephraim		#26	1900
BENDET	Yakov Tzadok		#26	1900
BERMAN	Shimon		#19	1897
BERMAN	Yerachmiel		#127	1897
BERMAN	Yerachmiel		#107	1898
BORSHTEIN	Chaim Yitzchok		#173	1898
CHAIKLOITZ	Dov Ber		#173	1898
DACHMAN	Aharon Leib		#117	1898
DAVIDOV	Pinchos		#173	1898
DAWIDOW	Pinchos		#26	1900
DAWIDZOHN	Nachman		#224	1895
DEITZ	Dov Ber husband of Ane Plot	wed 22 Av	# 192	1893
DOBRIA	Chaim ben Yosef father of Zanwil		#107	1898
DOBRIA	Zanwil ben Chaim husband of Rivka Tobias	wed	#107	1898
DORITZ	One		#26	1900
DOWIDZON	Rivka		#26	1900
DROIAN	Eliakum Eliezer	Rabbi	#173	1898
EDELMAN	Zelig		#173	1898
EDELSON	Zalman	from Rokishek	#127	1897
ELBAR	Ephraim		#173	1898
ELI	Hirsh Leib		#173	1898
EWENTSHIK	Eliahu Elias husband of Yente Elena Hirshowitz	wed	#142	1900
FARFEL	Shmuel		#127	1897
FARFEL	Shmuel		#19	1897
FARFUL	Chaim		#26	1900
FEINSHTEIN	Mordechai father of Yitzchok	rabbi gaon ABD	#224	1895

FEINSHTEIN	Yitzchok		#19	1897
FEINSHTEIN	Yitzchok		#173	1898
FEINSHTEIN	Yitzchok		#142	1900
FEINSHTEIN	Yitzchok son of Rabbi Mordehai		#224	1895
FEINSHTEIN	Yitzchok son of the Gaon, ABD		#26	1900
FELDSHER	Moshe		#26	1900
FIN	Ezriel		#173	1898
FLIGIL	Shlomo		#173	1898
GARBER	Feige mother of Miriam		#107	1898
GARBER	Mendil husband of Leah	wed 1896/7	#19	1897
GARBER	Miriam bas Feige wife of Moshe Plok	wed	#107	1898
GEFEN	Leib		#173	1898
GETZILIOV	Leib		#173	1898
GINTZBURG	Shimshon		#173	1898
GINTZBURG	Shmuel		#173	1898
GINZBURG	Shmuel		#26	1900
GLEH	Chana		#26	1900
GLIKMAN	Michal		#26	1900
GLINTERNIK	Reuven	Government Rabbi	#26	1900
GLOBASZKI	Bentzion		#173	1898
GORDON	Chaim		#26	1900
GORDON	Sarah sister of Aharon Leib Rachman		#274	1897
GOZ	Hirsh Leib		#173	1898
GRINBERG	Moshe		#142	1900
GRINMAN	yosef		#173	1898
HEILPEROWITZ	Reizil wife of Chanoch Henoch Itelmahn	wed	#107	1898
HIRSHOWITZ	Moshe Meir father of Yente Elena		#142	1900
HIRSHOWITZ	Yente Elene bas Moshe Meir wife of Eliahu Ewentshik	wed	#142	1900
HOCHENBERG	Mordechai husband of Sarah Olshwanger	wed 1896/7	#19	1897
HOFENBERG	Michal ben Mordechai	first son born 1898	#107	1898
HOFENBERG	Mordechai father of Michal		#107	1898

ITELMAHN	Chanoch Henoch ben Osher Shmaya husband of Reizel Heilperowitz	wed	#107	1898
ITELMAHN	Osher Shmaya father of Chanoch Henoch		#107	1898
KATZ	Chaya Sarah		#26	1900
KATZ	Feiwish		#173	1898
KATZ	Shraga Feiwish		#26	1900
KATZ	Yitzchok		#127	1897
KAPLAN	Shimon		#173	1898
LAPIDOS	Boruch		#173	1898
LAZAR	Dovid Eliezer		#173	1898
LAZER	Dovid Eliezer		#26	1900
LEWIN	Aharon Meir		#173	1898
LEWIN	Freidel bas Zalman wife of Menachem Mendel Parparow from Gewel	wed 2 Adar	#60	1895
LEWIN	Menachem Mendel		# 113	1893
LEWIN	Menachem Mendil		#19	1897
LEWIN	Mendel husband of Chana Biderman from Dvinsk	wed	#142	1900
LEWIN	Mendil		#19	1897
LEWIN	Moshe		#19	1897
LEWIN	Moshe		#173	1898
LEWIN	Yafne (?) sibling of Menachem Mendel in Daugavpils		#65	1897
LEWIN	Yehuda ben Asher		#173	1898
LEWIN	Yisroel Zelig		#173	1898
LEWIN	Zalman father of Freidel		#60	1895
LEWIN	Zelig Shmuel		#173	1898
LEWIT	Chaim		#26	1900
LEWITAN	Chaim		#173	1898
LIBERMAN	Zalman Aba		#173	1898
LIBKOWITZ	Avraham		#26	1900
LIFKOWITZ	Avraham brother of Moris		#173	1898
LIFKOWITZ	Moris brother of Avraham		#173	1898
LISH	Noach		#173	1898
LUTKER	Olga bas Z wife of Chaim Yakov	wed in St.	#173	1898

	Shtern	Petersburg		
LUTKER	Z father of Olga		#173	1898
MASIL	Y		#224	1895
MIZRACH	Yehuda		#173	1898
MIZRACH	Yehuda		#26	1900
MUSIL	Avraham Yitzchok		#26	1900
MUSIL	Yakov		#26	1900
NEIHOIZ	Hene Miriam bas Tzvi wife of Michal Sheinker	wed	#107	1898
NEIHOIZ	Tzvi father of Hene Miriam		#107	1898
OLSHWANGER	Sarah wife of Mordechai Hochenberg	wed 1896/7	#19	1897
PEN	Aba		#26	1900
PEN	Ezriel		#224	1895
PEN	Ezriel		#26	1900
PEN	Yitzchok		#26	1900
PERSON	Chaikel		#173	1898
PLOK	Moshe husband of Miriam Garber	wed	#107	1898
PLOT	Alechsander Ziskind		#142	1900
PLOT	Alechsander Ziskind		#26	1900
PLOT	Ane wife of Dov Ber Deitz	wed 22 Av	# 192	1893
PLOT	Chaya Sarah bas Meir Eliezer wife of Moshe Ozer Lewin of Dvinsk	wed	#26	1900
PLOT	Meir Ekiezer		#173	1898
PLOT	Meir Eliezer		#107	1898
PLOT	Meir Eliezer father of Chaya Sarah		#26	1900
PLOT	Prade Feige		#26	1900
POLITZ	Levi		#173	1898
POMIANSKI	Boruch		#26	1900
POMPIANSKI	Boruch		#173	1898
POPISKI	Zev		#26	1900
PORKOWIK	Avraham Shmuel		#19	1897
RACHMAN	A L		#224	1895
RACHMAN	Aharon Leib		#127	1897
RACHMAN	Aharon Leib		#26	1900
RACHMAN	Aharon Leib brother of Sarah		#274	1897

	Gordon			
RACHMAN	Aharon Leib s-i-l (?) of Raphel Shtern		#173	1898
RADUGAN	Dov Yitzchok		#173	1898
REN	Yitzchok		#173	1898
RING	Sarah		#26	1900
RODWAGIN	Dov Ber Yitzchok		#26	1900
ROZINKOWITZ	Aharon		#173	1898
SAPIR	Zelig		#173	1898
SHACHOR	Moshe		#173	1898
SHALMAN	Ephraim		#173	1898
SHALMAN	Ephraim		#26	1900
SHAPIR	Mendil		#26	1900
SHAPIR	Zelig		#26	1900
SHAPIRO	Leib		#173	1898
SHEINKER	Michal husband of Hene Miriam	wed	#107	1898
SHREIBER	Tzvi		#224	1895
SHTEIN	W		#127	1897
SHTEIN	Yehuda		#19	1897
SHTEIN	Yehuda		#274	1897
SHTEIN	Yehuda		#107	1898
SHTEIN	Yehuda		#173	1898
SHTEIN	Yehuda		#142	1900
SHTEIN	Yehuda		#26	1900
SHTEINMAN	Bentzion		#173	1898
SHTEINMAN	Chaim		#26	1900
SHTEINMAN	Dovid		#224	1895
SHTEINMAN	Dovid		#173	1898
SHTERN	Chaim Yakov ben Raphel wife of Olga Lutker	wed in St. Petersburg	#173	1898
SHTERN	Raphel father of Chaim Yakov f-i-l(?) of Aharon Leib Rachman		#173	1898
SHUB	Yitzchok Aharon		#19	1897
SOFER	Eliahu Chaim		#173	1898
TOBIAS	Rivka wife of Zanwil Dobria	wed	#107	1898
WEITZ	Beile		#26	1900
WEITZ	Eli		#173	1898

WEITZ	M	#224	1895
WEITZ	Menachem Mendel	#26	1900
WEITZ	Naphtali	#26	1900
WEITZ	Shimon	#19	1897
YAFE	Aizik	#173	1898
YAFE	Shaul	#173	1898
YAFE MICHEL		#173	1898
YECHIELTZIK	Yisroel Meir	#173	1898

Žagarė (Zhager)

Zagare (Zhager in Yiddish) is one of the oldest settlements in Lithuania. It lies on both banks of the Svete River on the Latvian border, about 40 km. (nearly 25 miles) from the district administrative center of Siauliai (Shavl), where an estate named Zagare was built and which eventually developed into a town. In 1495 the town received permission to hold markets. A hundred years later a church was built on the right bank of the river: houses were built around it and streets were paved according to a relatively modern plan. By the end of the seventeenth century there were one hundred homes. This area was called New Zhager and the older settlement on the left bank, Old Zhager, these two settlements being managed by different administrative units. A wooden bridge over the river Svete connected the two areas.

In time the population of New Zhager exceeded that of Old Zhager and the economic and social conditions as well as the quality of life were far superior to that in the older area. A noble family named Narishkin, who from 1850 was the owner of the Zhager estate and part of New Zhager, exerted great influence on its development as economic activity grew rapidly. In 1861 there were three small factories producing buttons, belts and sundry items. They employed ninety workers. More small industries for processing agricultural products and other foods were established. One of the workshops produced candles.

In contrast, the economic development of Old Zhager, whose land now belonged to the noble family Heiman, was slow. In 1897 there were 27 shops compared to 121 in New Zhager, while 90 artisans lived in the old town compared to 640 in the new.

Over the years Zhager residents suffered many adversities: the Russian-Swedish war in 1705; a cholera epidemic in 1848; the Polish rebellion in 1863; the great famine in the region in 1867, and inevitably, fires in 1864, 1881, 1909 and 1911. A Cossack battalion brought into the town to restore order during the revolution of 1905 caused many problems for the residents of Zhager. For a very short time the revolutionaries established a symbolic autonomic framework, called The Zhager Republic.

From the end of the nineteenth century until World War I New and Old Zhager combined and became a district administrative center: government and other institutions had offices there. There was also extensive commercial dialogue with Latvia and the town attracted buyers from Germany and England to its annual fairs. Not unexpectedly, Zhager's population increased. While Czarist Russia was in control (1795-1915), Zhager was in the Kovno Province (*Gubernia*) and in the Shavl (Siauliai) district.

However, from 1918 to 1940 under independent Lithuania, the absence of trade with Latvia and Russia was a severe blow to the local economy. The population decreased to its level of sixty years previously. During this period Zhager was a county administrative center, a status it kept during Soviet rule (1940-1941) and during World War II under Nazi rule (1941-1944).

Jewish Settlement until and after World War I

The Jewish community in Zhager was one of the first in Lithuania, in particular in the Zamut (Zemaitija). Its earliest development can probably be traced back to the sixteenth century. The first Jews in the town collected taxes for the authorities and rent for the landowners and traded in salt and metals that they imported from abroad. Others exported honey, wax and leather, while there were also active Jewish artisans. In 1766 there were 840 Jews and by 1847 the number had increased to 2,266.

The two separate communities each had its own rabbi, cantors, *shokhtim* and cemetery.

The Old Zhager Community

Because of overcrowding and difficult living conditions, sanitation was very bad, and when a cholera epidemic reached the town, 973 Jews succumbed. At the end of the nineteenth century Old Zhager had 1,629 (64%) Jews out of a total of 2,527 residents. There were 210 houses, of which 158 were Jewish owned.

Most Jews made their living from crafts (mainly tailoring and shoemaking) from agriculture (vegetable and cherry growing) and from small trades after the wholesalers had moved to New Zhager. There were then about 500 Jewish craftsmen. The synagogue, the *Beth Midrash* and the bath-house were among the few buildings constructed of stone.

Jewish children studied in its few *Hadarim*. In 1893 a Jewish school for girls with two classes opened in Old Zhager.

Despite the continuing economic deterioration, the community continued to extend help to other communities in trouble. For example, in 1884 a fire almost ruined the nearby town of Laizeve (Laizuva) and both Zhager communities donated 70 rubles for its restoration.

Among the rabbis who officiated in Old Zhager were:

> Yekutiel-Zalman, died in 1848
>
> Tsemakh Zaksh (1796-1863), served in Zhager 1815-1863
>
> Hayim Luria, from 1858 in Zhager
>
> Hayim-Tsevi-Hirsh Broida
>
> Yehudah-Leib Rif
>
> Yehudah-Leib Broida (official rabbi).

The New Zhager Community

About 50 Jewish families occupied the entire market square in New Zhager in 1790. These families operated 30 shops and bars in the town and its surroundings. The leasing fees for all these buildings totalled 900 rubles per annum. By this time the main institutions of the community, including prayer houses and the cemetery, were in use. The town's rabbi, Berl Itskovitz, was responsible for the payment of the Jews' leasing fees for their houses and business premises.

After the Napoleonic wars, the authorities, acting on Jewish requests, increased the number of market days and fairs. Some sources claim that the value of goods sold at each fair was about 4,000 rubles and the turnover for the Jews accounted for 900 rubles. The Jews established factories for candles; for a beverage made of honey (probably mead with malt); cords; leather; buttons, for processing pig bristles, etc. The flax processing plant, owned by Mosheh Elyashev, employed 100 workers.

In 1897 the Jews of greater Zhager totaled about 60% of the population: 5,443 Jews (1,629 in Old Zhager and 3,814 in New Zhager) out of 9,129 residents. They occupied 329 of the total of 450 plots. Most Jews made their living from crafts, small industry, agriculture and trade. In contrast to Old Zhager, in New Zhager the relatively large number of important merchants was significant. The New Zhager merchants exported flax (about 4,000 wagons per year) and grains (about 1,000 wagons per year) to Germany and other countries and imported goods (about 300 wagons) from abroad. The pleasant commercial center built in the center of the town was also occupied mainly by Jewish merchants.

The sound economic situation of most of the Jewish population encouraged a favorable attitude towards them by the authorities, who granted them considerable freedom to conduct their affairs through the Civic Management which was created in 1880. One of the heads of the Narishkin family opened his splendid garden to the Jews, a garden spread over an area of 80 hectares, which in time became the urban park.

During this time, there were four Jewish educational institutions: a boys' school with thirty pupils in 1897/98; a girls' school with fifty-three young ladies, a *Talmud Torah* located in a magnificent building built through donations by Zhager-born Klonimus Ze'ev Wissotzky (the founder of the tea firm in Russia) and another where a further 100 boys studied. In this school Hebrew, Russian, German and arithmetic were already being taught in 1900. For some of the time Nathan-Neta Vainberg was the teacher of the three languages.

The Russian government school had a complement of 154 Jewish boys and 24 girls. Boys and men studied religious subjects at the four *Batei Midrash* in town.

In the 1840s eighteen Jewish families from Yanishok (Joniskis) and Zhager (among them the K. Z. Wissotzky family) moved to Dubne, about 30 km. (20 miles) from Dvinsk, to establish an agricultural settlement on land that the government had allocated, without charge, for an experimental farm which eventually failed.

In autumn 1881 a raging fire broke out and the *HaMelitz* newspaper reported that "more than 400 buildings, including the synagogue and the *Beth Midrash*, burned down and about 1,000 families were left without a roof over their heads". Thanks to the newspaper *HaMelitz* appeal for assistance and other requests, help arrived in the form of money, food and clothes. A committee led by the local physicians Dr. Hertsberg and Dr. Hentch was very active in managing the restoration work, greatly helping the Jewish population for many years. It is noteworthy that Dr. Hentch was a Christian gentleman.

In the years 1880 to 1890 there was a surge of emigration from Zhager to South Africa and America. A society named *Rodfei Tsedek Anshei Zhager* (The Pursuers of Justice from Zhager) was established in Philadelphia in 1887. By 1895 there already was a large community of former Zhager Jews in Johannesburg: they generously supported their relatives back home. The list of donors was published in the Hebrew newspaper *HaTsefirah*.

The rabbis who officiated in New-Zhager were:

Berl Itskovitz

Shimon Hurvitz (1810-1900), later rabbi in Leipzig, published many books on Judaica

Eliyahu Shik (1809-1876), famous for his fight against conscription of poor Jewish children to serve in the Czar's army for twenty five years (according to an order which Czar Nikolai the First had issued in 1827): he died in Kobrin.

Uri-David Apiryon (lived in the nineteenth century)

Hayim-Yits'hak Korb (1870-1957), during 1930-1950 was head of a *Yeshivah* in Chicago. In 1952 he emigrated to Jerusalem, where he died.

Ya'akov-Josef Harif.

Many Jews in Zhager, and in particular in Old Zhager, were fanatically orthodox. For many years it was a center of the *Musar* movement initiated by the Zhager-born Yisrael Salanter. However, many merchants who traveled to Koenigsberg, Leipzig and other German towns on business imported, together with the goods, new ideas and many books representing the best of European literature. Among these travelers was a group of erudite religious people, not fanatics, who avidly read secular and scientific books. This group was the *Khahmei Zhager* (Zhager Scholars) and was formed soon after *Haskala.* Among its members and supporters were:

Hayim Zak, honored by all the town's people

Shneur Zaksh, researcher of Judaica

Refael Neta Rabinovitz, author of the book *Dikdukei Sofrim*

Rabbi Shimon HaLevi Hurvitz, later the rabbi of Leipzig

The writer Ya'akov Dinezon

The bibliographer Avraham Freidos

Ben-Zion Zaltsberg who published a research work on *Koheleth*

Eliezer Atlas, in due course one of the editors of the Hebrew periodicals *HeAsif* and *HaKerem*

Avraham Idelson, later the editor of the Jewish Russian periodical *Razsviet* which was published in St. Petersburg

Tsevi Kan, a specialist in Judaica

Simhah Hilman, a future workers leader in the USA

Tsevi Izakson, in time the chairman of the Agrarians Union in Israel, and many others.

The Synagogue

(Picture taken by and courtesy of Elkan Gamzu, July 2005)

The most prominent and erudite of the learned men of Zhager were the Mandelshtams. The family originated in Germany and its descendants were among the leaders of the *Haskalah* movement in Russia and among the great writers and scientists in that country. In particular Josef Mandelshtam and his three sons Benjamin, Aryeh-Leon and Yehezkel were famous, since, in addition to their chosen professions, they were also involved in Bible research, writing poetry and imparting their knowledge to the Jewish people. The son of Yehezkel, Max (Imanuel), whose education had its roots in a *Heder* in Zhager, eventually became a famous ophthalmologist in Kiev and assistant to Theodor Herzl in promoting Zionism. Hayim-Josef the son of Mosheh Mandelshtam published articles on Zhager in *HaMelitz*. It is worthwhile mentioning that Zhager, quite a small town, produced a long line of erudite men, intellectuals, writers, researchers and public figures who were well known in the Jewish world.

The Aron-Kodesh in New-Zhager

The Synagogue in Old-Zhager

Dr. Hertsberg, who had done so much after the devastating fire of 1881, contributed an important endowment to Zhager's cultural life. In July 1898 he opened a bookshop and a library in the main street of New Zhager which existed for many years. Shortly before World War I a branch of the Berlin *Yiddishe Literarishe Gezelshaft* (The Jewish Literature Society) was active locally, its main activities being to maintain reading evenings and lectures on literature and social subjects. Sh. Yakobzon was the chairman of the Society, V. Yakobzon, the secretary: they were supported by Aizik Novazenetz and Avraham Sheinfeld.

The *Bund*, with its many Jewish workers, had much influence, but later the *Hibath Zion* movement and Zionism became the strongest local social force.

There are at least five tombstones of Zhager Jews in the old cemetery in Jerusalem:

> Rabbi Tsevi, son of Zerakh, died in 1861
>
> Fruma, daughter of Shemuel, died in 1863
>
> Yehezkel, son of Ze'ev Katz, died in 1870
>
> Leib, son of Yisrael Be'eri, died in 1873
>
> Duber, son of Leib, died in 1899.

In lists of donors for the settlement of *Eretz-Yisrael* published in *HaMelitz* in the years 1894, 1895, 1897, 1898, 1900, 1902 and 1903, the names of 315 Zhager Jews appear. The fund raisers were B. Segal and B"Z. Goldberg (see **Appendix 1**). In a 1909 list there are another 18 donors (see **Appendix 2**).

The donors to the Persian famine victims in 1872 published in *HaMagid,* include 142 Zhager Jews. (see **Appendix 3**).

The religious anti-Zionist *Agudath Yisrael* party was also active in Zhager. In a list of yearly membership fees paid to this party dated 1914, 64 names from New Zhager appear and also 10 from Old Zhager (see **Appendix 4**).

Zhager Jews exhibited a strong solidarity with their Lithuanian neighbors. When Czarist rule prohibited the printing of books in Lithuanian, Zhager Jews helped the Book-carriers (*Knygnesiai* in Lithuanian) to smuggle Lithuanian literature from abroad into the country. Zhager Jews took part in the 1905 revolution and several were detained, exiled and even shot by the Russians.

During World War I most Zhager Jews left their town for Russia or emigrated elsewhere.

Zhager under Independent Lithuania rule (1918-1940)

After World War I and the delineation of the border between the two new independent states, Latvia and Lithuania, Zhager declined into one of the remotest and poorest towns in Lithuania. Many of its Jewish residents did not return and quite a few of those who did later emigrated to America, South Africa and *Eretz-Yisrael*. The major problem was that the nearest railway station was about 28 km. (17 miles) distant. This caused insurmountable problems for local commercial and social activity. There was no road to Zhager passable in winter and the only commercial activity was confined to the market days on Tuesdays and Fridays.

The first census by the new Lithuanian government, taken in 1923, counted 4,730 residents living in Zhager. Of these 1,928 (61%) were Jews.

Following the law of autonomies for minorities issued by the Lithuanian government, the minister for Jewish affairs, Dr. Menachem (Max) Soloveitshik, ordered elections for community committees (*Va'adei Kehilah*) to be held in the summer of 1919. In Zhager the elections took place in the first half of 1920 and a committee of eleven members was elected. In 1921 the committee consisted of one General Zionist, two *Tseirei Zion*, one artisan, two from the workers list and five non-party men.

In 1931 there were 59 shops, 51 (86%) of them in Jewish hands. The distribution according to type of business is given in the table below:

Type of business	Total	Owned by Jews
Groceries	5	5
Grain and flax	2	2
Butcher shops and Cattle Trade	21	19
Restaurants and Taverns	2	1
Food Products	1	1
Beverages	1	0
Textile Products and Furs	8	8
Leather and Shoes	7	6
Haberdashery and house utensils	1	1
Medicine and Cosmetics	5	2
Watches, Jewels and Optics	2	2
Radio, Bicycles, Sewing Machines	1	1
Hardware Products	2	2
Other	1	1

According to that Government survey (in 1931) there were twenty-five workshops and light industries owned by Jews: four barber shops, two workshops for processing pig bristles, two spinneries, two boot makers, two sewing workshops, one flour mill, one bakery, one sawmill, one weaving workshop, one chocolate and candy factory, one milliner, one felt factory, one dyeing plant, one offal-cleaning workshop, one tinsmith's workshop, one soda water factory and one power plant.

Youth from Old-Zhager, most of whom emigrated to South Africa

In 1937 there were fifty-five Jewish artisans: fifteen boot makers, ten tailors, eight butchers, five dressmakers, three tinsmiths, two bakers, two barbers, one hatter, one locksmith, one carpenter, one knitter, one painter, one photographer, one watchmaker and three others.

A group of Zhager men

The Jewish Popular Bank (*Folksbank*), with 287 members in 1927, played an important role in the financial affairs of Zhager's Jews.

Except for a few outbreaks of hostility by Lithuanians against their Jewish neighbors, there was, on the whole, fair surface amity between them.

The nine members of the municipal council included four Jews but in the 1934 elections only three Jews were successful.

In the early 1930s aggressive competition from Lithuanian cooperatives increased. Because of the difficult economic conditions, inevitable feelings of depression, and being cut off from Latvia, many Jewish merchants and also youth moved from Zhager, particularly to the nearest town of Joniskis (Janishok).

Despite the annulment of the autonomy in 1925, the end of the *Va'ad HaKehilah* and the continuing decrease in number of Jews, almost all institutions continued their activities: seven prayer houses; the old age home; the *Bikur Holim* society; two bath houses; two libraries (one Yiddish and one Hebrew) and two schools. 135 children studied in the school of the religious *Yavneh* network. In 1922 the *Tarbuth* society organized evening courses for adults, with fifty participants.

The market square

The town had two fire brigades, both manned by many Jewish volunteers. There were sport organizations *Maccabi* and *HaPoel* and also some Zionist parties and youth organizations (*HaShomer-HaTsair* was one). The table below shows the election results of Zhager Zionists for the Zionist congresses:

Cong No.	Year	Tot Shek	Total Votes	Labor Party		Rev	Gen Zion		Gro	Miz
				Z"S	Z"Z		A	B		
16	1929	33	10	---	1	4	4	----	----	1
18	1933	----	64	45		12	7	---	---	-- -
19	1935	288	261	161		-- -	46	52	---	2

Note: Cong No. = Congress Number, Tot Shek = Total Shekalim, Rev = Revisionists, Gen Zion = General Zionists, Gro = Grosmanists, Miz = Mizrahi

By 1939 there were 5,443 residents including about 1,000 (18%) Jews. Of 36 telephone subscribers 15 were Jews.

Despite the inevitable disruptions caused by World War I and thereafter, the rivalry between Old Zhager and New Zhager Jews remained unchanged. The Old Zhager people thought that they were more important: after all, the first Jewish settlement was established there. But the New Zhagers thought that they were superior because most of the Jewish community lived there. These differences caused unnecessary controversy at times. This old-time split was resolved and family relations preserved thanks to the actions of Rabbi Yisrael Rif, the rabbi of New Zhager and his son, Yits'hak-Zundl Rif, the rabbi in Old Zhager.

Zhager branch of *Maccabi*

Zhager in World War II and Afterward

During Sovietization (1940-1941), after Lithuania had been annexed to the Soviet Union, almost all Jewish institutions and all Zionist parties and youth organizations were disbanded and the Hebrew school closed. The Yiddish library founded by the *Libhober fun Visen* (Fans of Knowledge) association was one of the few institutions which continued to exist. Several shops were nationalized. A short time before the German invasion of Lithuania several Jewish families were exiled to Siberia, among them the teacher and Bible researcher Meir Kantorovitz (Elyoeini).

Three days after the outbreak of war between Germany and the Soviet Union, on June 25th, 1941, the Germans occupied Zhager, assisted by armed Lithuanians calling themselves Nationalist anti-Soviet Partisans. Together with the municipality they imprisoned hundreds of Jewish men in the synagogue and subjected them to great cruelty. The old rabbi, Yisrael Rif, a tall man, was insulted and assaulted violently. He and a short Jew were forced to harness themselves to a cart and pull it through the streets of the town to the amusement of the Lithuanian onlookers. Many Jews were shot in the Jewish cemetery and in a nearby grove.

In July all Jews were concentrated into one quarter, a so-called ghetto. They were joined by Jews from Zheimel (Zeimelis), Tirkshle (Tirksliai), Trishik (Tryskiai), Yanishok (Joniskis), Loikeve (Laukuva), Ligum (Lygumai), Linkeve (Linkuva), Pokroi (Pakruojus), Kelm (Kelme), Krok (Kriukai) and Radvilishok (Radviliskis). Altogether they comprised about 7,000 people. Each day the Lithuanians forced most of the men into various types of hard labor, all the while maltreating them. Before going out to work, the men were forced to spit in the face of Rabbi Rif and any man refusing to fulfil this order was killed on the spot. In order to avoid the slaughter the rabbi ordered them to obey. Humiliated and hungry, crowded into the small ghetto without sanitary facilities or medical help, they suffered greatly at the hands of these Lithuanians and Latvians. Gangs frequently burst into the ghetto to rob, rape and pillage.

The mass grave at the Narishkin Park

(Picture taken and supplied courtesy of Elkan Gamzu, July 2005)

On the day after Yom Kippur, 11th of Tishrei, 5702 (October 2nd, 1941), all Jewish men, women and children were ordered to the market square where the commander of a *Sonderkommando* (Special unit, a secondary unit of the operation Formation A) delivered a calming speech saying that they would be transferred to a new workplace where conditions would be better. Then the commander gave a signal, and from the surrounding yards, armed Lithuanians broke out shooting at the Jews with automatic weapons. During this action Alter Zagarsky shouted to others to escape and himself took out a knife and stabbed a Lithuanian to death. Another Jew, Avraham Akerman, also attacked a Lithuanian, biting him in the throat. These two were shot on the spot, but in the ensuing disturbance many Jews managed to escape. Additional armed Lithuanian groups were called in and rounded up the remaining Jews, capturing those who had escaped, and led them to the nearby Narishkin Park where pits had been prepared. There they shot and buried their victims, killing babies and small children by slamming their heads against the trees. Many Jews were thrown into the pits alive. Their clothing and other belongings were looted by their neighbors and by the murderers and local authorities.

Only a few Jews survived the gruesome bloodshed — those who had been exiled and a few others who managed to escape to Russia at the outbreak of war. The researcher Meir Kantorovitz died in exile in 1980.

The monument at the murder site

(Picture taken and supplied courtesy of Elkan Gamzu, July 2005)

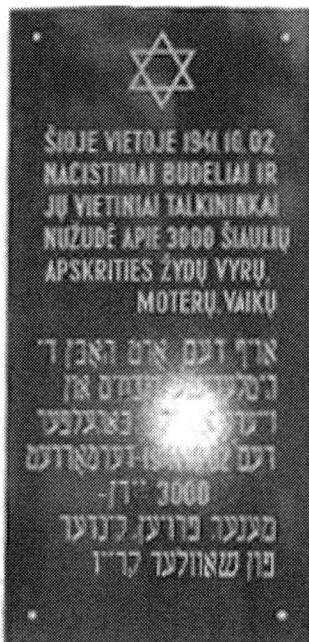

The inscription on the tablet of the monument in Lithuanian and Yiddish: "At this site Hitler's murderers and their local helpers murdered about 3000 Jewish men, women, children from Shavl district on 2nd October 1941."

A monument in memoriam of about 40 Zhager Jews who were slaughtered at the Jewish cemetery in 1941

At the beginning of the 1990s at the entrance to Narishkin Park two tablets were erected, bearing inscriptions in Lithuanian and Yiddish: "At this site Hitler's murderers and their local helpers murdered about 3,000 Jews from the Shavl district, men, women, children on 2nd October 1941".

The remains of the Zhager Jewish cemetery
(Picture taken and supplied by Elkan Gamzu, July 2005)

Sources:

Yad Vashem Archives, M-1/Q-1407/181; M1/E-1032/931, 1679/1556; M-9/15 (6); 0-4/1; 0-33/1261; Koniuhovsky collection 0-71, files 102, 115

YIVO, New York, Lithuanian Communities Collection, files 437-452

Oshri - Hurben Lite (Yiddish)

Oshri - Rabbi Yisrael Rif-Zhager (Hebrew)

Dinezon Ya'akov - *Erinerungen, Der Pinkas* (Yiddish), Vilna 1913

Vigoder Meir-Joel, *Sefer Zikaron* (Hebrew), Dublin-Liege, 1931

Yerushalmi Eliezer, *Pinkas Shavli* (Hebrew)

Slutsky Yehudah, Dr. Mandelshtam (Hebrew), *HaAvar* 4, 1977

Kantorovitz Meir (Elyoeini), Bible Research from the Soviet Captivity, (Hebrew), Jerusalem, 1984

Yiddisher Lebn (Yiddish) Kovno, #124, 13.4.1923

Dos Vort (Yiddish) Kovno, 10.11.1934

Di Yiddishe Shtime, Kovno, 26.6.1931

Di Tsait, Kovno, 4.10.1933

HaMelitz, (Hebrew), St. Petersburg, 6.2.1862; 10.6.1879; 14.10.1879; 20.9.1881; 23.2.1884; 5.1.1884; 29.8.1884; 17.12.1885; 17.1.1886; 1893 #66; 4.7.1895

HaAvar (Hebrew), Vol.4, 1956; Vol 21, 1972.

*Morgen Journal (*Yiddish), New York, 10.6.1946

*Kovner Tog (*Yiddish) 8.6.1926

Masines Zudynes Lietuvoje (Mass Murder in Lithuania) Vol. 2, pages 225-141

Janulaitis Augustinas - *Zydai Lietuvoje*, Kaunas 1923

Appendix 1

A list of 142 Zhager Jewish donors to the victims of the famine in Persia in 1872 (From JewishGen, Org. Databases, HaMagid, compiled by Jeffrey Maynard) Note below that Zagare* means Zagare (new)

Surname	Given Name	Comments	Town	Year
AHRENZOHN	Chaim	from old Zagare	Zagare*	1872
AHRENZOHN	Nachum		Zagare*	1872
ARKIN	Chaim Leib		Zagare*	1872
ARKIN	Dovid		Zagare*	1872
ARKIN	Mendil		Zagare*	1872
ARKIN	Shmuel		Zagare*	1872
ARKIN	Tuvia		Zagare*	1872
ARKIN	Yosef		Zagare*	1872
ASHRON	Ber		Zagare*	1872
ATLES	Eliezer Tzvi		Zagare*	1872
BALKIN	Eizik		Zagare*	1872
BARSHTEIN	Shmuel		Zagare*	1872
BASKIN	Dovid	from old Zagare	Zagare*	1872
BISKOWITZ	Yehoshua		Zagare*	1872
BLUMBERG	Simcha		Zagare*	1872
BORZOWSKI	Chaim		Zagare*	1872
BROIDA	Mordechai		Zagare*	1872
CHAITKIN	Avraham		Zagare*	1872
CHEZKELOWITZ	Yudel		Zagare*	1872
DISLER	Yeshiahu		Zagare*	1872
DOVIDOWITZ	Zalman	from old Zagare	Zagare*	1872
DWALEINKI	Eli		Zagare*	1872
DWOLEIZKI	Avraham		Zagare*	1872
DWOLEIZKI	Mendil		Zagare*	1872
EIZEKZOHN	Avraham		Zagare*	1872
EIZENSHTAT	Moshe Zalman		Zagare*	1872
EPSHTEIN	Cheikel	bridegroom	Zagare*	1872
EPSHTEIN	Leib		Zagare*	1872
FISHHOIT	Kalman		Zagare*	1872

FRIDMAN	Devorah	woman, mother of Yehuda Leib	Zagare*	1872
FRIDMAN	Dov Ber		Zagare*	1872
FRIDMAN	Eli Ber		Zagare*	1872
FRIDMAN	Eliezer	gvir	Zagare*	1872
FRIDMAN	Leib		Zagare*	1872
FRIDMAN	Nechamiah		Zagare*	1872
FRIDMAN	Raphel		Zagare*	1872
FRIDMAN	Shraga		Zagare*	1872
FRIDMAN	Tzvi	gvir	Zagare*	1872
FRIDMAN	Yechezkel		Zagare*	1872
FRIDMAN	Yechezkel Mendil		Zagare*	1872
FRIDMAN	Yechiel		Zagare*	1872
FRIDMAN	Yehuda Leib	son of Devorah	Zagare*	1872
FRIEDENZOHN	Yakov		Zagare*	1872
GOLDBERG	Hirsh		Zagare*	1872
GOLDBERG	Shalom Meir		Zagare*	1872
GOLDBERG	Tuvia	f-i-l of Bendet	Zagare*	1872
HOPSHA	Shraga Meir		Zagare*	1872
HORWITZ	Gitel	woman	Zagare*	1872
HORWITZ	Leib		Zagare*	1872
KANTOR	Hirsh ben Yoel		Zagare*	1872
KIWIN	Yosef ben Leib		Zagare*	1872
KOHN	Tzvi		Zagare*	1872
KOTZ	Leib		Zagare*	1872
KREZER	Moshe		Zagare*	1872
KWEITZ	Meir		Zagare*	1872
KWITZ	Mendil		Zagare*	1872
LANE	Wolf		Zagare*	1872
LEWIMAN	Zalman		Zagare*	1872
LEWIN	Tzvi	boy	Zagare*	1872
LEWITAN	Shlomo		Zagare*	1872

LIPSHITZ	Moishe		Zagare*	1872
LURIA	Nechemiah	f-i-l of Yakov	Zagare*	1872
LURIN	Yosef		Zagare*	1872
MANDELSHTAM	Tzvi		Zagare*	1872
MEINKIN	Dovid	bridegroom	Zagare*	1872
MENDELZOHN	Yakov		Zagare*	1872
MINKEN	Abba	father of Shalom	Zagare*	1872
MINKEN	Shalom ben Abba		Zagare*	1872
MIYANISHOK	Pesach	from Joniskis (Yanishok)	Zagare*	1872
MOLWIDZKI	Abba		Zagare*	1872
MOLWIDZKI	Shalom		Zagare*	1872
MOSHAT	Yosef	bridegroom	Zagare*	1872
MOZEZOHN	Yitzchok		Zagare*	1872
NACHUMZOHN	Lemel		Zagare*	1872
NATKIN	Ber		Zagare*	1872
NEIMARK	Avraham	from old Zagare	Zagare*	1872
NEIWIDAL	Beinish		Zagare*	1872
NEIWIDAL	Yitzchok		Zagare*	1872
NOIMESHZOHN	Shalom		Zagare*	1872
PINKUS	Yakov		Zagare*	1872
RABINOWITZ	Boruch		Zagare*	1872
RABINOWITZ	Zalman		Zagare*	1872
RITOW	Avraham		Zagare*	1872
ROZENBERG	Dovid Shlomo		Zagare*	1872
RUBIN	Shalom	father of Shephtil	Zagare*	1872
RUBIN	Shephtil	ben Shalom	Zagare*	1872
RUBIN	Zalkind		Zagare*	1872
SEGAL	Note		Zagare*	1872
SHAPIRO	Ber		Zagare*	1872
SHIK	Eli	Rabbi Gaon ABD	Zagare*	1872
SHLEZINGER	Eli		Zagare*	1872

SHMIDMAN	Shmuel Kopel			1872
SHNEIDER	Moshe		Zagare*	1872
SHUB	Shmuel		Zagare*	1872
TANKEL	Abba		Zagare*	1872
WEINBERG	Ber		Zagare*	1872
WEINER	Tzvi		Zagare*	1872
WEINERWITZ	Eli ben Hirsh Mendil		Zagare*	1872
WEINGEWER	Wolf		Zagare*	1872
WINDEROW	Yitzchok	bridegroom	Zagare*	1872
YAFE	Abba		Zagare*	1872
YAFE	Eizik		Zagare*	1872
YAFE	Leib		Zagare*	1872
YAFE	Moshe		Zagare*	1872
YAFE	Shalom		Zagare*	1872
YAFE	Yeshayahu		Zagare*	1872
YAKOBZOHN	Hillel		Zagare*	1872
YAKOBZOHN	Mordechai	bridegroom	Zagare*	1872
YAKOBZOHN	Nachum		Zagare*	1872
YAKOBZOHN	Nachum	bridegroom	Zagare*	1872
YAKOBZOHN	Yakov		Zagare*	1872
YERMAN	Meir	bridegroom	Zagare*	1872
YITZCHOK	Yafe		Zagare*	1872
YUDES	Yeshiahu		Zagare*	1872
ZAK	Chaim	gvir	Zagare*	1872
ZAKS	Hershil		Zagare*	1872
ZALELZOHN	Mendil		Zagare*	1872
ZALELZOHN	Shachna		Zagare*	1872
ZALELZOHN	Yitzchok		Zagare*	1872
ZALKIND	H	Apothecary	Zagare*	1872
ZELIKOWITZ	Leib		Zagare*	1872
	Abba ben Yehuda Leib	bridegroom	Zagare*	1872

	Ari ben Yehoshua		Zagare*	1872
	Bendet	s-i-l of Tuvia Goldberg	Zagare*	1872
	Hirsh ben Binyomin		Zagare*	1872
	Leib ben Yitzchok		Zagare*	1872
	Lesne	woman, mother of Nechama Hene	Zagare*	1872
	Menashe	g"sh	Zagare*	1872
	Nechama Hene bas Lesne		Zagare*	1872
	Note Yitzchok		Zagare*	1872
	Pesach Tzvi		Zagare*	1872
	Shephtil ben Boruch		Zagare*	1872
	Shraga Levi	bridegroom	Zagare*	1872
	Tzvi Levi	m"sh	Zagare*	1872
	Yakov	s-i-l of Nechamiah Luria	Zagare*	1872
	Yehoshua ben Abba		Zagare*	1872
	Yeshiahu son of Rabbi Dovid		Zagare*	1872
	Yeshiahu Tuvia son of the Rabbi	bridegroom	Zagare*	1872
	Zalkind	m"sh	Zagare*	1872
	Zalman	m"sh	Zagare*	1872
GOLDBERG	Yechezkel	businessman visiting Riga	Zagare, Lith.	1871
ZAKS	I	businessman visiting Riga	Zagare, Lith.	1871

Appendix 2
A List of Zhager donors (from 1909) to buy land in *Eretz-Yisrael*
New Zhager

Aizenshtat Yits'hak	Klein Ben-Zion
Grinblat Sheftl	Naividel Shalom-Tuviyah
Idelson Shraga	Tankel B.
Kantor Yeshaiya	Yakobson Hirsh
Kikon Yekutiel	Yavnovitz

Old Zhager

Kaplan Mosheh-Hayim	Shtein Ben-Zion
Klatskin Mendl	Trubik Nisan
Lamdan Ben-Zion, Rabbi	Yakobson Leib
Maldiner David	Yakobson Shabtai

Appendix 3
A List of Zhager Jews donors to the Settlement of *Eretz-Yisrael*

(From JewishGen. Org., Databases, *HaMelitz*, compiled by Jeffrey Maynard)

Surname	Given Name	Comments	Source in HaMelitz	Year
ABELSHON	Yitzchok		#167	1898
ABRAMZOHN	Leib		#167	1898
AIZIKOWITZ	T		#250	1894
AIZIKZOHN	Fani		#117	1898
ARKIN	D		#250	1894
ARKIN	Leib		#167	1898
ARONOW	Chaim		#118	1900
ARONOW	Chaim		#221	1903
ARONOW	Chaim ben Dov		#117	1898
ARONZOHN	Thereza		#274	1897

BALKAN	Aizik		# 228	1898
BALKIN	Aizik		#167	1898
BALKIND	Aizik		#250	1894
BALKIND	Aizik		#212	1895
BALKIND	Aizik uncle of Chaim Bentzion Balkind of Chwedana		#229	1899
BASKIN	Dovid		#167	1898
BIRZANSKI	Shmuel Eliezer		#195	1900
BIRZONSKI	Shmuel Eliezer	wed - from New Zager	#138	1897
BIRZONSKI	Yudel Kanter		#167	1898
BLOCH	Gitl Malka wife of Bentzion Nachum Tankel	wed 5 Ellul in Zager	# 206	1897
BLUM	Aharon Yakov		# 228	1898
BLUM	Avraham brother of Yosef in Shkod		#218	1894
BLUM	Avraham brother of Yosef of Shkod		#218	1894
BLUM	Frida		#117	1898
BLUMBERG	Alechsander Ziskind	wed in Kursenai 19 Av	#195	1900
BLUMBERG	Mordechai		#90	1898
BLUMBERG	Yitzchik	from Dvinsk	# 228	1898
BLUMBERG	Yitzchok ben Yona Ber husband of Ch E Shmuelowitz	from Dvinsk	#61	1897
BLUMBERG	Yona Ber father of Yitzchok	from Dvinsk	#61	1897

BOBIN	Dovid Shlomo	in Pretoria, SA	#288	1897
BROIDA	Boruch uncle of Shalom Tuvia Neiwidel		# 228	1898
BROIDA	Gnese bas Yehoshua wife of Aba Heisman from Woliz	wed in Shavel 1 Nisan	#82	1895
BROIDA	Y		#250	1894
BROIDA	Yehoshua uncle of S T Neiwidel father of Gnese	Rabbi Gaon	#82	1895
BROIDA	Zalman ben Boruch husband of Paie Yavneh	wed 1898	# 228	1898
BROIDE	Yitzchok		#167	1898
BRUCHMAN	Dovid		#195	1900
BRUCHMAN	Dovid husband of Motle Izraelshtam	wed 10 February	#90	1898
CHATZES	Doshe		#167	1898
CHATZES	Tzvi Hirsh		#142	1898
CHAWSHA	Ch A		#250	1894
CHAWSHA	M A		#250	1894
CHEN	Sh		#250	1894
CHLZ	Y		#250	1894
COHEN	Tzvi father of Shmuel & uncle of Moshe Yanowski in Shveksna		#225	1902
DONIE	Robert		#167	1898
DWILAITZKI	Yete		#117	1898

DWOLEITZKI	Avraham		#167	1898
DWOLEITZKI	Eli		#167	1898
DWOLEITZKI	Moshe		#167	1898
DWOLEITZKI	Shoshana		#167	1898
EDELSON	Shaweli husband of Zinote Hoppenkopf		#117	1898
EIDELMANN	Sh		#250	1894
EIDELSOHN	Shmarihu husband of Shifra Hirshberg of Dvinsk	dentist, wed 3 Elul in Amalia	#201	1897
EIDELSON	Tzvi		#221	1903
EIDELZOHN	Sh	Dentist	#117	1898
EITZIGZOHN	Moshe		#167	1898
EITZINSOHN	Aharon husband of Ida Segal of Taurage	wed 20 Elul	# 196	1893
EIZENSHTADT	Y		#250	1894
EIZENSHTADT	Y		#117	1898
EIZENSHTADT	Yitzchok		#167	1898
EIZENSHTAM	Yitzchok		# 228	1898
EIZENSHTAT	Yitzchok husband of Yete Hirshhorn	wed 15 March	#117	1898
ELIASHAW	Moshe		#230	1895
EPSHTEIN	Binyomin		#167	1898
EPSHTEIN	Chaim Fishel	Rabbi	#29	1898
EPSHTEIN	Ida		#167	1898
EPSHTEIN	Tzvi Ari ben Chaim Fishel	born 6 Kislev 1896	#29	1898
ESTERMAN	Dovid Yitzchok		#167	1898
FEINBERG	Miriam		#117	1898
FERKIN	Yisroel		#118	1900

FINKELMAN	Eli		#90	1898
FISHHOIT	Frida		#117	1898
FISHHOIT	K		#250	1894
FRIDMAN	Alechsander		# 228	1898
FRIDMAN	Boruch		#90	1898
FRIDMAN	Heshil		#250	1894
FRIDMAN	Lazer		#167	1898
FRIDMAN	M		#250	1894
FRIDMAN	Mendil		#221	1903
FRIDMAN	Nechamiah		#221	1903
FRIDMAN	Nechemiah		#250	1894
FRIDMAN	Nechemiah		#167	1898
FRIDMAN	Rochel		#90	1898
FRIDMAN	Shalom		#221	1903
FRIDMAN	Shraga		# 228	1898
FRIDMAN	Tzirle		#167	1898
FRIDMAN	Yisroel husband of Freida Yafe	wed 1903	#221	1903
FRIDMAN	Yudel		#118	1900
FRIEDMAN	Alechsander		#117	1898
FRIEDMAN	Nechemiah		#117	1898
GAFINOWITZ	Yisroel		# 228	1898
GARFINKEL	Yisroel		#195	1900
GAWRONSKI	Shabasai		#167	1898
GLAS	Eliezer		#274	1897
GLASNER	Leopold husband of Sheine Chanah Yafe	wed 3 Ellul in Frankfurt on Main	#195	1900
GLAT	Aharon husband of batia Menucha		#29	1898
GLAT	Batia Menucha		#29	1898

GLAT	wife of Aharon Moshe Tzvi ben Aharon	born 1 Tevet 1896	#29	1898
GLAZER	Aizik		#117	1898
GLAZER	Sarah Tane wife of Shalom Gotler	wed 8 Nisan	#117	1898
GOLDBERG	Hawsha Yechezkel		#167	1898
GOLDBERG	Tzvi		#167	1898
GOLDBERG	Y		#250	1894
GOLDBERG	Yakov		#167	1898
GOLDSHTEIN	Kalman	Rabbi	#250	1894
GOLDSHTEIN	Kalman	Rabbi	#167	1898
GOLDSHTEIN	Yitzchok		#117	1898
GOLDSHTEIN	Yitzchok		#221	1903
GOLDSHTEIN	Yitzchok		#221	1903
GORDON	Hine Mirl		#167	1898
GOTLER	Shalom		#221	1903
GOTLER	Shalom husband of Sarah Tane Glazer	wed 8 Nisan	#117	1898
GRIN	Yekutiel		#167	1898
GRINBLAT	M Sh		# 159	1893
GRINBLAT	M Sh		#250	1894
GRINBLAT	M Sh		#117	1898
GRINBLAT	Moshe		#274	1897
GRITZMAN	Miriam		#118	1900
GRITZMAN	Mordechai Yosef	son born 1900	#118	1900
HATZES	Tzvi		# 228	1898
HAWSHA	Chaim Aharon		# 228	1898
HELLER	Ch		#250	1894
HELMAN	Reuven		#167	1898

HERTZBERG	father of Hadassah	Doctor	#167	1898
HERTZBERG	Hadassah wife of Dr. Lowenshtein from Mitau	wed	#167	1898
HIRSHFELD	Chaim		#221	1903
HIRSHFELD	Shmuel		#221	1903
HIRSHHORN	Yete wife of Yitzchok Eizenshtat	wed 15 March	#117	1898
HOPPENKOPF	Eliezer father of Zinote		#117	1898
HOPPENKOPF	Zinote bas Eliezer wife of Shaweli Edelson	wed 3 March	#117	1898
HORWITZ	Feige		#167	1898
IZRAELSHTAM	Hinde		#90	1898
IZRAELSHTAM	Motle wife of Dovid Bruchman	wed 10 February	#90	1898
IZRAELSHTAM	Shalom		#90	1898
IZRAELSHTAM	Shmuel		#90	1898
IZRAELSTAM	Shmuel		#195	1900
KANTER	Ester		#167	1898
KANTER	Pesach		#167	1898
KANTER	Sh		#250	1894
KANTOR	Hane		#167	1898
KANTOR	Shlomo		# 228	1898
KAPLAN	Eliahu	in Pretoria, SA	#288	1897
KAPLAN	Helena		#167	1898
KAPLAN	Shmuel husband of Shula Hana Hawsha of Shkod	wed 3 Elul	#195	1900

KISMAN	Yehuda		#117	1898
KLEIN	Elimelech		#117	1898
KLEIN	M		#250	1894
KOHN	Hirsh		#167	1898
KOHN	Sh Y		#250	1894
KORNOWSKI	Ritow		#167	1898
KOTZ	L		#250	1894
KOTZ	Leib		#250	1894
KREMER	Rivka wife of Leib Gershon from Tukum	wed	#117	1898
LEIBSON	Tzvi		#142	1898
LEMGIN	Mordechai husband of Miriam Mandelshtam	wed 28th August 1898 in Dubbeln	# 228	1898
LEWI	Zalman		# 228	1898
LEWITAS	Avraham		#117	1898
LEWITAS	Chaya Sara		#117	1898
LEWITAS	Miriam		#117	1898
LEWITAS	Sh M		#250	1894
LISIS	T		#250	1894
LISIS	Tuvia		# 228	1898
LISOS	Aizik		#167	1898
LISOS	Leib		#167	1898
LISOS	Leib	New Zager	#29	1898
LISOS	Nite		#117	1898
LISOS	Rivka		#117	1898
LISOS	Shalom		#167	1898
LISOS	Toibe		#117	1898
LUNTZ	Chaya		#90	1898
LURIA	Leib		#167	1898
LURIA	Tz A		#250	1894

LURIA	Tzvi Ari		# 228	1898
MANDELSHTAM	Ch Y		#250	1894
MANDELSHTAM	Ch Y		#250	1894
MANDELSHTAM	Ch Y		#274	1897
MANDELSHTAM	Ch Y		#167	1898
MANDELSHTAM	Chaim Yosef		#195	1900
MANDELSHTAM	Chaim Yosef		#225	1902
MANDELSHTAM	Miriam wife of Mordechai Lemgin	wed 28th August 1898 in Dubbeln	# 228	1898
MANDELSHTAM	son of Chaim Yosef	wed	#225	1902
MANDELSHTAM	Tzvi Leib		#167	1898
MARGOLIOS	N		#250	1894
MAWSHOWITZ	Bertha		#167	1898
MEHL	Yitzchok Michel		#117	1898
MELAMED	Sh		#250	1894
MELAMED	Tzvi		#117	1898
MELER	Bentzion		# 228	1898
MELLER	Bentzion Shmuel		#227	1894
MENDELSHON	Nachum		#167	1898
MENDELZOHN	A		#250	1894
MENDELZOHN	N		#250	1894
MENDELZOHN	Nachum	in Pretoria, SA	#288	1897
MICHALOWITZ	Batia		#167	1898
MICHALOWITZ	Yette		#167	1898
MILL	Bentzion	Rabbi	#167	1898
MILWITZKI	Sheftil		#117	1898
MIRENOWITZ	Boruch		#221	1903
MORFLER?	Sh		#250	1894

MOZESZOHN	Y Y		#250	1894
NEIWIDEL	Sh T		# 159	1893
NEIWIDEL	Shalom Tuvia		#170	1897
NEIWIDEL	Shalom Tuvia		#198	1900
NEIWIDEL	Shalom Tuvia nephew of Boruch Broida		# 228	1898
NEIWIDEL	Shalom Tuvia nephew of Rabbi Yehoshua Broida		#82	1895
OSHRATZ	Chana wife of Avraham Yitzchok	wed Adar Sheni 5	#118	1900
PAKTMAN	Yitzchok		#221	1903
PEKIN	Moshe	from Shavel	#221	1903
PERKIN	Ete		#167	1898
PERKIN	Ete		#221	1903
PERKIN	Rivka		#221	1903
PERKIN	Yisroel		#117	1898
PERKIN	Yisroel		#35	1900
PERKIN	Yisroel		#221	1903
PERKIN	Yitzchok		# 228	1898
PILVERMACHER	Yosef		#221	1903
RABINOWITZ	Sh Y		#117	1898
RAZOMNE	Yosef Yakov		#168	1895
RIF	Yehuda Leib	Rabbi ABD	# 228	1898
RITOW	A		#250	1894
RITOW	Avraham		# 228	1898
ROZENBERG	Leib		#117	1898
ROZENFELD	Ch		#250	1894
ROZING	Nachum Zev		#29	1898
ROZOMNA	Y Y		#250	1894

ROZOMNI	Yete		#117	1898
ROZOTAI	Yosef Yakov		# 228	1898
ROZUMNA	Yosef Yakov		#195	1900
SEGAL	B	Official Collector	# 171	1893
SHAPOW	Eliezer		#117	1898
SHEIN	Gavriel		#167	1898
SHEIN	Leib		#167	1898
SHEIN	Yulius		#167	1898
SHEINIGZOHN	Moshe		#250	1894
SHER	Hinde Gite		#221	1903
SHIR	Eliezer		#221	1903
SHKOT	Y		#250	1894
SHLAPABERSKI	Eidel		#167	1898
SHLAPABERSKI	Polina		#117	1898
SHMUELOWITZ	Chana Feiga wife of Uri		#61	1897
SHMUELOWITZ	Chaya Ester bas Uri wife of Yitzchok Blumberg		#61	1897
SHMUELOWITZ	Uri husband of Chana Feiga father of Chaya Ester		#61	1897
SHMUELOWITZ	Y	in Dublin, Ireland	#61	1897
SHMULIA	N		#250	1894
SHOCHAT	Leib		#221	1903
SHOCHAT	Leib friend of Rabbi Chaim Shochat ABD Abel		#195	1900
SHTEIN	Bentzion		#221	1903
SHTEIN	P		#221	1903

SHTEIN	Sh M		#250	1894
SHTZUPOK	Avraham		# 228	1898
TANKEL	B		#250	1894
TANKEL	Bentzion		#250	1894
TANKEL	Bentzion Nachum ben Zelig Meir husband of Gitl Malka Bloch	wed 5 Ellul in Zager	# 206	1897
TANKEL	Benzion Nachum		# 228	1898
TANKEL	Chana Gitl wife of Zelig Meir		# 206	1897
TANKEL	Moshe Aharon		#221	1903
TANKEL	Moshe Bentzion		#118	1900
TANKEL	Zelig Meir		# 228	1898
TANKEL	Zelig Meir husband of Chana Gitl father of Bentzion Nachum		# 206	1897
TASKIN	A		#250	1894
TZALELSOHN	Mina wife of Tzvi Kurshan of Vieksna	wed 10 Elul	#195	1900
TZALELZOHN	Shlomo Chen		#167	1898
TZIONI	Rivka d-i-l of Rabbi Chaim Tzvi	wed 14 Av	#195	1900
WEINBERG	Ch		#250	1894
WEINSHTOK	Tzvi Hirsh	from Telshen	# 228	1898
WEIS	Eli ben Leib	wed 19 Av	#195	1900
WEIS	Leib father of Eli		#195	1900
WOLFSON	Shlomo		#118	1900

YAFE	A		#221	1903
YAFE	Aba		#118	1900
YAFE	Ari		#167	1898
YAFE	B		#250	1894
YAFE	B R		#221	1903
YAFE	Chana		#117	1898
YAFE	Emma		#221	1903
YAFE	Freida wife of Yisroel Fridman	wed 1903	#221	1903
YAFE	Frida		#117	1898
YAFE	Hillel brother of Freida	from Riga	#221	1903
YAFE	M		#250	1894
YAFE	Sarah mother of Sheine Chanah		#195	1900
YAFE	Sheine Chanah wife of Leopold Glasner	wed 3 Ellul in Frankfurt on Main	#195	1900
YAFE	Simcha		#134	1900
YAFE	Simcha fiance of Toibe Zegerman of Salant	engaged	#239	1899
YAFE	Y		#250	1894
YAFE	Yakov		# 228	1898
YAKOBSON	Avraham		#167	1898
YAKOBZOHN	Hirsh		#250	1894
YAKOBZOHN	Leib		#167	1898
YAKOBZOHN	Tzvi		# 228	1898
YAKOBZOHN	Y		#250	1894
YAVNEH	Paie wife of Zalman Broida	wed 1898	# 228	1898
YEDAKIN	Sh		#250	1894
YEGERMAN	A		#250	1894

YOWROWITZ	Moshe		#221	1903
YUDELOWITZ	Shalom		#90	1898
ZACHS	Y		#250	1894
ZAK	Hinda Gitl		#212	1895
ZAK	Hinde Gite		#167	1898
ZAKS	Heshil b-i-l of Rabbi Meir Michel Hawsha of Shkod		#195	1900
ZAKS	Tzesne		#117	1898
ZAKSH	Moshe		#221	1903
ZALTZBERG	B		#227	1894
ZALTZBERG	Bentzion		#250	1894
ZEGERMANN	Asher		#167	1898
ZENERMAN	Asher		#212	1895
ZIMAN	Avraham Menachem ben Heshil	born 1 Tevet 1896	#29	1898
ZIMAN	Choda Golda		#29	1898
ZIMAN	Heshil husband of Choda Golda		#29	1898
ZIMAN	Simcha	Motz	#117	1898
ZIMANSOHN	Folk uncle of Fani		#195	1900
ZOMSER	Shmuel		# 228	1898
ZUSMAN	Bentzion		#274	1897
	Chaim Tzvi f-i-l of Rivka Tzioni	Rabbi ABD Zager Yashan	#195	1900
	Fani daughter of sister of Folk Zimansohn	wed	#195	1900

Appendix 4   The 1914 list of Zhager Jews who paid annual membership fees to the *Agudath-Yisrael* party

New Zhager:

Apiryon Mendl

Arenov Tsevi

Arkin Mordehai

Asasin Leib

Blas Josef

Blidun Hayim

Blum Avraham-Ya'akov

Blum Josef

Brokhman David

Bruker Mendl

Dvoloitsky Shakhna

Eszon Shemuel-Khone

Esterman David

Fridman Yehudah

Goldberg Azriel

Goldberg Tsevi

Gitelson Peretz

Gotlib Shalom

Gotler Shalom

Helman Asher

Kantor Yudl

Kimelfeld Pinhas

Lan Ya'alov-Mosheh

Lerman Aizik

Levitas Leib

Lisus Mordehai

Lisus Aizik

London Meir

London Yits'hak

Maister Yehudah-Meir

Mandelshtam Josef

Markushevitz Yits'hak

Meler Ben-Zion

Melamed A.S.

Milvitsky Sheftl

Milvitzky Eliezer

Naividel Shalom-Tuviyah

Nurok Noakh

Peretsman Tsevi

Rabinovitz Leib

Rozenberg Leib

Rozenfeld Nahum

Sarok Josef

Shalamov Mordehai

Shapov Mordehai

Sheininzon Mosheh

Shikshtein Yehezkel

Shokhat David

Shor Elazar

Shtein Shelomoh-Mosheh

Tankel Mosheh-Aharon

Tankel Aba-Eliezer

Todes Shalom

Trumpeitsky Shalom-Tsevi

Vagenheim Mihah

Viner Josef

Volkin Avraham-Shimon

Yakobzon Tsevi

Yankelson Tsevi-Leib

Yavnovitz Mosheh

Yankelevitz Hayim Dr.

Zagarzky Yekutiel

Zlot Khone

Zegerman Asher

Old Zhager

Blidon Mordehai

Feldman Ben-Zion, Rabbi

Fishhoit Fishl

Hilman Shemuel

Hirshberg Shemuel-Eliyahu

Gavronsky Shabtai

Kahn Hayim-Mendl

Levitas Avraham-Elia

Olshvang Mosheh-Yits'hak

Pshedmeisky Tsevi, Rabbi

Žiežmariai (Zhezhmer)

Ziezmariai (Zhezhmer in Yiddish), in eastern Lithuania, is situated 1 km. (0.6 mile) south of the main Kovno-Vilna road and 8 km. (5 miles) from the railway station of Koshedar (Kaisiadorys), on the west bank of the Streva River.

Ziezmariai is mentioned in fourteenth century German records and known then as Sysmare or Sisemare. It received the status of a town in 1501. Thanks to its location the town developed as a commercial and administrative center. By 1600 it had about 100 houses, a liquor factory, two flourmills, a bakery, many shops and bars; by 1780 it had seven streets.

The nearby estate was in the hands of various noblemen for many generations: among them were the families Poniatovky and Tishkevitz.

The Northern War at the beginning of the eighteenth century, devastating fires in the nineteenth century and the arrival of Napoleon's soldiers successively caused much damage to Zhezhmer.

In the 1880s and thereafter, the town's population decreased as a result of continuing emigration, but despite this, economic development flourished and the number of market days and fairs increased. In 1897 there were 231 wooden houses, eight solidly built homes and four paved streets radiating out from the market square. Being a county administrative center, government offices, schools and central institutions were established there. Under Russian rule (1795-1915) Zhezhmer was included in the Vilna province (*gubernia*) and during the rule of independent Lithuania (1918-1940) Zhezhmer was a county administrative center. However its development slowed down, because it was cut off from Vilna and from its district administrative center at Troki (Trakai).

Jewish Settlement until after World War I

Zhezhmer was one of the oldest Jewish communities in Lithuania and its beginnings can probably be traced back to the sixteenth century. At that time and for a short period thereafter Karaites lived in Zhezhmer. By tradition, the princess who owned the Zhezhmer estate and the land on which the town was built, greatly reduced the Jews' taxes as well as providing other privileges. These were registered in golden letters in an official book given to the Jews and carefully preserved for generations. Later, probably at the end of the nineteenth century, the estate owner Graf Tishkevitz wanted to collect taxes again. He forced the Jew who kept the golden book to hand it over to him and so the proof of exemption from taxes was lost. From 1795 onwards, Jewish leaseholders had the exclusive right to produce and market liquor. The Jews also owned most of the local shops and workshops.

A street in Zhezhmer

In 1766, 482 Jews lived there and by 1847 there were 713. Of the 32 shops in the locality in 1897, 30 were in Jewish hands, despite the emigration of many.

In 1895 a fire caused much damage to Zhezhmer and the Alliance Izraelite Association in Paris sent 700 rubles in aid. The members of the distribution committee were Ya'akov Ratsky, Naftali-Hertz Shaker, Yits'hak Zerakh, Mosheh Rozenberg, A.M. Antselovitz, Pinhas Katz, Mosheh Beineshovitz, Naftali Beiles, Leib Ilinsky and Mordehai Rozenberg.

Religious and social life revolved around the three prayer houses and other public institutions. The Zhezhmer Jews developed an affinity to *Eretz-Yisrael* long before the rise of modern Zionism, and they sent a delegate to the conference of Russian Zionists in Warsaw in 1898.

In lists of donors to the settlement of *Eretz-Yisrael* published in *HaMelitz* in 1878 and 1900, many Zhezhmer Jews appear. The fundraiser was Uriyah Vainer.

The Hebrew newspaper *HaMagid* published a list of 126 Zhezhmer Jews who donated money to the victims of the famine in Persia in 1872 (see **Appendix 1**).

The correspondent of *HaMagid* and *HaMelitz* was Idl-Yehudah Shapira.

Tsevi-Hirsh of Zhezhmer was one of first ten to obey the request of the *Gaon* of Vilna, Rabbi Eliyahu to emigrate to *Eretz-Yisrael*. He arrived in *Tsefath* (Safed) in 1804 and became an honored person.

In Jerusalem's old cemetery there are two tombstones of Zhezhmer Jews, Tsivyah daughter of Mordehai (died in 1890) and Yisrael ben Reuven.

According to the government census of 1897 the population of Zhezhmer was 2,795, with 1,628 (58%) of them Jews.

This is a list of the rabbis who officiated in Zhezhmer:

> Yedidyah Ginzburg
>
> Yehoshua-Heshl Eliashzon (1799-1874)
>
> Mordehai Eliashberg (1817-1889), from 1851 until 1863. He published several books on Judaism and was one of the first rabbis to become a follower of the *Khibath Zion* movement.
>
> Ya'akov MiKruzh (until 1877)
>
> His son Leib-Yekutiel Elyon (1845-1900), for 22 years a rabbi in Zhezhmer, published several books on Judaism
>
> Joel-Yits'hak Ketsenelnboigen (1809-1891)

Personages born in Zhezhmer:

> Yits'hak-Mosheh Rumsh (1822-1894), writer and teacher. Together with his friend Yehudah-Leib Gordon in the government school in Ponevezh, he translated several books from German into Hebrew.
>
> Avraham-Shemuel Shvartz (1876-1957), doctor and poet, one of the first Hebrew poets in America. He died in New York.
>
> The cantors Yoke Bas and Shalom Tsemakhzon.

Zhezhmer in Independent Lithuania (1918-1940)

With so many wooden buildings in the town fire was an ever-present hazard. In 1918 a fire ruined many Jewish houses and the three prayer houses. Five years later another fire burned down a further 20 houses.

The law of autonomies for minorities issued by the new Lithuanian government resulted in the minister for Jewish affairs Dr. Menachem (Max) Soloveitshik, ordering elections for community committees (*Va'adei Kehilah*) to be held in the summer of 1919. In Zhezhmer the elections took place in 1920 and a community committee of eleven members was elected: five non-party men, four workers and two General Zionists. The committee was active until 1925, when the autonomy was annulled.

In 1922 Zhezhmer Jews voted in the elections for the first *Seimas* (Parliament) in independent Lithuania: the Zionist list garnered 406 votes, *Akhduth* 80 votes and Democrats 6 votes.

The first census of the new Lithuanian government in 1923 counted 2,198 residents resident in Zhezhmer. 1,205 (55%) were Jews.

Most Zhezhmer Jews made their living from small trade, peddling, agriculture, crafts and fishing. An important part of their livelihood was derived from the two weekly market days, Mondays and Thursdays. There were merchants who exported potatoes to Germany and also those who dealt in furs and leather.

According to the government survey of 1931 there were 44 shops, 41 (93%) under Jewish management. The distribution according to the type of business is given in the table below:

Type of business	Total	Owned by Jews
Groceries	6	5
Grain and flax	4	4
Butcher shops and Cattle Trade	4	4
Restaurants and Taverns	7	6
Food Products	3	3
Textile Products and Furs	5	5
Leather and Shoes	5	5
Medicine and Cosmetics	1	0
Hardware Products	4	4
Others	5	5

The same survey listed thirteen enterprises as Jewish owned: three photograph shops, one soda factory (owned by Strazh), four wool combing workshops, one workshop for men's hats, two workshops for leather processing and two saddler workshops. There was also a flourmill owned by Yits'hak Shugen.

After the market was relocated to the periphery of the town in 1939, Jewish merchants and shopkeepers were adversely affected financially.

In 1937 fifty Jewish artisans worked locally: six tailors, six bakers, six blacksmiths, five shoemakers, five hatters, five butchers, three carpenters, two oven builders, two tin smiths, two saddlers, one painter, one dressmaker, one textile dyer, one potter, one wood carver, one photographer and two others.

The stamp of the Jewish *Folksbank*

The Jewish Popular Bank (*Folksbank*) with its 156 members, directed by Dr. Sh. Sapir, played an important role in the economic life of Zhezhmer Jews. Up to 200 families were assisted by loans without interest from the local *Gemiluth Hesed* society, whose basic capital was estimated to have been 30,000 litas. There was also a branch of the United Credit Society for Jewish Agrarians. There were 28 telephones in 1939, 8 in Jewish houses or enterprises.

The *Beth Midrash*

In addition to the *Beth Midrash*, the *Shtibl* and other religious and social institutions common to most similar Jewish communities, there was an orphanage with about 20 children established in 1922 through the generosity of former Zhezhmer Jews in the USA. These emigrants helped to maintain it by donating $100 every month. From time to time they would also donate money to buy equipment for the Hebrew *Tarbuth* School, established in 1922 and directed by Mosheh Shofer. About 150 children studied in this school. The teachers were Zevulun Petrikansky (Poran) from Yurburg,, Shemuel Siderer and Havivah Siderer-Kaplan.

The *Aron Kodesh,* a gift from a former Zhezhmerer in America

Children and management of the Zhezhmer orphanage 1937

A drama society, a reading hall and the Y.L. Peretz library, with about 1,000 books, all opened in 1928.

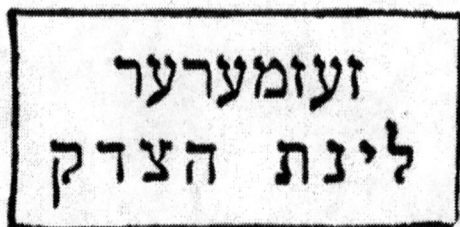

זעזמערער
לינת הצדק

The stamp of the Zhezhmer *Linath HaTsedek* society

Many Zhezhmer Jews were active Zionists and almost all Zionist parties had local members. The Zionist youth organizations were branches of *HaShomer HaTsair*, *Betar* and *Benei Akiva*. *Maccabi*, the sports organization, was active too. Despite continued emigration of Zhezhmer Jews to America, Uruguay and *Eretz-Yisrael* the number of voters for the Zionist congresses increased as can be seen in the table below:

Cong No.	Year	Shek	Total Voter	Labor Party		Rev.	Gen. Zion		Gro	Miz
				Z"S	Z'Z					
16	1929	63	48	2	4	40	1	----	----	1
17	1931	37	30	14	2	13	----	----	----	1
18	1933	---	175	177		49	8	----	4	1
19	1935	---	287	195		---	4	51	9	28

Cong No. = Congress; Shek = Shekalim; Revis. = Revisionists; Gro = Grosmanists; Miz. = Mizrahi

The rabbis who officiated in Zhezhmer during this time were Mosheh Shapira (1862-1930) from 1896 until 1930 and the last rabbi, Yisrael-Tanhum Fortman, who was murdered in 1941.

Between 1836 and 1903 there were 204 subscribers to rabbinic literature.

עשי
הזביירים
בזזמר
1932

The Zhezhmer *HaShomer HaTsair* branch
The "Sheveth of the Habirim" (The younger members "Tribe") 1932

During World War II and Afterwards

After Lithuania was annexed to the Soviet Union in the summer of 1940, intensive sovietization took place in Zhezhmer. Businesses, mostly Jewish, were nationalized and Jewish parties and organizations were disbanded. Many Jews joined government economic enterprises and security institutions. The Hebrew school was closed and all Zionist activities were forbidden. A limited amount of cultural activity on behalf of the *Comsomol* took place in the hall of the Y.L. Peretz library. At the same time the departure of the town's youngsters to Kovno and other towns continued, and just 200 families were left in Zhezhmer.

On June 24th, 1941 only two days after the German invasion of the Soviet Union, Zhezhmer was occupied by the German army. The town was already in the hands of Lithuanian nationalists who began their persecution of their Jewish neighbors. Among the first victims they murdered were three members of the Ilionsky family. On the pretext that Jews had shot Lithuanians and that they had hidden explosives under the floor of the synagogue, the LIthuanians searched Jewish houses and robbed them. They detained heads of families and other men and transferred them to Koshedar (Kaisiadorys), where they were killed together with the local Jews. At the same time the local authorities published orders forbidding Jews to be seen in the streets, to buy food and so on.

For several weeks many Jewish men were forced to dig peat in Palemonas and the women to do the same in Praveniskis.

In the second half of August 1941 all Jews were gathered into the synagogue and kept there without food and water for several days. On August 27th, 1941(4th of Elul 5701) all the men were taken to Strosiunai forest near the village of Vladikiskis, about 3 km. (nearly 2 miles) north of Zhezhmer. There they were executed and buried in previously prepared pits. The next day, August 28th (5th of Elul), the women and children were slain in the same forest. 2,200 men of Koshedar, Zhosly and Zhezhmer together with 1,800 women and children from those towns are buried in those mass graves. One of the women, Miriam Kotskin, who realized what was going to happen, set fire to her house and jumped into the flames before the murderers came to take her to the murder site.

Most of the local residents did nothing to help their Jewish neighbors and only a few helped Jews to survive. Their names are inscribed in the archives of *Yad Vashem* in Jerusalem.

In 1943 Nazi military rulers established a working camp in Zhezhmer, intended for hundreds of Jews from small ghettos between Lithuania and Belarus. In May of that year 700 people from this camp were transferred to the Kovno ghetto where they were absorbed by the local authorities.

In the autumn of 1991 the local authority erected a metal fence around the mass graves and placed new marble slabs on the monuments. On them is written in Lithuanian and Yiddish: "Here on August 28th, 1941, Nazi murderers and their local helpers tortured and buried alive 2,200 Zhezhmer, Zhosly and Koshedar Jews."

On the nearby mass grave the same inscription was engraved with a slight variation to its wording: "...1,800 women and Jewish children..." There the Lithuanian sculptor V. Kapaciunas erected three wooden sculptures named "Pain."

The massacre site of the men in the forest of Strosiunai
At the left of the photograph stand the three wooden sculptures

The massacre site of the women and children

A group of survivors at a commemoration service beside the monument

Sources:

Yad Vashem Archives - Jerusalem: M-1/E-122/50; 633/531, 1313/1274, 1493/1403, 1763/1635, 2129/1908, 2452/1514; M-9/15(6); M-33/383; M-35/80; 0-3/3681, 3870.

Koniuhovsky Collection 0-71, file 85; 0-57 Zhezhmer file, testimony of Yits'hak Kalmitsky.

YIVO New York, Lithuanian Communities Collection, file 1519

Garfunkel, Leib, *Kovna HaYehudith BeHurbanah* (Hebrew), Jerusalem, 1949

Levin, Dov - Zhezhmer: *Pinkas HaKehiloth-Lita, Yad Vashem*, Jerusalem 1996

Ghetto *Yedioth* (Yiddish), Vilna, #33, 4.4.1943; #42, 6.6.1943

Di Yiddishe Shtime - Kovno, 16.7.1922

HaMelitz - St. Petersburg #68, 135, 158

Folksblat - Kovno, 25.10. 1937, 26.7.1939, 13.11.1940

Kaisiadoriu Aidai, #76, 21.9.1991

Appendix 1

List of Zhezhmer Jews donors to the Persian famine sufferers in 1872 listed in Hamagid.

(From JewishGen.org. data bases compiled by Jeffrey Maynard)

Surname	Given Name	Comments	Source	Year
	Breine	woman from Ziezmariai (Zezmer)	#12	1872
BATZKAN	Eidil		p169	1872
BEILES	Yosef Tzvi ben Avraham		#17	1872
BEILESH	Yosef Tzvi ben Avraham		p169	1872
BEISHTRIK	Moshe Avraham	brother of Zev	p169	1872
BEISHTRIK	Zev	brother of Moshe Avraham	p169	1872
BINSH	Yitzchok		p169	1872
BROIDA	Tzvi		p169	1872
BROIDA	Yakov		p169	1872
CHAYAT	Leib		p169	1872
CHAYAT	Meir		#17	1872
DONOWKE	Moshe		p169	1872
EIZELMAN	Yitzchok		p169	1872
ELIAN	Yekutiel Leib		#17	1872
ELIAN	Yekutiel Leib	Rabbi	p169	1872
GARBER	Chaim Hirsh		p169	1872
GLEZER	Boruch	brother of Yekil & Gedalia	p169	1872
GLEZER	Gedalia	brother of Boruch & Yekil	p169	1872
GLEZER	Moshe	old	p169	1872
GLEZER	Shimon		p169	1872
GLEZER	Yekil	brother of Boruch & Gedalia	p169	1872
HEILPER	Yisroel		*p169*	1872
KA"TZ	Yudil ben Ch		p169	1872
KATZ	Avraham		p169	1872
KATZ	Chaim		p169	1872
KATZ	Eidel	brother of Eliezer	p169	1872
KATZ	Eliezer	brother of Eidel	p169	1872
KATZ	Peretz		p169	1872
KATZAV	Feivish		p169	1872

KIRZNER	Aharon		p169	1872
KIRZNER	Avraham		#17	1872
KIRZNER	Eli		#17	1872
KIRZNER	Yakov		#17	1872
KIZANSKI	Yitzchok		p169	1872
KOMINER	Aharon		#17	1872
MAILIAN	Moshe		p169	1872
MAILIAN	Yosef		#17	1872
MALIVOWITZ	Moshe		p169	1872
MELAMED	Leib Ber		p169	1872
MERETZ	Mordchai		p169	1872
MERETZ	Moshe		p169	1872
MIOEWIA	Tzvi		p169	1872
MIZASLI	Yosef		p169	1872
MONES	Eli		p169	1872
NEPHACH	Eli		p169	1872
NEPHACH	Leib		p169	1872
NEPHACH	Michel		p169	1872
PERETZ	Leib	his wife	p169	1872
POLIMS	Moshe		#17	1872
POM	Raphel	father of Yudil	p169	1872
POM	Yudil ben Raphel		p169	1872
POMIANSKI	Zev		p169	1872
POMPIANSKI	Aharon		p169	1872
PRENSKI	Dovid		p169	1872
RABINOWITZ	Zev		p169	1872
RATZKI	Yitzchok		p169	1872
ROZINBERG	Eliezer		p169	1872
ROZINBERG	Yosef		p169	1872
RUBINOWITZ	Zev		#17	1872
SANDLER	Mina		p169	1872
SANDLER	Yakov Moshe		p169	1872
SANDLER	Yosef		p169	1872
SEGAL	Yitzchok Leib		p169	1872
SEGAL	Zalman		p169	1872
SHACHOR	Niv		p169	1872
SHACHOR	Shmeriahu		p169	1872
SHACHOR	Yakov		p169	1872
SHAFER	Leib		p169	1872
SHAMAI	Yedidia Eliezer		p169	1872
SHAPIRO	Eidil		p169	1872
SHINBIT	Yitzchok		p169	1872
SHWART	Dovid Leib		#17	1872
SIFER	Leib brother of Reuven		p169	1872
SIFER	Reuven brother of Leib		p169	1872
STRASHUN	Chaim ben		p169	1872

	Yosef			
STRASHUN	Note		p169	1872
STRASHUN	Yosef	father of Chaim	p169	1872
TEPER	Anshil		p169	1872
TEPER	Beinish		p169	1872
TEPER	Note		p169	1872
TKATZ	Kopil		p169	1872
TRILISHOK	Binyomin		p169	1872
YANOWER	Leib		p169	1872
YETILIN	Moshe		p169	1872
YEZNERKE	Sarah		p169	1872
	Aharon ben M		p169	1872
	Aharon Chaim		p169	1872
	Ari Tzvi		p169	1872
	Avraham Meir		#17	1872
	Avraham Yitzchok ben N Sh		p169	1872
	Dov	k"b	p169	1872
	Eli Eidil		p169	1872
	Eliakum Hertz		p169	1872
	Falk	nephew of Zalman	p169	1872
	Gedalia	from Kaunas (Kovno)	p169	1872
	Heshil ben Y P		p169	1872
	Leib ben A		p169	1872
	Leib ben Ch		p169	1872
	Leib Mendil		#17	1872
	Mordechai ben Z B		p169	1872
	Mordechai Eli		#17	1872
	Moshe	a"ch	p169	1872
	Moshe ben Y P		p169	1872
	Moshe Bentzion		#17	1872
	Moshe Hirsh		p169	1872
	Moshe Yitzchok		p169	1872
	Naphtali ben Y Tz		p169	1872
	Peretz	the old	p169	1872
	Risha	woman	p169	1872
	Shimshon bven Dov		#17	1872
	Shmuel	k"b	p169	1872
	Tzvi ben N Sh		p169	1872
	Tzvi Gershon		p169	1872
	Tzvi Matitiahu		p169	1872
	Yakov Shmuel		p169	1872
	Yehoshua		p169	1872

Lipman Yekutiel Nechamiah	f-i-l of Zelig	p169	1872
Yisroel	k"b	p169	1872
Yitzchok	ly"m	p169	1872
Yitzchok ben A Ch	bridegroom	p169	1872
Yona	k"b	p169	1872
Yosef Dovid		p169	1872
Yosef Tzvi	hach"m	p169	1872
Zalman ben A		p169	1872
Zalman uncle of Falk	from Jurbarkas (Yurburg)	p169	1872

9 780976 475910